Key Concepts in
Ethnography

KAREN O'REILLY

Key Concepts in
Ethnography

Los Angeles • London • New Delhi • Singapore • Washington DC

First published 2009

Apart from any fair dealing for the purposes of research or
private study, or criticism or review, as permitted under the
Copyright, Designs and Patents Act, 1988, this publication
may be reproduced, stored or transmitted in any form, or by
any means, only with the prior permission in writing of the
publishers, or in the case of reprographic reproduction, in
accordance with the terms of licences issued by the Copyright
Licensing Agency. Enquiries concerning reproduction outside
those terms should be sent to the publishers.

SAGE Publications Ltd
1 Oliver's Yard
55 City Road
London EC1Y 1SP

SAGE Publications Inc.
2455 Teller Road
Thousand Oaks, California 91320

SAGE Publications India Pvt Ltd
B 1/I 1 Mohan Cooperative Industrial Area
Mathura Road, New Delhi 110 044

SAGE Publications Asia-Pacific Pte Ltd
33 Pekin Street #02-01
Far East Square
Singapore 048763

Library of Congress Control Number: 2008924903

British Library Cataloguing in Publication data

A catalogue record for this book is available from the
British Library

ISBN 978-1-4129-2864-9
ISBN 978-1-4129-2865-6 (pbk)

Typeset by C&M Digitals (P) Ltd., Chennai, India
Printed in Great Britain by The Cromwell Press Ltd, Trowbridge, Wiltshire
Printed on paper from sustainable resources

contents

key concepts in
ethnography

Introduction

Please read this first

WHY DO WE NEED ANOTHER BOOK ON ETHNOGRAPHY?

Social research methods texts have been growing in number incrementally in the past decades. It seems that every methodology, analytical approach, technique, and stage of the research process has its own dedicated book, and ethnography is no exception. There are books on visual ethnography, virtual ethnography, organisational ethnography, ethnography and education, ethnography and health, writing ethnography and so on (apparently ad infinitum). Perhaps this is precisely why a book like this one is called for.

This book clearly and succinctly summarises a broad range of issues relevant to ethnography. It is not quite an encyclopaedia but is more than a dictionary. It is comprehensive yet brief. It is small and neat and easy to hold and flick through. It covers methodological techniques, advances, debates, concepts, and research fields. Time-honoured themes traditionally explored in qualitative methods textbooks are included, such as key informants, access, participant observation, and rapport. Issues sometimes excluded from older texts, such as reflexivity, writing, fieldnotes, and ethics are also covered. But, more exciting, recent developments such as virtual and multi-sited ethnography also have their place. No other book covers all these themes of direct relevance to ethnography in one place.

Each concept is presented comprehensively yet critically, with examples from ethnographic fieldwork accounts, and with references for students to follow up if they want to pursue a topic in more depth. Cross-references to concepts covered in the book are indicated by the use of bold. The examples are enjoyable to read and are collated from a range of books and articles. However, I have tried to use several examples from a few of the same projects, so that as the student dips into the concepts over time, he or she will gradually become familiar with the work of a few authors in some depth.

The book draws on my own reflexive-realist perspective. I am a sociologist with intellectual ties to both social anthropology and human geography.

I have a background in qualitative and quantitative methods and have taught ethnographic methods for a number of years to undergraduates and postgraduates from a range of social science disciplines. This unique perspective impacts on my interpretation of the concepts addressed. I enjoy postmodern accounts for their creativity and passion but I am concerned that ethnographers should also remain faithful to what they set out to do when access was first obtained. It is crucial that we conduct ethnography reflexively with constant awareness of our role in the research enterprise. However, this does not mean abandoning any sense that there is a real world we wish to learn about, and which our research participants live in, experience, feel constrained by, and help create.

The book can be dipped into as required, to learn about individual concepts, or consulted in its entirety, as a treatise on current issues and debates in ethnography. I have indicated where concepts are linked or can be read together. It is a useful didactic tool for teachers, who can prepare an entire session around one, or a group of, concepts and indicated further reading. The book is for students who are learning about ethnography as part of research methods training or in order to prepare for the field themselves. And it is for practising ethnographers to take with them into the field (and back), as a sort of comfort blanket, a resource to turn to in difficult times. It is meant to be consulted at every stage of the research process, being a first port of call before taking the ideas further in your own work or by consulting that of others. Enjoy! But first I would like to clarify the distinction between fieldwork, the field, and ethnography.

FIELDWORK, THE 'FIELD', AND PARTICIPANT OBSERVATION

The term 'fieldwork' is often confused with participant observation and ethnography, as if they were all one and the same thing. To be clear: *ethnography* is a methodology, *participant observation* is a method, and *fieldwork* refers to the period of primary data collection that is conducted out of the office or library. Fieldwork is also used in survey research where it refers to the period of data collection when questionnaires are distributed or face-to-face interviews are conducted. For ethnographers, fieldwork is the phase of data collection when the ethnographer is 'in the field'. The term 'fieldwork' also acknowledges that there is a beginning and end to the fieldwork part of the research process, and that this phase is distinct (at least to some extent) from other phases such as the research design, review of the literature, analysis, and writing stages.

Ethnographic fieldwork may involve any or all of the following elements and considerations (all covered elsewhere in this book): gaining **access**, recruitment of participants, establishing an insider role and gaining an **insider** (emic) perspective, deciding the extent to which to be overt or **covert**, building **rapport**, using gatekeepers, **key informants**, or research assistants, getting out, retaining an objective (etic) perspective, and avoiding **going 'native'**. It may draw on the following methods: participation, observation, document collection, group and individual interviews, asking questions, taking photographs, even survey research, or collection and construction of audio tape and film. What is essential is that it remains faithful to some sort of definition of ethnography.

WHAT IS ETHNOGRAPHY?

Ethnography is a methodology – a theory, or set of ideas – about research that rests on a number of fundamental criteria. Ethnography is iterative-inductive research; that is to say it evolves in design through the study (see **analysis, coding, fieldnotes, grounded theory**, and **induction**). Ethnography draws on a family of methods, involving direct and sustained contact with human agents, within the context of their daily lives (and cultures), watching what happens, listening to what is said, and **asking questions** (see **interviews, participant observation**, and **visual ethnography**). It results in richly written accounts that respect the irreducibility of human experience (see **writing**), acknowledges the role of theory (see **generalisation**), as well as the researcher's own role (see **reflexivity**), and views humans as part object/part subject (see also O'Reilly, 2005; Willis and Trondman, 2000). Beyond this, each ethnographer will choose whether or to what extent he or she wishes to consider historical and/or macro factors, the extent to which to be critical or to engage in cultural politics (see **critical ethnography** and **feminist ethnography**), and the range of methods employed beyond direct and sustained contact, watching, listening, and enquiring. Similarly, ethnography tends to be small-scale and tends not to include much in the way of quantification, but these are not to be taken as limitations (see **multi-sited**).

Ethnography has its roots in British social anthropology and in American cultural anthropology as well as (later) in the **Chicago School** of sociology. It has not been possible to include much discussion here of early anthropology, its development, its roots in biological field sciences and the salvage of native cultures, and its subsequent crises in the face of postmodern and poststructuralist critiques. For more on these, I direct readers to MacDonald (2001) and Faubion (2001).

REFERENCES

Faubion, J. D. (2001) 'Currents of cultural fieldwork', in P. Atkinson, A. Coffey, S. Delamont, J. Lofland and L. Lofland (eds) *Handbook of Ethnography*. London: Sage, pp. 39–59.

Macdonald, S. (2001) 'British social anthropology', in P. Atkinson, A. Coffey, S. Delamont, J. Lofland and L. Lofland (eds) *Handbook of Ethnography*. London: Sage, pp. 60–79.

O'Reilly, K. (2005) *Ethnographic Methods*. London: Routledge.

Willis, P. and Trondman, M. (2000) 'Manifesto for ethnography', *Ethnography*, 1(1): 5–16.

Access

Ethnographic research properly begins once one has entered the field. This involves gaining access to the people and places being studied.

Outline: First steps in ethnography. The general gathering stage. Deciding where to study. Introductions and 'recruitment', and persuading participants to take part. Negotiating sensitive access. Deciding whether to be overt or covert. Choosing a role and presentation of self. Getting out, and avoiding 'a case of the Pyles'.

GENERAL GATHERING

One of the first steps one has to consider when embarking on a piece of ethnographic research is how to gain access to people and places in such a way that the ethnography successfully achieves its outcomes. However, I think it is important to note that most research projects actually begin in the library and surfing the Internet, with what Paul Thomson (1988) has called the 'general gathering stage'. Here the ethnographer swots up on his or her topic, collecting background information, reading substantive and theoretical works related to the field and, of course, learning more about the research participants themselves. This might involve, for example, collecting background statistics on migration for ethnography with a migrant group, or learning about policies towards homelessness for an ethnographic study with homeless women. The next step is actually getting into the field and this involves gaining access to the group or setting.

FIRST STEPS

Though it may seem a simple point, it is actually crucial to take this first step tentatively and carefully. Many an ethnographer has been hampered or curtailed by the means of direct access to the group. The means through which access is gained will affect whom the ethnographer can

access

5

speak to about what, and how the research participants respond. The knock-on effects of the way the initial approach is handled can be devastating and long-lasting, barring the ethnographer forever from certain aspects of the group or from addressing certain questions or issues. More than this, access is not something achieved once and for all. It has to be negotiated and renegotiated all along to different groups, different people, for different topics (Berg, 2004). It is not always obvious where to do the research, and as Laud Humphreys (1970: 18) points out, there is often a tendency to avoid difficult access issues by simply using 'that beleaguered, captive population, students in our classrooms'. It is far better to begin with a research interest or intellectual puzzle and then to ask where the action is. For his study of behaviour in *'certain men's conveniences in an American city'* (tearooms, in American slang), Humphreys says he did not want to simply research homosexuals but 'participants in homosexual acts', which was an important distinction for him and helped him think about where to begin. First of all he had to find out which tearooms, or public lavatories, were actually used in the ways he was interested in.

Some researchers are already members of the group they are studying or are already familiar with the people. Patricia Adler (1985) and her husband, in their study of a community of drug dealers and smugglers, sort of fell into their research through having inquisitive minds, wanting to get to know the neighbours and, rather sensationally, through their own use of recreational drugs. Their research then simply followed instincts and developed leads in an ongoing process driven by the pursuit of meaning. Matthew Desmond (2006) had worked as a wildland firefighter in northern Arizona for several seasons prior to collecting data on why people choose such high-risk occupations. And Jason Ditton (1977), when he began work on his study of fiddling and pilferage, was already working in the bakery where he did ethnographic fieldwork.

Others will set off to distant places to do ethnographic research amongst people who are completely unknown to them. For example, in order to explore the simple, everyday acts of resistance such as foot dragging, false compliance, pilfering, and feigned ignorance that are used by relatively powerless groups in their everyday struggles against dominance and exploitation, James Scott (1985) spent two years living in a small Malaysian village. In such circumstances, and even in more familiar surroundings such as a school or factory, persuading people to accept a researcher into their daily lives, to live amongst them, to spend time watching, listening, and asking questions, can be daunting. Paul Rock (2001) says it can feel awfully like cold calling; like trying to sell something to those who neither need it nor can afford it. On the other hand, generally speaking, most ethnographers have found it surprisingly easy to gain access. People generally have accepted the presence of a researcher hanging around with them, asking them questions, as long as they understand why and are permitted to offer insights of their own. Indeed, many are flattered and will enjoy taking part. Sue Estroff (1981: 8), in her research on psychiatric outpatients, found respondents surpassed her expectations with their helpfulness, allowing her to observe and take part in their lives often under extreme and unhappy circumstances.

Of course, ethnographers are now conducting ethnography in multiple locations, online, virtually or historically (**multi-sited and mobile ethnographies, virtual ethnography**). These each raise their own issues for access, but it remains useful to distinguish between public and private settings. In public settings it is easier in some ways to gain access but more difficult to engage in-depth with participants and to be entirely overt about the study. Private settings require more careful negotiation but are likely to yield more interesting and rich data. Humphreys (1970) began his research in public settings but as he became more familiar with the gay scene, he wanted to understand the individuals on whom more conventional studies were based. As he conducted interviews and built relationships with participants, so he came to understand how their activities are driven underground but are not so seedy or dangerous as they first appear to an outsider.

INTRODUCTIONS AND RECRUITMENT

A good way to begin what we might call recruitment is to provide participants with a brief explanation of the research and the reasons why it might be important. This could be written down or spoken, or both. I like to offer participants a written explanation that they can take home with them and read at their leisure. When this is nicely presented on headed paper, people realise they are taking part in something the researcher, at least, feels is worthwhile. It is important to present this explanation in a way the participants can understand; that is, in language they are familiar with. In any attempt to emphasise the value and relevance of the research, we should avoid intimidating the very people we hope will participate in it. When Daniel Murphy (1986) did his ethnography of shoplifting, he used to first write to shop owners, personnel, or police to ask for a meeting at which the research could be discussed. I have found this approach very useful in my own work, and I tend to follow up my

access

7

letters with a phone call asking if the letter arrived safely. Murphy also suggests ethnographers construct some sort of *cover story* for their work. This is not so much meant for deceit as an attempt to describe loosely, and in a language participants can relate to, a research proposal that may be quite complex or that may actually evolve in practice. Murphy also says he used a 'rhetoric of science' to gain authority for his work, especially when presenting it to officials. I think this might be a useful technique for some participants but I would not want to take it so far as to be intimidating, because of the ethical implications (**ethics**) as well as the likely impact on the quality of relationships we can then build.

In some approaches to ethnography, such as action research, participants can be assured that the work will have direct impact, but not everyone needs or can be given such firm assurances. Murphy used to take the opportunity to point out that at least his research can do no harm and that it was possible, at some stage, it might even do some good! Similarly, William Foote Whyte (1993: 293) told his key informant that the best he could hope for was that when he wrote up his research someone might read it and act on it later. That, it seems, was good enough for Doc, who replied, 'I think you can change things that way. Mostly that is the way things are changed, by writing about them.'

BARRIERS TO ACCESS

It is important to remember that the researcher's own personal attributes – gender, age, religion, ethnicity – may affect access. Bernadette Barton (2007) found it very difficult as a woman alone to gain access to clubs for her study of exotic dancers. One bouncer told her: 'we don't want any hookers here'. Becoming part of a group, participating in their daily activities, and attempting to blend into the background are not easy when the one thing that sets the group apart from other groups is skin colour or sex. This is not to say one has to be the same as the research participants. Difference can be a resource in ethnographic research, enabling the researcher to ask naïve questions that an insider (**insider ethnographies**) would never consider. The point is only that there will always be some places and groups to which some people will never gain access. However, this need not mean abandoning one's research interests. Stephen Moore (2000), for example, employed younger, what he calls 'cool' researchers, to do the fieldwork for his ethnographic study with youths who 'hang around' street corners, because he did not imagine he would gain access to rural gang life himself.

Sometimes a setting or topic can be very sensitive and access has to be negotiated carefully. It is always important to demonstrate empathy and understanding with the group, and to understand that occasionally access will not be permitted for reasons of privacy. Elite or powerful groups can be particularly difficult to access because they have the power and knowledge to obstruct access in subtle ways, and perhaps have more reason than others not to want to be exposed.

BEING COVERT OR OVERT

One decision that has to be made is the extent to which one will remain covert. Overt research means openly explaining the research to the participants, its purpose, who it is for, and what will happen to the findings. It means being open. **Covert** research is undercover, conducted without the participants' knowledge or without full awareness of the researcher's intentions. Patricia Adler's (1985) research in a drug dealing community involved juggling covert and overt roles; a balancing act that was both difficult and dangerous.

Many ethnographers believe that for ethical reasons no one should do covert research unless it can be completely justified. Others ask that we consider carefully whom we protect when we always protect anonymity and confidentiality. How else can covert and illegal activities be researched other than through covert means (see Scheper-Hughes, 2004)? However, **participant observation** is very often undertaken in such a way that we are open about our research plans (open at the point of gaining access) but hope the participants will forget we are studying them and will 'act naturally'.

Gaining access, then, will usually involve explaining about the research overtly and then settling in to a semi-overt role, where participants know what we are doing but do not always have it in the forefront of their minds. Alternatively, some ethnographers begin in a covert manner, gathering information in a range of settings in a passive way, then becoming overt later on in the study as they explain their research to participants from whom they need a longer time commitment or some more in-depth involvement (see Estroff, 1981).

CHOOSING A ROLE

It is important to carefully consider, prior to accessing the group, what role the researcher will take. This can affect how people see us and therefore how they act towards us, and it may also affect whom we subsequently gain access to. When doing research in a school, for example, a potential role might be as a support teacher, with daily access to the classroom, to teachers and pupils, to the playground and staffroom. However, once the role of teacher is established, informal access to student groups may prove problematic. Sometimes a role is chosen by gatekeepers (**key informants and gatekeepers**), but it is possible to learn from this experience about the culture and unwritten codes and rules of the group we are studying.

Implicit attitudes, about gender and age for example, are often revealed when one is assigned to a role. Jason Ditton (1977), whose research began in a bakery, changed his role during his research in order to improve access. He became a salesman in order to ask more questions and delve more deeply. Sue Estroff (1981) wanted to understand the way of life of psychiatric outpatients both inside and outside of institutional settings. She began by spending time in the clinical setting, joining in therapy sessions and recreational activities in the hospital, where access was granted by the clinic staff not the patients. As they got to know her better, she gradually gained overt access to the patients as they lived their lives out of the clinic. Gaining access for her involved thinking very carefully about how she would be seen by the patients, and considering not only her dress but also her manner of speech, posture, and general presentation.

People often find it much easier to relate to someone in terms of a role they understand and which is accepted in the setting. This role may be that of ethnographer, or it may be as mother, daughter, or stranger. It may well change during fieldwork or as one moves through different settings within the overall place or organisation. Lee Monaghan (2002) studied bouncers, or door security staff, in Britain's night-time economy. As a body-builder in a previous life and study, he adapted quite easily and comfortably to the role of bouncer, to the extent that his participants, though they knew full well he was doing academic research, found it easier to relate to him as a bouncer than an academic.

PRESENTATION OF SELF

An ethnographer may also have to think about how to present his or her ideas and opinions on given topics, as this will affect the quality of access to others. This leads to worries about deception, that are discussed more under **ethics**. But always there is some control or thought about our presentation of self. The best approach is to appear both naïve and knowledgeable.

Knowing too much can foreclose in-depth conversations; knowing too little can appear rude and disinterested. In Monaghan's participant observation as night-club and pub doorman, he says that his physical capital and informal local networks were far more important and relevant than formal qualifications, signed contracts, and pre-arranged interviews. In other words, the fact that he was male, young and muscular turned out to be the best resource for 'getting in and getting on with the study' (2002: 409). These attributes could just as easily be a hindrance in other settings.

It is always important to consider the impact of your own attributes. When Joan Gross (2001) set out to undertake an ethnographic study of Walloon Puppet theatres (in Belgium), she discovered that it was not just her age, gender, and perceived class background that influenced people's relations towards her, but also the historical and political relations between her country and theirs. In other words, as the daughter of an American soldier, people related to her in terms of the nation she represented and her family background rather than simply her own personal attributes.

As discussed briefly above, there are some places that will never be accessed. An ethnographer who is determined to access difficult places should be sure whose interest it is in. It is not necessary to insist on gaining access to a given group or event, when often other approaches or other places would yield similar information. I do not believe an ethnographer should insist on getting access as if it were an inalienable right. The best approach is to consider why anyone should participate and use that to try to persuade them. An ethnographer should check the approach is not biased in anyone's favour and should show due respect. Always remember that, if we are lucky, our participants will tell us about and show us their lives. They are only likely to do this if we appear interested in them and open-minded about their way of life.

GETTING OUT

Finally, it may be worth our while to think a little about how our ethnographic research is completed, or how indeed we get out at the end. This can raise all sorts of interesting issues. In my own research in Spain, going home was a bit like letting the side down. I had shown a lack of commitment to the group by admitting I was going home at the end of my research period. This mistake, if you like, revealed to me the importance of a sense of continuity for migrant groups whose lives were essentially temporary and tentative, their futures uncertain, and their pasts severed

(O'Reilly, 2000). On the other hand, if we don't go home, we run the risk of going 'native', of losing all sense of distance or objectivity, or of forgetting why we went there in the first place. Many ethnographers find they do not want to go home because they have adapted so well and the participants have become their friends. Ditton (1977: 5) humorously calls this 'getting a case of the Pyle's'. He draws on a discussion by someone called Pyle, to explain his own yearning to get back into the field after he left, which was exacerbated by their furious pleas to him to stay on and help them during the summer labour shortage period. The lure of acceptance in the field, the dangers of over-rapport and the lack of objective distance, and the problem of getting out when research is conducted on your own doorstep are discussed under the concepts of **going 'native'** and **insiders**.

See also: *covert; ethics; participant observation; the participant observer oxymoron*

REFERENCES

General

Berg, B. L. (2004) *Qualitative Research Methods for the Social Sciences*, 5th edn. Boston: Pearson.

Rock, P. (2001) 'Symbolic interactionism and ethnography', in P. Atkinson, A. Coffey, S. Delamont, J. Lofland, and L. Lofland (eds) *Handbook of Ethnography*. London: Sage, pp. 26–38.

Thompson, P. (1988) *The Voice of the Past*, 2nd edn. Oxford: Oxford University Press.

Examples

Adler, P. A. (1985) *Wheeling and Dealing: an Ethnography of an Upper-Level Drug Dealing and Smuggling Community*. New York: Columbia University Press.

Barton, B. (2007) 'Managing the toll of stripping: boundary setting among exotic dancers', *Journal of Contemporary Ethnography*, 36(5): 571–96

Desmond, M. (2006) 'Becoming a firefighter', *Ethnography*, 7(4): 387–421.

Ditton, J. (1977) *Part-Time Crime: an Ethnography of Fiddling and Pilferage*. London: Macmillan.

Estroff, S. E. (1981) *Making it Crazy. An Ethnography of Psychiatric Clients in an American Community*. Berkeley, CA, and London: University of California Press.

Gross, J. (2001) *Speaking in Other Voices. An Ethnography of Walloon Puppet Theatres*. Amsterdam/Philadelphia: John Benjamins.

Humphreys, L. (1970) *Tea-Room Trade*. Chicago: Aldine.

Monaghan, L. F. (2002) 'Regulating "unruly" bodies: work tasks, conflict and violence in Britain's night-time economy', *British Journal of Sociology*, 53(3): 403–29.

Moore, S. (2000) 'Research, reality and "hanging around"', *Sociology Review*, 10(3): 8–13.

key concepts in ethnography

Murphy, Daniel J. I. (1986) *Customers and Thieves: an Ethnography of Shoplifting.* Aldershot: Gower.

O'Reilly, K. (2000) *The British on the Costa del Sol.* London: Routledge.

Scheper-Hughes, N. (2004) 'Parts unknown: undercover ethnography of the organs-trafficking underworld', *Ethnography*, 5(1): 29–73.

Scott, J. C. (1985) *Weapons of the Weak: Everyday Forms of Peasant Resistance.* New Haven, CT: Yale University Press.

Whyte, W. F. (1993) *Street Corner Society: the Social Structure of an Italian Slum*, 4th edn. Chicago: University of Chicago Press.

Analysis

> *Ethnographic analysis is not a stage in a linear process but an iterative phase in a spiral where progress is steadily made from data collection to making some sense of it all for others.*

> *Outline: The messy business of making some sense of it all. Analysis as an iterative-inductive, reflexive process. The spiral approach to analysis in which further data are collected as analysis proceeds. The search for insider perspectives and broader patterns, for meaning and process. The role of theory.*

THE MESSY BUSINESS OF MAKING SENSE OF IT ALL

Ethnographic analysis is something of a messy business that ethnographers learn through practice and experience. Largely, it comes down to having an inquisitive mind and imaginative sensibility, as well as a strong desire to explore various aspects of the social world and *make some sense of it all*. Making sense of it all is the stuff of analysis, and involves summarising, sorting, translating, and organising (**coding**). Analysis means moving from a jumble of words and pictures to something less wordy, shorter and more manageable, and easier for an outsider to understand. It involves exploring deeply to see what is there that might not be obvious; standing back to see what patterns emerge; thinking and theorising to draw conclusions that can be generalised in some way or other, and **writing**.

THE REFLEXIVE PROCESS OF ANALYSIS

Broadly speaking, ethnography is about exploring, uncovering, and making explicit the detailed interactive and structural fabric of the social settings that social researchers suspect to be sociologically interesting. This is a reflexive process where we often find ourselves assuming, to begin with, a naïve, almost childlike perspective, as we gather information from everything we encounter to build a stock of detailed knowledge, accounts, events, and so on, as a means of enhancing our own understanding of the setting and presenting this to others.

During fieldwork we participate and observe, we note conversations we have both engaged in and overheard; we record (in writing, on tape, or even in photograph and video, see **fieldnotes**) activities, events, stories, formulae; we collect news articles or anything of interest that tells us more about our topic; and we conduct interviews for subsequent transcription. This is done reflexively (**reflexivity**), with a research puzzle guiding us, and with constant reflection on what we are seeing and hearing. But, at some point we eventually reach a stage where we feel we have collected enough information to say something significant about our findings, and where we feel we have sufficiently explored the various issues that excited our interest.

We then turn our attention to organising and presenting the data in a form that is both accessible to the reader and which provides them with both detailed information and some general observations, usually of a theoretically relevant nature, regarding the significance of what we have uncovered. In ethnographic research this process is rarely as linear as the use of such terms as 'data collection', 'analysis', and 'writing up' suggest. Ethnographic analysis presents us with some distinctive theoretical and practical issues when compared with other approaches, such as survey research.

A SPIRAL APPROACH TO ANALYSIS

In survey research the usual aim is to provide some fairly broad generalisations regarding some clearly defined issues which, in many instances, have been identified in advance of the data collection. In short, researchers often have a theory or hypothesis, a 'hunch', that they wish to test to find out whether their assumptions are supported by evidence. In this type of study, a data set is summarised, reporting how many respondents of certain ages did certain things or had certain attitudes, for example. In this way, a mass of information is summarised to offer some broad generalisations. However, a good deal of survey data is also analysed in greater depth. For example, researchers may look at a number of variables together and see how they correlate (doing multivariate analysis), as a means of providing some insight with respect to the complex interaction of factors that combine to influence social phenomena.

In ethnographic research, in very general terms the process is somewhat similar, given that all social research, to greater or lesser extent, follows the general 'scientific' model of collecting data, analysis, and then presentation suggested above. However, for ethnographers, this straightforward formula is often applied very flexibly in practice. This is because though an initial idea will inform data collection, the collected data will then raise questions about theory, which in turn leads to more data collection, analysis, writing, and the ongoing development of ideas. A fieldworker is able to be much more flexible than a survey researcher. The focus of the research does not have to be predetermined as the questions are designed and set. Different people can be asked different questions depending on the emergent analysis. People, settings, groups, and themes can be included or excluded as the research develops. Unlike in much survey research, the data collection phase of the research is not a discrete phase. Indeed, analysis is so tangled up with every stage of the research process that it is difficult to talk of an analysis phase. Rather than proceeding in a linear fashion, it is far more likely that the ethnographer will progress as in a spiral, moving forward from idea to theory to design to data collection to findings, analysis, and back to theory, but where each two steps forward may involve one or two steps back (**inductive and deductive**). In other words, we analyse and collect data almost simultaneously.

This, to a large extent, is consistent with the specific theoretical and epistemological perspective from which qualitative investigation generally, and ethnographic study specifically, is associated (see **interpretivism**). This type of progressive spiral approach is common in ethnographic work, where the very broad straightforward progression, from initial interest, recording, analysis, and writing up, is constantly interspersed with periods where we turn back on ourselves, retrace our steps, and mix one stage with another (Ezzy, 2002). In one sense we move from the naïve, childlike perspective of the initial exploration to gradually become more like detectives, systematically sifting through very general evidence, looking for clues and reflecting on their significance. The aim is to narrow the scope of our enquiry to

analysis

15

the most significant issues, whilst constantly retracing our steps where something of interest becomes evident and where greater exploration might provide dividends. All of this is consistent with what has been referred to as the *iterative-inductive* approach to ethnographic analysis (O'Reilly, 2005; see Glaser and Strauss, 1967). Gary Shank (2006) has labelled it 'abduction'. See the discussion in **inductive and deductive**.

THE SEARCH FOR MEANING

Many quantitative and, to some extent, survey approaches are informed by a positivist standpoint, where social life is believed to be governed by various structural patterns and even general laws (**positivism**). By contrast, ethnographic research and analysis emerge from the interpretive, phenomenological, and hermeneutic traditions within the social sciences (**interpretivism**). This latter perspective takes greater account of the reflexive and highly variable nature of human existence and seeks to *understand* the motivations, thinking, and ideas that generate the patterned mosaic of social life. In a very general sense, quantitative and survey methodologies tend to focus on reporting, summarising, and analysing *what* people do and say, to identify broad patterns; on the other hand, qualitative and ethnographic research tends to probe more deeply into *why* people act and talk about the things that they do. However, in practice, most social science research mixes elements of both of these approaches and merely leans, to greater or lesser extent, towards either end of the spectrum.

As ethnographic research leans towards the latter, however, the approach to both study and analysis is highly sensitive to the malleable and, often, idiosyncratic nature of social life. For example, the influence of the *phenomenological* perspective is integral to the way in which we gather accounts and seek to uncover the ideas and meanings, the common-sense knowledge (*first-order categories*), that inform the activities of individuals and groups within social settings (Schutz, 1972). A key task of the ethnographer is to make explicit the ways in which people draw upon and deploy this social knowledge, as well as documenting the outcome of ensuing social action in the research setting.

THE SEARCH FOR PATTERNS

However, the ethnographer within the social sciences must be more than merely a biographer or diarist, as another key aim of this type of research is to identify and comprehend some of the recurrent patterns and relationships that emerge from the web of specific events. Thus, we look to identify structured routines and relationships in the hope of identifying a framework that might be relevant to understanding similar settings or which, in some cases, may be broadly generalisable (**generalisation**). As we uncover information and insights with respect to specific occurrences, we seek to identify patterns within them that might increase our understanding of what we are observing, and revise these assumptions in the light of continuing observation and data collection. If we are successful, we find ourselves applying increasingly sophisticated classifications (*second-order categories*) that fit well with what we observe and that provide us with the means to gain deeper insights which, in turn, further advances the sophistication and efficacy of our theoretical framework. This is the essence of what theory is about: rationally and objectively defined models are developed that can be applied to aid our exploration and understanding of the social world. Thus, we move back and forward between applying theory and observation and data collection, and even theorising ourselves, and reflect upon the fit and usefulness of this theoretical framing with respect to what we experience and observe. For some interesting discussions about analysis and theory development see Whyte (1993), Becker et al. (1961), and Fine (2003).

See also: coding; generalisation; grounded theory; writing

REFERENCES

General

Ezzy, D. (2002) *Qualitative Analysis: Practice and Innovation*. London: Routledge.
Glaser, B. G. and Strauss, A. L. (1967) The *Discovery of Grounded Theory: Strategies for Qualitative Research*. Chicago: Aldine de Gruyter.
O'Reilly, K. (2005) *Ethnographic Methods*. London: Routledge.
Schutz, A. (1972) *Phenomenology of the Social World*. London: Heinemann.
Shank, G. (2006) 'Praxical reasoning and the logic of field research', in D. Hobbs and R. Wright (eds) *Handbook of Fieldwork*. London: Sage.

Examples

Becker, H. S., Geer, B., Hughes, E. C. and Strauss, A. (1961) *Boys in White. Student Culture in Medical School*. Chicago: University of Chicago Press.
Fine, G. A. (2003) 'Towards a peopled ethnography: developing theory from group life', *Ethnography*, 4(1): 41–60.
Whyte, W. F. (1993) *Street Corner Society: the Social Structure of an Italian Slum*, 4th edn. Chicago: University of Chicago Press.

analysis

Asking Questions

> *Asking questions, and listening, are central to ethnography and can involve bringing a discussion around to your topic, opportunistic questioning, or simply taking an interest.*

> *Outline: Interviews need not be formal, pre-arranged meetings between two or more people but can simply take the shape of informal, opportunistic questions and answers. Taking time and beginning passively. Direct and indirect questions. Responding to emergent themes and becoming more directed and focused. Factist versus interactionist approaches. Who to talk to.*

BACKGROUND

There may not always be a clear distinction between doing **participant observation** and conducting an interview (**interviews and conversations**). Ethnography not only involves participating and observing, watching and hearing, but also asking questions and listening to the answers. Conversations are a normal part of daily behaviour and talk goes on around us all the time, in a variety of contexts. Ethnographers in search of respondent understandings and interpretations of events and actions will take every opportunity to listen in to ongoing conversations, to slot in relevant questions that address their research questions, or to gradually and subtly bring a conversation around to their topic of interest. Interviews need not be formal, pre-arranged meetings between two or more people but can simply take the shape of informal, opportunistic questions and answers. An ethnographer will find that things they are interested in are discussed in the field all the time and they should take the opportunity to ask people to elaborate and explain, to reflect on what they are doing, or to describe how they feel about it. The ethnographer should not be surprised to find others chipping in, offering their little bit of information or their own opinion. In fact, fieldwork is really one long conversation with people and 'a field' you are fascinated with.

key concepts in ethnography

18

THE IMPORTANCE OF TIME FOR ETHNOGRAPHY

However, one hopes the ethnographer will also know when *not* to ask questions, when *not* to probe or delve, and when to simply listen and observe. It is very important that the researcher always remains sensitive to the context and to the research participants' feelings, as well as being knowledgeable enough about the context to avoid asking questions that appear ignorant. Questioning in ethnography therefore usually begins passively and becomes more active with **time**. It is best to begin slowly and carefully. As we learn more about the setting, we can ask more in-depth and meaningful questions and we will know who to ask them of and how to ask them sensitively. Time allows us to build **rapport** with research participants, and to gain their trust and confidence. Time also allows us to become sensitised to the rules of speech and action and to learn what we can say or ask without upsetting someone or breaking taboos. Barbara Sherman Heyl believes that the duration and frequency of contact along with the quality of the relationship are what make ethnographic research distinctive. Ethnographic interviews therefore take place under conditions where:

> researchers have established respectful, ongoing relationships with their interviewees, including enough rapport for there to be a genuine exchange of views and enough time and openness in the interviews for the interviewees to explore purposefully with the researcher the meanings they place on events in their worlds (Heyl, 2001: 369)

It stands to reason these goals for ethnographic interviewing can be achieved through conversations taking place at different times and places, within **participant observation**, as successfully as through in-depth interviews. Time also enables a deeper understanding of the conversations that are heard and the discussions in which we take part. All conversations are governed by a variety of cultural conventions and expectations which need to be learned to be understood (Kemp and Ellen, 1984). It is not just what people say that is interesting, but how they say it, to whom, when, where, what they don't say, and who they will and will not talk to about what. These are only gleaned through long-term participant observation and by treating fieldwork as a long conversation, rather than simply through direct interviewing.

DIRECT AND INDIRECT QUESTIONING

Ethnographic research tends to become more directed and focused over time, leading from brief questions and interjections, to more in-depth probing and even, sometimes, to fairly structured questionnaires. In the early stages, as the ethnographer settles in, he or she usually wants to merge quietly into the background. Overt interviewing reminds participants of our role as researchers and can alter participant observation relationships. But as the research progresses and ideas are honed, and analyses developed, it is essential to come out of one's shell to ask more pertinent questions. As fieldwork draws to a close, it is common to be quite determined in approach in order to confirm ideas or fill gaps in data.

That said, however, for some groups, an attempt at direct questioning might be completely futile and it may be necessary to glean information in other ways. Nigel Barley (1983) found he had to be very imaginative in dealing with Africans in Ghana who would not answer any question directly, and even considered it rude to be asked. While this is an extreme example, some people do make it very difficult to ask some things and it may be necessary to be very sensitive and indirect. When Sue Estroff began her ethnographic study with psychiatric outpatients, she asked too many questions, talked too much, and generally expected too much in terms of in-depth responses. She says, 'If I did push for precision and reflection, the responses became. "I don't know", or nothing at all related to my questions' (1981: 5). Instead Estroff learned to simply drop into her participants' apartments for a chat from time to time, to take them shopping or for a ride in her car, to visit hospital with them and join them in the café. Her data therefore consist not in interview transcripts but in reconstructed conversations, descriptions of events, and synopses of discussions.

Children, especially, are seldom asked to think about and reflect on their actions, and so indirect techniques are being creatively and imaginatively developed in this field. See, for example, the work by Patricia Henderson (2006) with AIDS orphans in South Africa. On discovering that children in KwaZulu-Natal are taught to demonstrate respect for elders by *not* initiating conversations or responding in depth to questions, she devised a series of theatre games to use in the classroom settings in which ethnographic interviewing took place. By introducing fun, unpredictability and a sense of immediate accomplishment into their daily lives, children thus became gradually more relaxed and expressive. Eventually, during a week-long trip, they produced a drama which used bodily performance to 'talk about' their life experiences.

ASKING QUESTIONS RELEVANT TO EMERGENT THEMES

An iterative-inductive ethnography (O'Reilly, 2005) will begin questioning in a passive and indirect way not only in order to leave time to become sensitised to the group but also because themes are emergent rather than forced onto the setting. Jim Thomas (1993: 37), for example, began his study of prison culture by 'simply asking prisoners, staff, and administrators in casual conversations what they perceived to be the most difficult part of their prison experience'. As the themes of control and resistance emerged, Thomas began more direct questioning around the topic of prisoner adaptation.

FACTIST AND INTERACTIONIST APPROACHES

Interviews combined with participant observation can result in being told different things at different times. Interviews often yield superficial answers or the formal line, or what people *say* they do or *should* do in certain circumstances rather than what they actually do. This is not problematic if your epistemological position is that society's rules and individual actions do not always coincide. You are thus learning about the society's structure – the rules, institutions, formal organisation, the norms, customs and myths people live by – and, through participant observation, how these rules and norms are interpreted in practice. On the other hand, in-depth interviews will lead to more ambiguous data, and to the private realm of ideas, thoughts, opinions and feelings, to what people actual do/did in given circumstances and how they felt about it.

It is useful to distinguish factist and interactionist approaches (Alasuutari, 1995). A *factist* approach sees interview data as yielding the one truth, which can only be obtained by sitting and talking to someone in depth, getting at what they really think. Many researchers treat interview data as the 'real' data and other data as marginal or problematic. An *interactionist* perspective, on the other hand, depends on a combination of methods and sees confessional-type statements as one type of discourse among many, and questions whether there is really one true way/thing that a person really thinks. These ethnographers therefore ask questions, have in-depth interviews and conversations, conduct **focus groups and group discussions**, and use all forms of data.

WHO TO TALK TO?

Sometimes it is difficult to decide who to talk to, ask questions of, or interview. Should the whole thing be opportunistic or should people be sought out for their thoughts and opinions? In ethnographic research, **sampling** of respondents or participants is ongoing, iterative, theoretically informed, and practically limited. It is important to try to include in fieldwork conversations those who are in some ways representative of the group and of its important divisions and differences, but also those who do not seem to fit any conceptualisation or categorisation we might develop. But rather than begin by delimiting the approach, I believe we should try to talk with anyone and everyone, of all types and personalities, of all roles, in all settings possible. The cleaner may have more insights than the doctor, and the doctor's husband or wife may be even more interesting. It is also important to talk (and listen) to those who are a little less forthcoming or are shy or hidden, rather than just the most vociferous and inquisitive. These quieter people may have some very important things to say that could easily be missed. **Key informants** are therefore useful in that they are normally happy to help and full of information and advice. However, **gatekeepers** are also useful in as much as they may enable us to contact the hidden groups and individuals.

See also: *focus groups and group discussions; interviews and conversations; participant observation*

REFERENCES

General

Alasuutari, P. (1995) *Researching Culture. Qualitative Method and Cultural Studies.* London: Sage.

Kemp, J. H. and Ellen, R. (1984) 'Informal interviewing', in R. Ellen (ed.) *Ethnographic Research. A Guide to General Conduct.* London: Academic Press, pp. 229–36.

O'Reilly, K. (2005) *Ethnographic Methods.* London: Routledge.

Thomas, J. (1993) *Doing Critical Ethnography. Qualitative Research Methods Series*, 26. London: Sage.

key concepts in ethnography

Examples

Barley, N. (1983) *The Innocent Anthropologist. Notes from a Mud Hut*. London: Penguin.

Estroff, S. E. (1981) *Making It Crazy. An Ethnography of Psychiatric Clients in an American Community*. Berkeley, CA and London: University of California Press.

Henderson, P. C. (2006) 'South African AIDS orphans: examining assumptions around vulnerability from the perspective of rural children and youth', *Childhood*, 13(3): 303–27.

Heyl, B. S. (2001) 'Ethnographic interviewing', in P. Atkinson, A. Coffey, S. Delamont, J. Lofland and L. Lofland, (eds) *Handbook of Ethnography*. London: Sage, pp. 369–83.

Case Study

A case study investigates a few cases, or often just one case, in considerable depth. In ethnography, case studies are used in various ways to illuminate themes or draw inferences.

Outline: Comparing case studies and ethnographies. Defining a case study. Case studies and generalisation. Cases that are intrinsically interesting. Instrumental case studies and theoretical inference. Collective and comparative case studies and their role in generalisation. The role of in-depth case analysis in ethnographic analysis and writing.

CASE STUDIES AND ETHNOGRAPHIES

I have included this concept because of the tendency to equate 'case study' and ethnography. Ethnographies are often, at least to some extent, studies of a given case. However, a case study is not necessarily ethnographic. A key difference between them is that *ethnography is defined by its methodology*, whereas a case study can be highly quantitative or statistical and use no ethnographic methods at all. As Robert Stake (2003:134) has argued: 'Case study is not a methodological choice but a choice of what is to be studied'. Ethnography, on the other hand, always implies a methodology and set of methods. But, more than that, a case study is a study that sees its focus as representing, or being a case of, something else. Thus the edited volume on *Case Study Method* (Gomm et al., 2000), brings together a range of articles under the two main themes of generalising and the role of theory. I recommend readers consult it especially for its fully annotated bibliography, which is particularly useful as a starting point for comparing Robert Yin's (2002) more scientific approach to case studies, with Robert Stake's constructivist approach where he calls for 'naturalistic generalisation', and then with Clifford Geertz's (1973) interpretive analysis and thick description.

The meaning of 'case study' overlaps with ethnography, participant observation, fieldwork, and even qualitative research broadly conceived, so that the distinction is complicated. Many of what are now considered classical *case* studies are indeed ethnographies, such as Thomas and Znaniecki's *The Polish Peasant* (1927), and other famous Chicago studies (**Chicago School**). A case study can be of a person, a group, an event, an institution, or even a process. It is used in all sorts of fields such as psychology, social work, and legal and detective work. Roger Gomm and colleagues (2000) define 'case study' in the following way (to paraphrase): usually 'case study' refers to research that investigates a few cases, or often just one case, in considerable depth. Case study researchers construct cases out of naturally occurring social situations, unlike the manipulation of variables that occurs in experimental research. And case study research frequently implies the collection of unstructured data, and the qualitative analysis of those data.

CASE STUDIES AND GENERALISATION

Several authors have attempted to compare case studies in terms of what they are attempting to achieve or what the purpose of the case selection is. I would argue that the language or terminology of 'case' implies that the thing being selected is in some ways seen as a case or instance of something else, broader or more general. So, when Gary Alan Fine (2004) describes his study of self-taught artists as an ethnographic case study of an embedded market, he is implying that we can learn something more general from this small number of individual stories and their relationship to the world of art. However, Stake (2003) has argued that some researchers do not aim to generalise from their case at all. He says that some people study a given case simply because it is intrinsically interesting. I still suspect it is considered interesting because it illuminates broader themes, or at least themes with which a reader can identify, but Stake distinguishes such intrinsic case studies (which are studied for their own intrinsic interest) from instrumental and collective cases (which are studied in order to build knowledge or broader processes). Of course, most studies do not fit neatly into such typologies. The types of case study are merely a way of thinking about what one is doing when one selects a case to research.

Intrinsic case studies

In what Stake calls the *intrinsic case study*, no attempt is made to generalise or to build theories or relevance beyond the case. The research is undertaken because of an intrinsic interest in the given group, institution, organisation, class, or whatever. As Roger Gomm and colleagues (2000: 99) point out, there are some rare cases that are worth studying in their own right: 'a study of decision making procedures in the Cabinet Office of the British government would surely have sufficient intrinsic relevance, obviating any need to try to generalize the findings to other governments.' But this is a fairly unusual example, and as they say, anonymising immediately wipes out any intrinsic benefits in most cases. However, more often cases are chosen expressly so that **generalisation** or wider inferences can be made, as in what Stake calls instrumental and collective case studies.

Instrumental case studies

A case study is instrumental when the actual case (organisation, class, individual, or event) is of secondary importance to the issue for which it is providing an example or enabling a generalisation. In other words, the ethnographer begins with something they are interested in for example, religion, social class, or gender) and selects a case to focus on because of what areas of the topic the case will illuminate. In ethnography, a case (or topic, field, or group) is often selected for its intrinsic interest in the first place but in the writing-up the study is often linked to broader social processes. Hence we end up with titles of monographs such as: *Transnational Lives. Expatriates in Indonesia* (Fechter, 2007) or of papers such as 'The international production of authoritative knowledge: the case of drought-stricken West Africa' (Moore, 2001). In these works, ethnographic accounts have been used to make arguments about processes beyond the given and closely studied situation.

John Brewer (2000) argues that both case studies and ethnographies share the same problem of small sample size and ability to extrapolate from the case, or make generalisations. Nevertheless, he says generalisations are possible using theoretical inference. We do this by employing concepts that explain complex phenomena and building theoretical explanations that link concepts together. These are applied to the specific case and then to other cases, as theoretical resources that might enable the deeper understanding of broader, or universal, themes. This involves the collection or analysis of further cases.

Collective and comparative case studies

When an ethnographer is interested in a given issue to the extent she compares several cases, then Stake refers to this as a *collective case study*. This is more common in quantitative than qualitative research, but **multi-sited ethnographies** could sometimes be seen as a form of collective case study. John Brewer, alternatively, describes comparative studies. Although ethnography is so involved and time-consuming that it is unusual to cover several cases or do comparative analysis, nevertheless, cases can be sampled (**sampling**), he argues, with comparison in mind. Here cases can be fieldwork sites, individuals and situations within the field, or even events. Brewer gives the example of his own research with the Royal Ulster Constabulary (1991). Here the actual design of the study followed the pattern of previous ethnographies of routine policing, so that the new study became part of a tradition, enabling not only the comparison of cases but the accumulation of a (longitudinal and historical) body of research in a given field.

Another approach is to sample cases that can be compared within one field or study, and even within one gender. Brewer gives the example of Paul Willis's (1977) *Learning to Labour*, which explores the processes of cultural and class reproduction which lead working-class kids to end up in working-class jobs. Willis conducted all his research in Birmingham, with male respondents, but added a comparative dimension to his study by including five additional groups to his non-conformist 'lads'. These included conformist children from the same and from a 'rougher' school, non-conformists from a single-sex grammar school, and a group similar to the lads from a different part of the district. Unfortunately, these groups receive scant attention in the published text.

key concepts in ethnography

CASE ANALYSIS

One of the most exciting and constructive uses of ethnography's ability to generate such abundant data is to use a given case to illuminate the analysis. Here a particular event or person can be focused on in detail, giving a comprehensive description or providing what Brewer calls an interesting vignette (or in-depth story) illuminating various themes central to the analysis. Clifford Shaw's (1966) autobiographical study of Stanley, the mugger, is a fine example that should be read in conjunction with other works by Shaw and Chicago sociologists of deviance (**Chicago School**). Another is Geertz's (1973) elaborate depiction of a Balinese cockfight, which not only illustrates his thick description but also his theoretical interpretation that the cockfight is a dramatic playing-out of status concerns in Bali; a space where mobility can appear to take place while in fact nothing really happens. Here, cases are taken from the ethnography and used as focal points or for discussion and elaboration, rather than being something that was initially selected as a case. For further discussion of the role of such key events see the discussion in **key informants**.

Overall, the language of 'case' should be used carefully, thoughtfully and intentionally within ethnography. I cannot see why an intrinsically interesting study should be called a case at all. For me, a 'case' is always a case of something and so should be used with that meaning.

See also: access; generalisation; sampling

REFERENCES
General

Brewer, J. (2000) *Ethnography*. Buckingham: Open University Press.
Geertz, C. (1973) *The Interpretation of Cultures*. New York: Fontana.
Gomm, R., Hammersley, M. and Foster, P. (eds) (2000) *Case Study Method: Key Issues, Key Texts*. London Sage.
Stake, R. E. (2003) 'Case studies' in N. K. Denzin and Y. S. Lincoln (eds) *Strategies of Qualitative Inquiry*. Thousand Oaks, CA, and London: Sage, pp. 134–64.
Yin, R. K. (2002) *Case Study Research: Design and Methods*: 005 (Applied Social Research Methods), 3rd edn. London: Sage.

Examples

Brewer, J. D. (1991) *Inside the RUC: Routine Policing in a Divided Society*. Oxford: Clarendon Press.

Fechter, A. M. (2007) *Transnational Lives. Expatriates in Indonesia*. Hampshire: Ashgate.

Fine, G. A. (2004) *Everyday Genius. Self-Taught Art and the Culture of Authenticity*. London and Chicago: University of Chicago Press.

Moore, S. F. (2001) 'The international production of authoritative knowledge: the case of drought-stricken West Africa', *Ethnography*, 2(2): 161–89

Shaw, Clifford (1966 [1930]) *The Jack Roller. A Delinquent Boy's Own Story*. Chicago: University of Chicago Press.

Thomas, W. I. and Znaniecki, F. (1927) *The Polish Peasant in Europe and America*. New York: Dover.

Willis, P. E. (1977) *Learning to Labour. How Working Class Kids Get Working Class Jobs*. Farnborough: Saxon House.

Chicago School

The Chicago School of sociology originated from the University of Chicago during the first half of the twentieth century and is famous for its ethnographic heritage.

Outline: Background and history of the Chicago School of sociology. The city as a natural laboratory. The influence of formalism, pragmatism, and social ecology on the development of an empirical methodology: the intimate study of everyday life. The Chicago heritage, and some Chicago ethnographies and life stories.

BACKGROUND

Sociology at the University of Chicago has a long and distinguished history. The top-rated journal, the *American Journal of Sociology*, was founded in Chicago in 1895, and in 1905 the department established the American Sociology Society (later the American Sociological Association). However, the Chicago School of Sociology was arguably most influential between the 1890s and 1940s, towering at this time over the intellectual and professional landscape of sociology and responsible for training more than half of the world's sociologists (Deegan, 2001). A key explanation for the School's particular eminence is a combination of external factors and the influence of some key figures in the field of social science. At the turn of the twentieth century Chicago was going through a period of rapid social change, with mass immigration, huge population growth, and a vast growth and development of urban areas, attended by the now-predictable social problems of increased crime rates, poverty, and social inequality. Social researchers influenced by pragmatist and formalist philosophies of those such as John Dewey and Georg Simmel, and the developing interactionism of George Herbert Mead, began to see their city as a sort of natural laboratory in which social life could be studied first-hand.

The first sociologist at Chicago to hold a Chair in Sociology was Robert Park. Park began his career as a newspaper reporter, but turned towards sociology as a means to address his interest in social reform; to look for ways not only to witness but also to understand living societies. In direct contrast to some other North American sociologists who tended towards abstractions and theorising, Park advocated direct, empirical, first-hand study and famously told his students to:

> Go and sit in the lounges of the luxury hotels and on the doorsteps of the flophouses; sit on the Gold Coast settees and on the slum shakedowns; sit in the Orchestra Hall and in the Star and Garter Burlesk. In short, gentlemen, go get the seat of your pants dirty in real research. (Park, cited in Bulmer, 1984: 97)

FORMALISM

Robert Park had previously worked in Europe and had been very impressed by the work of Georg Simmel, even returning to the US and translating some of Simmel's work in the *American Journal of Sociology*. He was particularly impressed by Simmel's formalism. Formalism looks at how interaction between humans seems to take on certain overarching forms. These forms of life are distinct from their content and are the patterned result of the interaction between individuals and society. In other words, what makes up social life can be variable but how it takes form in actions tends to be universal.

Social life contains individual drives, interests, purposes, inclinations, and psychic states around which individuals come together in interactions that take on certain forms (Ritzer, 2000). Simmel wanted to overcome both methodological individualism (which emphasises the primacy of the individual or actor) and what he termed sociologism (which emphasises the social or structure). For Simmel, neither society nor the individual is thinkable without the other. Individuals engage with one another and thereby constitute the social. Society is not just the sum total of individual acts, but refers to individuals interconnected through social interaction. This approach demands a research methodology that enables access to social life as it is lived and experienced, such as ethnography and biography.

PRAGMATISM

A further key influence on the Chicago School was the philosophy of pragmatism that emerged in the US in the 1870s. Pragmatism suggests that social life contains a plurality of shifting realities, grounded in concrete experience, and thus rejects the search for fundamental and absolute truths. It says the truth of a statement or belief is to be found in its consequences or use value. 'Pragma' means action, and is where the terms 'practice' and 'practical' come from. So pragmatism asks if a theory is practical.

William James, a psychologist and theorist of religion who has been associated with the term pragmatism, argued that it is only possible to establish if an idea or statement is right by first asking what impact it being right would actually make in someone's life, and how different that would be if the idea/assumption were wrong. In other words, all theoretical claims should be able to be verified in practice. Again, this implied a grounded, practical methodology. John Dewey is another key pragmatist. He believed that the mind is a set of processes, not a structure. Individuals thus define things in the world in terms of their use for them, determine their action based on what they understand about things, imagine the consequences of various forms of action, and select the optimal mode of conduct. A research methodology thus involves understanding how people make sense of their world (define the situations they are in) and act accordingly.

SOCIAL ECOLOGY

The Chicago School often drew on ecology and applied it to the urban setting. Ideas therefore more commonly applied in biology were used to explain the distribution of certain groups throughout the city. Groups that occupy 'natural areas' (which are homogeneous within themselves, in class or race or cultural terms, but different to the next group) compete with each other for space in a city, just as organisms in a pond compete for space. A new group moves in (or emerges), and competes for space with the other groups; some emerge as dominant and push out the weaker organisms or groups. Competitive pressure thus leads to relocation of groups to new areas. Robert Park used the term 'natural area' for any segregated racial or cultural group and the local zones they inhabited, believing that each zone has its own culture and form of life that distinguished it from the zone next door. Several of Park's students thus conducted ethnographic work in these zones, or natural areas, mapping the social life of the city and rendering it as a sort of mosaic of cultures. *The Gold Coast and The Slum* (Zorbaugh, 1929), for example, were clearly demarcated city zones with their own lifestyles and cultures, yet physically next to each other.

Park also saw cities as naturally merging into assimilation. Park said cities would eventually iron out differences and diversity through processes of social change. Race, for example, would eventually become less meaningful as differences merged into a melting pot of cultures and traditions. However, on the way, differences would be apparent. Other Chicago ethnographers emphasised the differences and people who crossed groups, for example the 'mulatto', or person of mixed race, who Park believed helped societies move towards homogeneity and mutual understanding. Park, of course, had his supporters and his challengers.

CHICAGO ETHNOGRAPHIES

The Chicago School has left sociology with a rich heritage which includes: a focus in research on the concrete experience of human interaction; the first-hand, intimate study of daily life (often of lower-status groups); a series of rich ethnographic studies of city life; urban sociology; and symbolic interactionism. The Chicago sociologists used a combination of methods including statistical data, mapping, diaries, case analysis, life histories, secondary analysis of documents, and even their own autobiography. But overwhelmingly these researchers studied face-to-face interaction in everyday settings, and produced descriptive narratives of social worlds. The ethnographers 'often lived in the settings studied, walked the streets, collected qualitative and quantitative data, worked for local agencies, and had autobiographical experience emerging from these locales or ones like them' (Deegan, 2001: 20).

A swathe of ethnographies (though they were not identified as such by name) were produced between 1917 and 1942, often conducted by students of Robert Park and his colleague Ernest Burgess and clearly influenced by the ideas of formalism, pragmatism, symbolic interactionism, and urban ecology (Bulmer, 1984). The Chicago School heritage includes a number of classical studies, including case studies on geographical areas (such as Zorbaugh, *The Gold Coast and The Slum*, 1929), on organisations and institutions (such as Cressey, *The Taxi-Dance Hall*, 1932), and even on individuals and small groups (such as Anderson, *The Hobo*, 1923, and Shaw, *The Jack Roller*, 1930). Below, I recount a little about two of my own favourites in order to illustrate Chicago ethnography.

The Polish Peasant in Europe and America (Thomas and Znaniecki, 1927)

Between 1899 and 1910 Poles accounted for a quarter of all migrants to the US, and Chicago could be described as the third largest Polish city after Warsaw and Lodz. *The Polish Peasant* is the result of eight years of work in both continents amounting to 2,200 pages over five volumes. The researchers collected and analysed letters (one volume presents 764), life histories (one volume is Wladek's story), newspaper archives, documents from migration and other social agencies, and third-person accounts from courts and agencies. But essentially it was, like many studies from the Chicago School, a microscopic study of daily life. Thomas is famous for having said 'If men define situations as real, they are real in their consequences.' That is to say, it is important to realise that what people think affects what they do. The book thus deals with migration but also wider social issues: What happens to community and family in periods of social change? Which social forms can successfully enable individualism? Martin Bulmer (1984) calls it a landmark study that moved sociology away from abstract theory and library research and towards the study of the real world, and Ken Plummer (2001) considers it a classic that has shamefully fallen into obscurity.

The Jack Roller: A Delinquent Boy's Own Story (Shaw,1930)

This is the story of Stanley, a mugger, in his own words (edited by Shaw). It is one of several life stories by Shaw, which he undertook as part of a wider study of delinquency that also drew on fieldwork, case studies, court records, and statistics. Shaw and Stanley became very close friends, and the story of Stanley is based on at least eight years of interaction between them. But this is not just a story, or even an autobiography. Collected and edited by a sociologist, with a clear purpose in mind, *The Jack Roller* illuminates a range of theories such as the power of stigma and labelling theory, and theories around learning crime. Its value thus stands in its relation to Shaw's other work and to work by other Chicago sociologists. Nevertheless, the rich depiction of Stanley's experiences, influences, and feelings, raises issues of continued relevance, and some we still have to address today.

See also: *case studies; covert; insider ethnographies; interpretivism; interviews and conversations; participant observation*

REFERENCES

General

Bulmer, M. (1984) *The Chicago School of Sociology*. Chicago: University of Chicago Press.
Deegan, M. J. (2001) 'The Chicago School of ethnography', in P. Atkinson, A. Coffey, S. Delamont, J. Lofland and L. Lofland (eds) *Handbook of Ethnography*. London: Sage, pp. 11–25.
Plummer, K. (2001) *Documents of Life 2*. London: Sage.
Ritzer, G. (2000) *Sociological Theory*, 5th edn. New York: McGraw-Hill.

Examples

Anderson, N. (1961 [1923]) *The Hobo*. Chicago: University of Chicago Press.
Cressey, P. G. (1969 [1932]) *The Taxi-Dance Hall. A Sociological Study in Commercialised Recreation and City Life*. Montclair, NJ: Patterson Smith.
Shaw, Clifford (1966 [1930]) *The Jack Roller. A Delinquent Boy's Own Story*. Chicago: University of Chicago Press.
Thomas, W. I. and Znaniecki, F. (1927) *The Polish Peasant in Europe and America*. New York: Dover.
Zorbaugh, H. W. (1976 [1929]) *The Gold Coast and the Slum. A Sociological Study of Chicago's Near North Side*. Chicago: University of Chicago Press.

Coding

> *Coding is a euphemism for the sorting and labelling which is part of the process of analysis.*

> *Outline: Coding as part of the ongoing process of interpretive analysis. First steps, close exploration of data, and initial line by line coding. Memo-writing as initial stages of writing up. Focused coding and focused memos. Keeping good records. How to find some examples of coding in practice.*

THE PURPOSE OF CODING

Coding is analysis. To review a set of field notes, transcribed or synthesized, and to dissect them meaningfully, while keeping the relations between the parts intact, is the stuff of analysis. (Miles and Huberman,1994: 56)

Coding is a euphemism for the sorting and labelling which is part of the process of **analysis**. It involves close exploration of collected data and assigning it codes, which may be names, categories, concepts, theoretical ideas or classes. It also involves writing memos or thoughts and ideas, associated with given codes, elaborating and linking codes, and thinking about what they mean in the context of a broader argument or story. It is the first step in analysis. In ethnographic analysis the ethnographer will normally have started to make some sense of it all as she went along. She will have thought about the research questions, decided who to ask what questions, and where to do the next piece of participant observation or interview, will have started to pull together disparate threads and pursued theoretically informed leads in the pursuit of an answer to the initial puzzle. By the time she reaches the analysis phase, she should have some idea of what it is she wants to convey, what story will be told, what pictures painted, and for which audiences.

Nevertheless, there comes a time when something has to be done with all the data collected, and most ethnographers find this over-whelming and daunting. One of the first stages of analysis involves moving from a chronological order to another kind of order. **Fieldnotes**, interview transcripts, and other kinds of data have been collected chronologically, as research progressed, but it is unlikely that they will be presented in this way. Analysis therefore involves some kind of sorting and sorted sections need coding or labelling. Data are coded into categories that suit the ethnographer's requirements, and these can be thematic or descriptive or both. How this is achieved involves a creative, reflexive (**reflexivity**) and interpretive (**interpretivism**) interaction between the researcher, the data, the literature, theoretical ideas that framed the research as well as those that emerge from close analysis of the data, and the researcher's feelings, emotions, experiences, and memory. There is no formula for coding ethnographic data (although, increasingly, researchers are trying to develop prescriptive techniques such as the Framework Approach described by Ritchie, et al. 2003).

It is crucial to consider the *purpose* of coding. It is not so that the data can be minutely explored in search of instances of phenomena; it does not amount to counting occurrences or utterances. Data were collected by someone who decided what to write down and when, how often to note something, and when to ignore it. Fieldnotes are not direct records of events and interview transcripts are not all there was to say on a subject. Something that happened numerous times may never have been recorded, while something else that happened a few times was written about at length. This does not make the latter more important. Using a computer to count how many words are said on a certain topic or how many times something happened will simply count those things the ethnographer thought relevant to note or to code into categories as the data were sorted. Coding is not content analysis.

READING

On the other hand, when coding, the ethnographer examines the data minutely, sometimes word by word and line by line, and in the process all sorts of patterns emerge. We might notice, for example, that every time one topic is discussed the subject gets subtly changed by the respondent; or that each time two people meet, they use one of a possible range of greetings that may reveal something about

coding

their relationship. This might only come out with close examination of transcripts and fieldnotes. As Ian Dey (1993) suggests, we seek patterns in data like putting together building blocks: moving, aligning, re-aligning, and building until patterns emerge that make some sense.

The first step then is to closely explore, wade in, minutely examine, and ask questions about the data. It will be useful to go back to the initial research question and remember what that was and how it developed as research progressed. Robert Emerson and colleagues (1995) recommend that this close analysis be undertaken line by line, at least initially and on a range of data, until it seems nothing new is emerging. It is important, also, that the data are viewed at this stage as a whole, so that the ethnographer can begin to make links across categories, between events, and among individuals. However, it should also be remembered that certain things will never have been recorded, and that memory remains a powerful research tool. The emotions and experiences that accompany the observation of an event – the smells, the sounds, the background noise, emotions, participants' comments, the background whispers, the misunderstandings that came clear later – none of these may be recorded and yet any or all may prove to be illuminating at this stage of analysis.

OPEN CODING AND OPEN MEMOS

This first examination (whether it occurs in the field or later) will generate any number of ideas and thoughts, flashes of inspiration, questions, doubts, and puzzles. These should be openly coded and then expanded with the use of memos. *Open coding* and writing *open memos* means jotting down labels (in the margins, using a computer, highlighting, or however) and making notes about them. The labels are names or phrases that label phenomena. The memos are notes by and for the ethnographer expanding on these labels: where they came from, what they might mean, what the ethnographer was thinking when she decided to use a given code. Nothing should be chopped up and divorced from its context. In other words, paragraphs or events should be assigned to a certain category without removing them from the rest of the fieldnotes, interview transcripts and data that were collected simultaneously. Most **computer software** programs allow this, but it can also be achieved by hand using multiple photocopies or coloured pens.

Open coding is essentially inductive (**inductive and deductive**), which means that the ethnographer is open to surprises, to discovering new ideas or fresh insights, which may even challenge the initial research focus, or take the ethnographer in new directions. It may yield expected and unexpected analytic categories. However, it is not naïvely inductive, but iterative-inductive. That is to say, what codes emerge will depend to some extent on the ethnographer's research interests, reading, and theoretical/epistemological framework. Essentially we are interpreting the data, relating them to wider frameworks and broader processes (Ezzy, 2002). Open coding and memo-writing involve some level of **generalisation** or thinking out of the specific instance to a more general theme or concepts, such as 'making friends' or 'hiding emotions'. Memos are the opportunity to work out ideas in more depth. It is where the ethnographer begins to move from data and labels and link to other ideas, theories, memory, and other data. Since the process of open coding can be overwhelming at times, generating unlimited, apparently unrelated themes, Emerson et al. (1995) advise beginning with systematic open coding on some of the data, and then moving on to more focused coding, before coming back to further phases of open coding for brief periods on new sections of the data. This ensures a balance between inductive and deductive theorising and is similar to the techniques described by **grounded theory**.

FOCUSED CODING AND FOCUSED MEMOS

The ethnographer rarely writes up everything that emerges from the data, but determines themes to work up into chapters or papers. For this reason, the same data can be coded very differently by different people and for different purposes. Open coding leads to *focused coding* and *focused memos* where the same ideas, categories, and/or insights are explored in more depth and links made between them, with a specific analytical argument (or story or picture) increasingly in mind. Themes will emerge that the ethnographer will want to write about in more depth and this will lead to returning to the data and re-coding in the light of these more focused themes. Focused memos (or what Emerson et al., 1995, term 'integrative memos') really begin to elaborate ideas and focus themes, making links between disparate codes and sets of ideas. Gradually, analysis leads to reduced sets of codes and memos and longer written pieces, first as an aid to analysis and, eventually, to present to an audience.

DATA COLLECTION FOR CODING

Given the demands of coding as described above, it is essential to keep good records that can be easily put into a computer or sorted and coded by hand. It is more common to regret *not* having collected a certain piece of information or noted down some crucial details than to regret having too much data. Ethnographers who bear the needs of analysis in mind as they conduct research collect data in a directed way, coding and contextualising as they go along. This can include audio and video tape, photographs, texts of myths, events, music, gossip, or whatever else seemed important at the time (see **fieldnotes**).

EXAMPLES OF CODING IN PRACTICE

I found the section on 'processing fieldnotes' in Emerson et al. (1995) invaluable for discussing the concept of coding. Their chapter recognises the debt the authors owe to techniques used by grounded theorists, but argues that grounded theorists tend to attempt to 'discover' theory. Kathy Charmaz (2006), on the other hand, has more recently accepted the more constructive nature of the social world and therefore of social theory, and acknowledges the role of the fieldworker at every stage of the research process. Emerson et al. (1995), Charmaz (2006), and Miles and Huberman (1994) provide some concrete examples of actual coding in practice which readers might find useful. However, in the end it is far better to attempt this process in practice than to read (or write) about it, and it is crucial to consider it in relation to all other stages of the fieldwork process, especially analysis.

See also: analysis; computer software; generalisation; grounded theory: writing

REFERENCES

General

Charmaz, K. (2006) *Constructing Grounded Theory. A Practical Guide through Qualitative Analysis*. London: Sage.

Dey, I. (1993) *Qualitative Data Analysis*. London: Routledge.

Emerson, R. M., Fretz, R. I. and Shaw, L. L. (1995) *Writing Ethnographic Fieldnotes*. Chicago: University of Chicago Press.

Ezzy, D. (2002) *Qualitative Analysis. Practice and Innovation*. London: Routledge.

Miles, M. B. and Huberman, A. M. (1994) *Qualitative Data Analysis. An Expanded Sourcebook*. London: Sage.

Ritchie, J., Spencer, L. and O'Connor, W. (2003) 'Carrying out qualitative analysis', in J. Ritchie and J. Lewis, (eds) *Qualitative Research Practice*. London: Sage, pp. 219–62.

Computer Software (Caqdas)

> Computer-assisted data analysis software (CAQDAS) is continually being developed and used in innovative ways by ethnographers.

> Outline: An overview of the logic of using computer-assisted qualitative data analysis software (CAQDAS) to aid data management. What CAQDAS can and cannot do: software does not do the analysis for us. The relationship between CAQDAS and grounded theory. Summary points and websites in relation to software packages. Manual techniques for sorting and coding.

WHAT CAQDAS CAN DO

Computer-assisted qualitative data analysis software (sometimes simply called CAQDAS or QDA software) is continually being developed and advanced, and the use of such software for assisting in the **analysis** of ethnographic data is becoming much more common. The best way to think about the uses of such programs is to consider how data might be managed by hand – using lots of photocopying, cutting, pasting, and sorting – and then imagine a computer doing this instead. Then consider what a computer might do that could not be achieved manually. The initial aim of CAQDAS was to enable researchers to store, search, code, annotate, and retrieve data (**coding**). Textual data are stored in the program, closely analysed, and sorted into categories, which are then marked with the assignment of codes or annotations. The researcher is able to retrieve all segments that share a particular code, combine coded sections with others, or organise codes into tree and branch structures. The individual segments of data assigned to a given code can be brought together while remaining in their initial context, and can have additional information, such as name, and place and date of record, added to the coded section. Most programs also enable the attachment of memos and analytical notes to segments and passages, and increasingly can include a link to visual and audio data.

CAQDAS programs can speed up the sorting process, enabling the exploration of complex pathways that would be difficult using cut and paste. They also provide a formal structure for storing the many forms of collected and created data and the ability to audit the ongoing analyses, and are particularly useful for **team ethnography**. As far as qualitative researchers go, ethnographers have been more reluctant than most to use technology to aid analysis, perhaps fearing that their craft will be undermined by the use of computers which may distance them from the field in which they have become so immersed. Nigel Fielding (2001) counters with the argument that instead CAQDAS can simply make more transparent a process that has been rather illusory. This is true, as long as we are careful to avoid so-called 'intelligent strategies' offered by programs such as Qualrus, which suggest coding systems based on previously noted coincident codes. Ethnographers must always remain close to the data and data collection conditions. However, software can be used to reflect the process of ethnography rather than simply being used at the end of data collection. I find it useful for storing my ongoing thoughts and reflections and being able to link this to quotations or passages of text, to photographs, and even to analytic diagrams.

A potentially exciting development in CAQDAS is the hypertext facility that many programs are now able to offer. Hypertext works like using the Internet, enabling links to other parts of the data set and thereby the construction of some complex pathways to various forms of data (see **visual ethnography** and **postmodern ethnographies**). Increasing interest in visual elements of culture and in the role of embodiment in understanding culture, structure, and action encourage the use of different media for data collection and storage and these, in turn, have implications for sorting and analysis (Gibbs et al., 2002b). Programs such as NVivo and Atlas-ti, can now usually store a range of file types, including audio and visual, and some enable labelling and attaching analytic memos to pictures, sections of film, or passages of sound. Searching and coding of the data using hypertext can be more interactive and creative than CAQDAS previously implied, and can be useful in the early stages of a project for simply browsing through what has been recorded (Fielding and Lee, 1995 and 1998). Some programs enable the linking of codes in creative ways and even the ability to visualise the emerging analytical connections. Of course, innovative uses of these facilities for the presentation of the data are being developed as I write, especially by postmodern and reflexive (**reflexivity**) ethnographers attempting to address issues of representational authority (see Gibbs et al., 2002a).

WHAT CAQDAS CANNOT DO

It is important to remember that computer programs merely aid the management and analysis of data, they do not do the analysis. In fact Kelle (1997) says CAQDAS programs could more correctly be called 'tools for data storage and retrieval' rather than for data analysis, and Ezzy (2002) argues that CAQDAS is just one tool to help store, search and retrieve, in order to aid analysis; it is not *the* tool, and not *for* analysis. Beware any books or articles that claim they analysed their data with whatever piece of software. It demonstrates a serious lack of understanding of the process of analysis. The researcher conducts analysis: determines categories, assigns notes to categories, and allocates segments to codes. The researcher then decides what to present to which audience and how, selecting the illustrations considered apt. The computer cannot do this work alone, just as it did not make observations, ask questions, listen to conversations, take notes, and decide what to include or ignore. The researcher is inextricably linked to the entire research process, from selecting a topic to presenting findings, and this includes the analysis. Some people use CAQDAS to bring ethnographic analysis closer to quantitative analysis, as they count instances of phrases or events, or even interpretations. This seems to me a rather worrying development, tending to reify socially constructed data. It is important to avoid the veneer of objectivity that using a computer can lend.

It is also important for the researcher to remain intellectually close to the research context throughout the analysis phase. Few CAQDAS programs can store all forms of data, and even those that store multimedia cannot store one's memory. Finally, one should not be afraid to stop using software, or to use some additional techniques, where it does not suit requirements, is not compatible with one's epistemological approach, not practical, or is in any way unsatisfactory.

CAQDAS AND GROUNDED THEORY

There has been considerable debate regarding the extent to which CAQDAS is associated with **grounded theory**, so that Amanda Coffey and colleagues (1996) worry about the neglect of other approaches in the development and use of software. In other words, grounded theory assumptions are arguably built into the design of the software. Fielding and Lee (1998), on the other hand, believe the link has been overdrawn. Their research has shown that CAQDAS users take many different approaches and, furthermore, that those who claim to be using grounded theory often deviate so far from the original exposition of the method by Glaser and Strauss in 1967 that it is now barely recognisable as a single approach. CAQDAS therefore supports not only a grounded theory approach, but also narrative, discourse and semiotic analyses, for example.

SOFTWARE PACKAGES

Reviews of CAQDAS software packages are quickly out of date so, for further information on each, it is best to consult the websites of those who produce the software as well as browsing the latest independent reviews that have been published. I can highly recommend the web pages of the CAQDAS Networking Project (http://caqdas.soc.surrey.ac.uk) which aims to provide practical support, training and information in the use of a range of software programs. The project has been funded for six years by the UK Economic and Social Research Council (ESRC) and has platforms for methodological debate, information on training events, links to online articles and other websites, and an updated bibliography. There are links to the sites of software developers, where free demonstration versions can be downloaded. The bibliography includes some useful reviews of such programs. There are over twenty CAQDAS packages available as I write. Commonly used ones are QSR NVivo, The Ethnograph, Atlas-ti, HyperRESEARCH, Max QDA, and Qualrus. You might also visit the website of QSR International (http://www.qsrinternational.com/) to see screen shots and download demo versions of the packages they publish. Clearly, of these, The Ethnograph is the one with the clearest historical links to ethnography.

A disadvantage of CAQDAS is the time it can take to learn to use a program, and with ethnographic research the storing and sorting of data usually begins not long after the first data are collected. For this reason, it is recommended to decide on a program as early as possible in the research process. I also recommend a visit to the website of Online QDA (http://onlineqda.hud.ac.uk/), which offers training and support materials addressing many common problems experienced by users of CAQDAS.

MANUAL TECHNIQUES

CAQDAS does not replace careful analysis by the ethnographer, and should not replace the systematic and considered reading and re-reading, remembering, thinking, sorting, looking, and listening that are part and parcel of analysis. And any number of techniques may be used to enable this process, including manual cutting and pasting, as well as the use of databases and index files. The latter are particular useful for logging certain repetitive details, for storing standardised segments of information on participants or institutions, on events or actions. I used a database to record everything I knew about all the different people I had spoken to over the years and on whom, on reflection, I was able to note several details such as age group, ages of children, home ownership, health insurance, time in Spain, and so on (O'Reilly, 2000). Having compiled the database, I was able to go back and fill in the gaps where I had forgotten to ask people something. This has been an invaluable resource to me over the years. As a result of technological advances and digitisation of all forms of data, such manual procedures may eventually become obsolete, but before that time comes, I think it is important to consider what they offer so that they may be preserved in some form. Technology should be used to aid not replace other techniques, in my opinion, otherwise we are in danger of being determined by it.

See also: analysis; coding; grounded theory

REFERENCES

General

Coffey, A., Holbrook, B., and Atkinson, P. (1996) 'Qualitative data analysis: technologies and representations', *Sociological Research Online*, 1(1).

Ezzy, D. (2002) *Qualitative Analysis: Practice and Innovation*. London: Routledge.

Fielding, N. (2001) 'Computers in qualitative research', in P. Atkinson, A. Coffey, S. Delamont, J. Lofland and L. Lofland (eds) *Handbook of Ethnography*. London: Sage. pp. 453–67.

Fielding, N. and Lee, R. (1995) 'The hypertext facility in qualitative analysis software', *ESRC Archive Bulletin*.

Fielding, N. and Lee, R. (1998) *Computer Assisted Qualitative Research*. London: Sage.

Gibbs, G. R., Friese, S. and Mangabeira, W. C. (eds) (2002a) 'Using technology in the qualitative research process', *FQS: Forum Qualitative Social Research*, 3(2) (special edition).

Gibbs, G. R., Friese, S. and Mangabeira, W. C. (eds) (2002b) 'The use of new technology in qualitative research. Introduction to issue', *FQS: Forum Qualitative Social Research*, 3(2).

Glaser, B. G. and Strauss, A. L. (1967) *The Discovery of Grounded Theory: Strategies for Qualitative Research*. Hawthorne, NY: Aldine de Gruyter.

Kelle, U. (1997) 'Theory building in qualitative research and computer programs for the management of textual data', *Sociological Research Online*, 2(2).

Weitzman, E. A. and Miles, M. B. (1995). *Computer Programs for Qualitative Data Analysis: a Software Source Book*. Thousand Oaks, CA: Sage.

Example

O'Reilly, K. (2000) *The British on the Costa del Sol: Transnational Communities and Local Identities*. London: Routledge.

Covert

> *Covert research is research that has not gained the full consent, and is not conducted with the full knowledge, of the participants.*

> *Outline: Some classical and contemporary studies that use covert methods. Ethical and practical issues with covert research. The covert–overt continuum and difficulties for ethnography in being entirely overt. The distinction between lies, evasiveness and white lies, and the ubiquitous practice of 'ethnographic cloaking'.*

CLASSICAL COVERT STUDIES

In the past, covert research was common and some very important studies came out of the tradition. Several of the **Chicago School** ethnographers undertook covert studies. Paul Cressey (1932) remained covert in the taxi-dance halls. And Nels Anderson (1923) never told his subjects he was studying them. He didn't really see it that way since he was himself living as a Hobo (homeless person), struggling to get by day to day, and from that vantage point decided to write it all down (Bulmer, 1984). One of the most infamous covert studies is David Rosenhan's (1973), in which eight researchers from different backgrounds gained access to an institution for the insane simply by claiming that they heard voices. Once hospitalised they then acted 'normally' in the settings (as far as they could, given the nervousness they experienced), no longer alluding to the voices or displaying any other unusual behaviours, in order to test the effects of labelling and the subjective nature of diagnosis. Regardless of the fact they made their symptoms up, they found themselves detained for an average of 19 days (the range being from seven to 52 days). Rosenhan concludes:

> A psychiatric label has a life and an influence of its own. Such labels, conferred by mental health professionals, are as influential on the patient as they are on his relatives and friends, and it should not surprise anyone that the diagnosis acts on all of them as a self-fulfilling prophecy. (1973:25)

Another study that is now infamous is that of Laud Humphreys (1970), who made a covert study of behaviour in *'certain men's conveniences in an American city'* (tea rooms in American homosexual slang). In other words, he studied anonymous sexual encounters in a men's toilet in a public park in Chicago. He achieved this by taking on the role of 'watchqueen', an acceptable role within this community where individuals who enjoy watching the activities inside the tea room compensate for this privilege by also watching the door to warn when police or youngsters approach. It is clear that Humphreys abused his position as covert researcher when later he noted down the car registration numbers of the participants and then pursued them to their homes to conduct a survey. And for this reason, the study is more often used to illustrate transgression of social research ethics than for its other achievements (see Warwick, 1982). However, in his defence, the study was nevertheless a successful attempt to understand some of the complex issues around, and to gain an insider perspective on, a very difficult to access and misunderstood form of 'deviant' behaviour.

Humphreys chose to be covert because he wanted the acts he observed to remain as 'normal' as possible. He argues it is only possible to observe some things by being covert, and by pretending to be 'in the same boat'. This reflects Humphreys' desire to be scientific and to affect the research setting as little as possible. Since the reflexive turn and the rise of interpretivist approaches, ethnographers participate as much to learn from the experience as to observe in a detached way (see **reflexivity** and **the participant observer oxymoron**), and as a result of this, and some tortuous ethical debates, covert research has become less common.

I also want to mention Nigel Fielding's (1981) ethnographic study of the National Front, an extreme right-wing and (in his own words) unlovable organisation, in which Fielding conducted **participant observation** in order to understand the participants' own rationalisation for what they do and believe in. I include this not only because of its achievement, again, in providing an insider perspective on a 'deviant group' but also because Fielding was actually overt; his respondents knew he was conducting research on their organisation. But Fielding's overt status was an ambiguous one in that it did not stretch to his personal opinions. He says he could not like or feel any sympathies for this group whose ideology was completely alien to him, but of course he did not want them to know this. So, although he was overt in a way, he actually kept his feelings to himself.

ETHICAL DIFFICULTIES

Covert research has now become far less common, partly as a result of a series of heated debates about ethical implications that were conducted both in the US and the UK during the 1980s. Some of this debate arose as direct criticism of the studies above. Humphreys, for example (see Warwick, 1982), was accused of causing serious damage to the reputation of the social science community because of his blatant disregard for the rights of his research participants (if one can call them participants in covert research!).

The criticism of covert research centres around a few themes which are covered in more depth with the concept of **ethics** (and see O'Reilly, 2005). They are: the impossibility of acquiring informed consent to participate; exploitation of people who cannot have agreed to take part and therefore can have no control over how they are represented; the problem of misrepresentation and deception of research participants; difficulties for the researcher (who is often a graduate student) of keeping up the pretence, and the related possibility of getting caught; and the ongoing damage to the wider research community caused by the undermining of trust. Later, it was argued that covert research is only acceptable in some extreme circumstances, since it is so difficult, if not impossible, to justify. The International Sociological Association Code of Ethics, approved in 2001, for example, suggests:

> Covert research should be avoided in principle, unless it is the only method by which information can be gathered, and/or when access to the usual sources of information is obstructed by those in power. (ISA, 2001)

CONTEMPORARY COVERT STUDIES

However, some work is still being done undercover, especially when it can be justified on the grounds of scientific or moral value, or when studying powerful groups who themselves engage in lies, deceit and misrepresentation (Brewer, 2000). I will describe two. Barbara Ehrenreich's (2001) bestselling book, *Nickel and Dimed*, is based on her covert participant observation in the US, where for two years she worked in some of the lowest-paid jobs in the country and tested out the experience of living solely on poverty-level wages. Ehrenreich ended up working covertly as a waitress, a cleaner, a care assistant, and a shop assistant. She found the wages woefully inadequate and the work gruelling, and discovered that in many cases one job was inadequate to fund normal daily living expenses. Ehrenreich concludes that, rather than withdrawing welfare or social security benefits to encourage people into work, what states should be doing is ensuring a decent minimum wage and the opportunity to work hard to improve living conditions.

Nancy Scheper-Hughes (2004) has recently undertaken covert research on organs trafficking and discovered that an abundant source of organs is provided by the living bodies of the poor, naïve, illiterate, frail, mentally ill, and children. Like most covert studies, her work is powerful and engaging, drawing the reader into an underworld of shady deals, exploitation, dangerous liaisons, sickness, hardship and even death. She says:

> My basic ethnographic method – 'follow the bodies!' – brought me to police morgues, hospital mortuaries, medical-legal institutes, intensive care units, emergency rooms, dialysis units, surgical units, operating rooms, as well as to police stations, jails and prisons, mental institutions, orphanages and court rooms in North and South America, the Middle East, Africa and Asia. (Scheper Hughes, 2004: 32)

LIES, DAMNED LIES, AND WHITE LIES

Some researchers consider any deception within the long-term relationship-building process of ethnography as unacceptable. However, the distinction between covert and overt research is not as straightforward as it might seem, and openness is often a matter of degree. Many ethnographers are what Jason Ditton (1977) would call *interactionally deceitful*. That is to say, in our interactions with our research participants we are not entirely honest and open. Sometimes because we cannot be – we may not even know what the final focus of the research will be and cannot say what will happen to the material, especially if it is archived for secondary analysis. We may well hope that our participants forget we are researching them and 'act naturally'. Even overt researchers often pretend to 'be in the same boat' as their respondents. Lee Monaghan for example, informed many of his respondents of his research interests, yet, having been a weight-lifter and boxer in the past, they primarily treated him, and he was happy to be treated, as a working doorman:

> Most of the time I have been and continue to be successful in using my body to research other bodies. Usual comments from ethnographic contacts, upon initially learning that I am an academic have been of the type: 'Oh, you don't *look* like a lecturer!' (Monaghan, 2002: 410)

Other ethnographers, like Fielding above, may be overt with respect to their research but might keep their own feelings and opinions to themselves. Indeed, this might be the only safe and sensible option in some situations. And openness might not extend to everyone in a given setting. In public settings such as a hospital or street, negotiating access from everyone would be impractical and futile, as well as completely undermining the behaviour one wishes to observe (Punch, 1994).

In presenting our research to others, as well as revealing our own opinions and feelings, Brewer suggests that we avoid blatant lies by recourse to the employment of *general statements* that avoid detail and yet are generally true.

> On one occasion, when I wanted to interview conservative evangelicals about their anti-Catholic views, I surmised that they would be reluctant to give consent knowing this intent, so I presented the interview as one about the modern church and conducted it as such. (Brewer, 2000: 97)

key concepts in ethnography

This was about gaining consent through blurring or avoidance, but not being so deceitful as to lie or to then conduct a very different interview than what had been agreed to. However, it may be necessary at times to actually lie – to protect yourself or your research participants, or to maintain confidentiality. I think we should consider these *white lies* – lies with justification – and use them wisely.

THE COVERT–OVERT CONTINUUM

Overt research therefore most often occurs on a continuum between covert and overt, and can involve lies, white lies, general statements (or evasiveness), and interactional deceit. In an extreme example, when Patricia Adler (1985) and her husband found themselves embroiled in the murky dealings of a drug-smuggling community, they saw the opportunity to develop research in this field and there-fore began covertly developing leads. They did eventually explain their research to some of the members with whom they had estab-lished a good rapport and found them happy to be of help, to the extent they were able to go on to conduct in-depth interviews. However, they continued to juggle covert and overt roles, finding it increasingly difficult to remember who knew about the study and who did not (incidentally, putting those with whom they had shared the truth in considerable danger, as well as themselves). And though Humphreys' (1970) research was admittedly covert, he did disclose his real intentions to some. Outside of the tearooms, he says he was able to get talking to 12 of the participants with whom his face and car had become familiar and, after relationships had been built with some sharing of meals and drinks, he was able to persuade them to agree to interviews.

Ethnographic cloaking

Interestingly, Herrera criticises covert research not on ethical grounds but on the grounds that the researcher cannot give any evi-dence that she was where she says she was, and cannot give full details of who took part in the research. Indeed, he believes most ethnographers engage in some form of *ethnographic cloaking*, or the disguise of details such that work cannot be validated, verified, or replicated.

covert

[L]ike most fieldworkers, covert researchers work to prevent anyone from identifying the subjects or locales described in the research by using fictionalized descriptions and portraying John and Jane Does in published reports. (Herrera, 2003: 353)

Given that most covert research is justified on the grounds that potential harm to participants is balanced by the gains of scientific rigour, this is a serious accusation. It is also an ethical issue, since no research participant should be expected to take part in poorly conceived or executed research, yet covert research cannot demonstrate its rigour. So, while we may want to do undercover research, we need to think carefully about how to retain its scientific validity. Undercover should not mean sloppy, and a gentleman's agreement (as Herrera calls the notion that the research community has a shared understanding about how research should be done) is not enough. We need to consider what evidence or information can be given to convince readers it is valid and therefore justified. However, on the other hand, some researchers, like Scheper-Hughes, who argues for a scholarship with commitment, an engaged and militant anthropology, would consider it even more unethical to refrain from doing research simply because it is difficult or dangerous.

See also: access; ethics; participant observation; virtual ethnography

REFERENCES

General

Brewer, J. (2000) *Ethnography*. Buckingham: Open University Press.

Bulmer, M. (1984) *The Chicago School of Sociology*. Chicago: University of Chicago Press.

Herrera, C. D. (2003) 'A clash of methodology and ethics in "Undercover" social science', *Philosophy of the Social Sciences*, 33: 351–62.

ISA (2001) International Sociological Association Code of Ethics. Approved by the ISA Executive Committee, Fall. Available online: http://isa_sociology.org/about/isa_code_of_ethics.htm

Lugosi, P. (2006) 'Between overt and covert research: concealment and disclosure in an ethnographic study of commercial hospitality', *Qualitative Inquiry*, 12(3): 541–61.

O'Reilly, K. (2005) *Ethnographic Methods*. London: Routledge.

Punch, M. (1994) 'Politics and ethics in qualitative research', in N. Denzin and Y. S. Lincoln (eds) *Handbook of Qualitative Research*. London: Sage.

Warwick, D. P. (1982) *Tearoom Trade: Means and Ends in Social Research Ethics. An Examination of the Merits of Covert Participant Observation.* London: Macmillan.

Examples

Adler, P. A. (1985) *Wheeling and Dealing: an Ethnography of an Upper-Level Drug Dealing and Smuggling Community.* New York: Columbia University Press.

Anderson, N. (1961 [1923]) *The Hobo.* Chicago: University of Chicago Press.

Cressey, P. G. (1969 [1932]) *The Taxi-Dance Hall. A Sociological Study in Commercialised Recreation and City Life.* Montclair, NJ: Patterson Smith.

Ditton, J. (1977) *Part-time Crime: an Ethnography of Fiddling and Pilferage.* London: Macmillan.

Ehrenreich, B. (2001) *Nickel and Dimed. On (not) Getting by in America.* New York: Metropolitan Books.

Fielding, N. (1981) *The National Front.* London: Routledge & Kegan Paul.

Humphreys, L. (1970) *Tea-Room Trade.* Chicago: Aldine.

Monaghan, L. F. (2002) 'Regulating "unruly" bodies: work tasks, conflict and violence in Britain's night-time economy', *British Journal of Sociology*, 53(3): 403–29.

Rosenhan, D. L. (1973) 'On being sane in insane places', *Science*, 179: 250–8.

Scheper-Hughes, N. (2004) 'Parts unknown: undercover ethnography of the organs-trafficking underworld', *Ethnography*, 5(1): 29–73.

--- Critical Ethnography ---

> Critical ethnography is an approach that is overtly political and critical, exposing inequalities in an effort to effect change.

Outline: The goals of a critical ethnography to expose hidden agendas, challenge oppressive assumptions, describe power relations, and critique the taken-for-granted. Critical ethnographers and the role of reform: from indirect to direct action. An inductive, interpretive and reflexive methodology combined with a critical analysis: looking beyond the surface of appearances. Some critical ethnographies described.

WHAT IS CRITICAL ETHNOGRAPHY?

Critical ethnography is not so much a way of doing ethnography as a way of understanding the role of social science. It begins with the premise that social science can and ought to be relevant to contemporary issues, and is based on a history of ideas in which different writers (beginning perhaps with Karl Marx) have asked why we should be content to understand the world without attempting to change it. Critical ethnographies therefore attempt to expose the hidden agendas, challenge oppressive assumptions, describe power relations, and generally critique the taken-for-granted. They are explicitly political and critical but do not consider this to undermine the scientific nature of what they do. Indeed, critical ethnographers argue that every attempt at representation has consequences and that there is no neutrality (Madison, 2005).

Critical ethnographers rely on the same sets of methods and even to an extent the methodology of conventional ethnography. So the definition of ethnography I have used in the introduction applies here, in as much as ethnography involves at least (and see O'Reilly, 2005):

- iterative-inductive research (that evolves in design through the study), drawing on
- a family of methods
- involving direct and sustained contact with human agents
- within the context of their daily lives (and cultures)
- watching what happens, listening to what is said, asking questions
- producing a richly written account
- that respects the irreducibility of human experience
- that acknowledges the role of theory
- as well as the researcher's own role
- and that views humans as part object/part subject.

However, critical ethnography goes a little further, enabling the ethnographer to actually choose between competing ways of seeing the world and judging some world views better (fairer, more just, even more truthful) than others. However, it should not be confused with Frankfurt School critical theory, which is a critique of capitalist society, and which *may* inform *some* critical ethnography but not others. It expresses, rather, any attempt to use knowledge for social change, but

key concepts in
ethnography

especially to expose and deal with systematic social disadvantage and unequal access to resources such as health, wealth, education, and jobs.

In terms of making sense of observations, critical ethnographers do not simply look to explain the meanings of actions within a given context, to ask how they make sense for the participants, but they also look for the meanings of meanings (Thomas, 1993) and how they connect to broader structures of power and control. They thus see ethnography as providing unique methods for looking beyond the surface, for really questioning the taken-for-granted, for seeing what Pierre Bourdieu (1977) has called the everyday acts of symbolic violence in which all members of a culture are complicit.

> Critical ethnography takes seemingly mundane events, even repulsive ones, and reproduces them in a way that exposes broader social processes of control, taming, power imbalance, and the symbolic mechanisms that impose one set of preferred meanings or behaviors over others. (Thomas, 1993: 9)

ETHNOGRAPHY AND REFORM

Just like other ethnographers, critical ethnographers rely on the collection of rich data through direct and sustained observation as well as the collection of other forms of data. They also look to objectively report the subjective views of the subjects. The key difference is that they do this *critically*. Critical ethnographers do, however, vary in the extent to which they seek reform, with some looking to actual and direct outcomes that change the world for the participants of the study (as in participatory action research), while others argue for a more radical overthrow of the status quo in the society as a whole (as in Marxist approaches). Some are less direct, for example demonstrating the role of language on social control (as in some poststructural and **postmodern ethnography**). Others are more direct in defining and tackling community problems. Most at least demand 'changes in cognition', or effecting a new way of seeing the world as a first step to changing it.

METHODS

Critical ethnography begins with an ontological argument, based on a vast array of previously collected empirical evidence, that some social groups are more disadvantaged than others, and with 'a compassion for the suffering of living beings' (Madison, 2005: 5). This does not mean, however, that ethnographers should begin with a research question that predetermines its outcome, such as 'I am going to demonstrate racism in the police force'. It is more open and exploratory than that, exploring what ethnographers and those around them *think* they know with an open mind and prepared to be wrong. Thomas suggests, for example, that ethnographers simply begin their time in a setting with the question: 'I wonder what's there?' However, once established in the field, critical ethnographers attend to speech and action, and to discourse (because naming things shapes how they are perceived). They interpret the data to show how they make sense for the participants, then reframe the data, using images and metaphors that show them in a new way, to reveal the hidden depths of exploitation, power, and disadvantage. And they do all this reflexively (**reflexivity**), with an eye to the way their own ideas have affected their work. Finally, they look to their study and ask 'so what?'

CRITICAL ETHNOGRAPHIES

Nancy Scheper-Hughes is a medical anthropologist who has spent her career engaged in critical ethnography. Her work focuses specifically on the violence of everyday life. *Death without Weeping: the Violence of Everyday Life in Brazil* (1993) explores the lives of women and children living in a hillside town (*favella*) in Brazil, where she worked on and off for 25 years. It introduces the disturbing and controversial idea that motherly love, as westerners might understand it, is something of a bourgeois myth, a luxury for those who can reasonably expect, as these women cannot, that their infants will live.

More recently she has been engaged in long-term undercover ethnography looking at the world of organs trafficking which took her around the world following the trade routes. She says the goal of anthropology is to problematise the received and conventional wisdoms of the day, to turn perceptions upside down, to comment as outsiders on the power relations as we see them. In her paper for *Ethnography*, Scheper-Hughes (2004: 36) outlines some of the responses to her work to date. She rather incredulously reports that reviewers highlighted in her work the 'exciting new landscapes where good and bad guys and goods are distributed in both expected and unexpected places'. And she angrily protests: 'with all due respect for the changing face of late modern capitalism, the human organs markets still conform to an earlier model of mercantile global capitalism, one that bears some resemblance to the Atlantic slave trade'. There are donor, recipient and transfer nations. The donors are poor and the recipients are rich and privileged. The circulation of kidneys, for example, follows that of economic capital – from south to north, from black to brown and white bodies, from females to males, and from poor males to affluent males. While this may illustrate what reviewers called 'novel intersections in geographical spaces', Scheper-Hughes believes it is rather more important to emphasise the global inequalities this market reproduces.

Jim Thomas has undertaken ethnographic fieldwork in prisons in the US. One critical theme that emerged from a large collection of prisoner narratives was that of racial identity, through which Thomas identified *institutionalised racism*. 'Racism in prison occurs not only because of discriminatory practice, but also because one's race connotes and denotes sets of meanings that define how one "does time"' (1993: 52). In other words, one's whole prison experience is circumscribed by one's race. For whites, 'race' is a resource that can be used to acquire privileges but, because whites in this case are usually in the minority, Thomas argues, race is also a symbol for the terror or danger of prisons. For non-whites, the implicit assumption that white culture dominates in the prison, the fact that 'white is right' as one prisoner puts it, drives many to join gangs in which they feel they have a place and are part of a culture they understand. The result in many prisons is tension bordering on warfare (see Thomas 1992 and 1988).

Paul Willis's (1977) *Learning to Labour* is arguably a critical ethnography. It is a now-classic study of counter-culture in schools, arguing that the rebellion of young working-class boys was actually a living-out through apparent choice of the inevitability that was their future. In many ways anticipating Bourdieu's later work, Willis believed that cultural practices tend to trap us into reproducing the status quo. Barbara Ehrenreich's (2001) *Nickel and Dimed* could also be described as critical ethnography. Describing her ethnographic research into low-paid jobs in the US, it is as much a critique of welfare reform and rhetoric as a rich ethnography of lives lived in poverty.

See also: ethics; feminist ethnography; inductive and deductive; realism; reflexivity

critical ethnography

REFERENCES

Key text

Thomas, J. (1993) *Doing Critical Ethnography.* Qualitative Research Methods Series, 26. London: Sage.

General

Bourdieu, P. (1977) *Outline of a Theory of Practice.* Cambridge: Cambridge University Press.

Madison, D. S. (2005) *Critical Ethnography: Method, Ethics and Performance.* London: Sage.

O'Reilly, K. (2005) *Ethnographic Methods.* London: Routledge.

Examples

Ehrenreich, B. (2001) *Nickel and Dimed. On (not) Getting by in America.* New York: Metropolitan Books.

Scheper-Hughes, N. (1993) *Death without Weeping: the Violence of Everyday Life in Brazil.* Berkeley, CA: University of California Press.

Scheper-Hughes, N. (2004) 'Parts unknown. Undercover ethnography of the organs-trafficking underworld', *Ethnography,* 5(1): 29–73.

Thomas, J. (1992) 'The meaning of race in prison culture: snapshots in black and white', in M. Lynch and E. B. Patterson (eds) *Race and Criminal Justice.* New York: Harrow and Heston, pp. 126–44.

Thomas, J. (1988) *Prisoner Litigation: the Paradox of the Jailhouse Lawyer.* Totowa, NJ: Rowman & Littlefield.

Willis, P. (1977) *Learning to Labour. How Working Class Kids Get Working Class Jobs.* Farnborough: Saxon House.

key concepts in
ethnography

Ethics

An ethical approach to ethnography attempts to avoid harm to, and respect the rights of, all participants and to consider the consequences of all aspects of the research process.

Outline: The need to be aware of guidelines and review boards. The extent to which covert research can be defended. Thinking about power and status and avoiding exploitation. The responsibility of the ethnographer to remain faithful to (implicit) promises. How to retain confidentiality. The need to reflexively attain an ethical approach by addressing dilemmas on a case-by-case basis.

INTRODUCTION

Every social researcher must consider the ethical implications of conducting research which in myriad predictable and unpredictable ways may impact on the social world, on those involved in the research (including oneself), as well as on those not directly involved. Ethnography is no exception and, indeed, because of the intimate and long-term nature of the method, it raises important and profound ethical issues of its own.

ETHICAL GUIDELINES AND COMMITTEES

Each discipline, academic department, institution, or organisation within which a researcher is involved may have their own set of guidelines or ethical committees which work together to determine correct procedure in given cases. Some of these act as gatekeepers (**key informants and gatekeepers**), controlling access to the field, and determining procedures that have to be met before research can proceed. Educational and medical institutions, especially, will often insist that all researchers fill in extensive questionnaires outlining and explaining their research procedures and how they will take account of and deal with ethical implications of their research. Potential researchers may need to attend committee meetings where their work is discussed in great depth before ethical clearance can be given. It is therefore essential that each and every ethnographer is aware of and adheres to the guidelines and committees that govern their own situation.

Examples of ethical guidelines of relevance to ethnography are available from the American Anthropological Association (AAA); and the Association of Social Anthropologists of the UK and Commonwealth (ASA). The guidelines tend to cover the same or similar issues to those I will address here. But it must be remembered that they are guidelines. Ethical dilemmas or considerations must usually be addressed on an individual case-by-case basis, interpreting guiding principles with a heavy dose of common sense, especially given that some people believe institutional guidelines, committees, and review boards tend inadvertently to end up serving the interests of powerful groups (Douglas, 1976). My own position is that any decision to abandon research, or to alter an intellectually justified research design, must be taken with as much care as the decision to proceed.

COVERT RESEARCH AND ENCOURAGING PARTICIPATION

A crucial decision for ethnographers is whether to conduct their study covertly or overtly. As a result of a series of heated debates that took place during the 1980s (see Punch, 1994; Warwick, 1982), as well as developments in feminist, critical, and reflexive ethnography, most ethical guidelines or textbook advice now suggests that completely **covert** research is rarely justified and should only be undertaken where the research is considered essential on moral or scientific grounds and where overt access is in some ways restricted. Patricia Adler (1985: 11) for example, believed that investigative research of the type she undertook is essential with deviant groups whose occupation makes them 'secretive, deceitful, mistrustful, and paranoid'. Nancy Scheper-Hughes (2004) also justifies her covert research on human organs-trafficking, on ethical grounds. John Brewer (2000), alternatively, does not believe it is the ethnographer's job to conduct undercover exposés.

In contemporary ethnography, research participants should be given as much information as possible in order to ensure their informed consent to our intrusion in their lives. Indeed, to take this even further, rather than passive 'informants' or 'subjects', research *participants* are now often encouraged to take an active part in the research process, empowered where possible to contribute, direct, redirect, and guide the research in ways that ensure their own perspective is given due weight. Such *participatory research* is considered particularly important in the field of health in majority world settings; for example, where the gap between professional and community conceptions of health and illness may be quite profound (de Koning and Martin, 1996). If the research is covert (conducted without the participants' knowledge) such conscious and active participation is impossible. Covert research is also considered somewhat risky for the ethnographer (often a research student or early-career researcher) who has to work to keep up the pretence and who faces the constant danger of being found out. Finally, covert research, when discovered or published, can be very damaging to the research community as a whole, undermining trust in the transparency, honesty, and openness of our endeavours.

In practice, however, the decision to be covert or overt is usually one of extent. It is often difficult to decide to what *extent* we should inform participants about the nature of the research project, and our own interpretations of the data. It is even more problematic to inform participants fully as to what might happen to the findings, given that we may have no control over secondary analysis of archived material or mass media interpretation and publication of our results (see Mauthner et al., 1998). It can also be difficult to be informative about a research project that develops as it proceeds, as in iterative-inductive research. As discussed in depth under the concept of **covert,** ethnographic research most often occurs somewhere on a continuum between covert and overt, and may well involve some white lies, evasiveness, or interactional deceit. This can raise its own difficulties. Daniel Murphy (1986), for example, for his study of shoplifting, was partly covert in that store detectives and police knew about his research but staff and shoppers did not. This became problematic when he found himself left alone with a member of staff who was accused of 'fiddling' the till. The man was anxious and frightened and turned to Murphy, asking 'What should I do?' No matter how he chose to respond (unless he admitted he was doing research) it would involve some form of deceit. He resorted to sophistry, mumbling 'I'm new here', which was in fact true, but he was left feeling very uncomfortable.

POWER AND STATUS

Some people feel that as researchers they are in a powerful position in relation to their research participants. They choose the topic, direct the

ethics

research, decide what to record and how, decide what to ignore or over-look, and determine what is written and where it is published. Some of these issues are being addressed in the move towards more ethical, reflexive, and participatory research (see Murphy and Dingwall, 2001). The politics of representation is a crucial issue for (not only critical and feminist) ethnographers, especially since 'the authority of the anthro-pologist and the authorizing power of fieldwork has come under attack' (Skeggs, 2001: 428).

Awareness of the potential for exploitation and the role of represen-tation is a first step in trying to avoid it. Ethnography is arguably less exploitative than other methodologies in that it is long-term, engaged, involves careful access, and the establishment of long-term reciprocal relationships built on trust and rapport. It listens to participants and attempts to understand their worlds from their own points of view (even those ethnographers who later stand back and engage in critical or realist (**realism**) interpretations of these emic perspectives). Ethnography avoids reductionism in its presentation of findings, includ-ing rich depth as well as theoretical and hermeneutic understanding. Nevertheless, anthropology has been accused of ignoring the power structure within which the discipline was able to take shape (Gledhill, 1994) and a great deal of traditional ethnographic work has been accused of 'othering' and exoticising its object. It is important to recog-nise the extent to which we do have control over the data and can influ-ence outcomes (see **reflexivity**), for scientific but also ethical reasons. Furthermore, the extent of engagement itself can raise ethical issues in relation to the instrumental nature of close relationships which the research participant might consider more long-term and reciprocal than we had thought.

On the other hand, it is important to direct one's ethical stance towards as much as against the ethnographer. My students often laugh when I remind them how powerful and influential they can be, arguing that on the contrary what they experience in the field is powerlessness, timidity, apprehension, and even fear. As discussed in **access**, those first forays into the field can be daunting and intimidating. Students, espe-cially, may feel overwhelmed by competing pressures to collect good data, write good fieldnotes, build quality relationships, establish **rapport**, negotiate ongoing **access** sensitively, and remain at least to some extent objective. Joan Gross, rather than being high status in the field was a 'poor young thing', away from her family; a student with no job to go back to and few worldly possessions. She gives a wonderful example of how her gatekeeper, Mr Dufour, treated her more like a daughter than an academic:

> He shouted at me, often poking me in the middle of the chest as he did so and berated me for associating with certain people, sure that I would be led astray. He coached me on how to make the most of my limited funds and quizzed me about my diet to make sure I was eating enough red meat to keep healthy. (Gross, 2001: xx)

Ethnographers can also find themselves in dangerous or tricky situations that can be difficult to negotiate. Some might find it morally imperative to try out for themselves the drugs that are having a daily and profound impact on their research participants (Estroff, 1981), while others would find this ethically indefensible, not to mention risky and perhaps illegal. I doubt many ethnographers would go so far as to break the law for the sake of research, so how does an ethnographer of criminal behaviour negotiate participant observation? See Hobbs (1988) and Giulianotti (1995) for some discussion.

RESPONSIBILITY

Ethnographers have to take responsibility for their own actions as well as those of others they implicate in their research such as research assistants, **key informants** and **gatekeepers**. We might take this sense of responsibility as far as to argue that all ethnographic research should have explicit policy implications. Daniel Bates (1996) points out that ethnographers not only gain rich data and deep, factual understanding of the given field, but they also read and draw on other studies in other places. They are therefore able to offer a broader, sociologically informed perspective than that of the participants themselves which should, ethically, be employed to advantage. Willis and Trondman (2000) similarly believe all ethnographic work should critically engage in cultural politics. I am not convinced we need to do this overtly but do concur in as much as we have the responsibility to do with the material we collected what was expected of us by the participants. In other words, if they thought we were writing an autobiographical account that gives no priority to the authorial or any other voice, then we can do that (see **postmodern ethnographies**). If on the other hand, they believed we were engaging in a serious, scientific endeavour that might have general implications for a broader population, then we should think carefully about how what we gather and interpret is presented to others.

ethics

61

CONFIDENTIALITY

It is always best to use people's real names and details where possible, as long as permission has been granted. Indeed, it seems quite unethical to delete participants from the record to which they have happily contributed. However, it is important to ensure that participants' comments, thoughts, feelings, and private experiences are kept as confidences between ourselves unless they have been expressly offered as material for the record. This may involve anonymising details in some way, by changing names, places, and other identifying particulars. If or where anonymity is required, we need to think carefully how to do it. I changed the names of *all* participants because some wanted me to, and to change some and not others might lead readers to assume a name was real when it was not. However, when I first started to write papers I chose pseudonyms arbitrarily, only to find later that in different papers and reports I have attributed different names to the same quotes. I subsequently attributed just one pseudonym to each individual, recording them with the real names on a separate file. I also, like Lee Monaghan (2002), had to alter some personal details and backgrounds so that people could not be identified by where they worked or their biographies.

Retaining confidentiality, as with many issues discussed here, is not straightforward. Consider what you might do if someone tells you in confidence some information that might make someone else's life much easier if you were to pass it on. One of my students who was doing ethnography with families of cancer patients was told by a man that he wished his sister could be more honest with him. The sister told her she wished she could be more honest but believed her brother did not want to hear! My student did not want to break confidences but encouraged the pair to sit together and discuss issues they had shared with her. Sue Estroff (1981) went so far as to break some confidences: when one of her 'clients' told her she intended to commit suicide, she reported it. She was concerned that this would undermine trust in her but felt the moral imperative to report the intended act outweighed her own research demands. As a result it is possible that she saved a life.

ONGOING DILEMMAS AND A REFLEXIVE DIALOGUE

I have not attempted to cover the complete range of ethical issues a researcher must consider, but have raised a few of relevance to ethnography specifically. Murphy and Dingwall (2001) cover a much broader range than I have been able to include and draw on some interesting examples, such as Blee's (1993) study of former Klu Klux Klan members and Bolton's (1995) covert ethnography of the gay scene in Brussels. I have also been able to go into this topic in more depth in my own *Ethnographic Methods* (O'Reilly, 2005), where I introduce a debate between students engaged in ethnographic fieldwork in order to illustrate the complexity of an ethical approach and the dangers of too prescriptive a set of principles. Ethical issues are best resolved via an ongoing reflexive dialogue between ourselves, the research participants, other academics and friends, and the field context. Concerns must be addressed on a case-by-case (moment-by-moment) basis.

See also: *covert; critical ethnography; feminist ethnography; rapport; reflexivity*

REFERENCES

General

AAA. Code of Ethics of the American Anthropological Association http://www.aaanet.org/committees/ethics/ethcode.htm

ASA. Association of Social Anthropologists of the UK and Commonwealth: Ethical Guidelines for Good Research Practice http://www.theasa.org/ethics/guidelines.htm

Bates, D. (1996) *Cultural Anthropology*. Boston and London: Allyn & Bacon.

Brewer, J. (2000) *Ethnography*. Buckingham: Open University Press.

de Koning, K. and Martin, M. (1996) 'Participatory research in health: setting the context', in K. de Koning and M. Martin (eds) *Participatory Research in Health*. London: Zed Books.

Douglas, J. (1976) *Investigative Social Research: Individual and Team Field Research*. Beverley Hills, CA: Sage.

Gledhill, J. (1994) *Power and its Disguises. Anthropological Perspectives on Politics*. London: Pluto Press.

Mauthner, N., Parry, O. and Backett-Milburn, K. (1998) 'The data are out there, or are they? Implications for archiving and revisiting qualitative data', *Sociology* 32(4): 733–45.

Murphy, E. and Dingwall, R. (2001) 'The ethics of ethnography', in P. Atkinson, A. Coffey, S. Delamont, J. Lofland and L. Lofland (eds) *Handbook of Ethnography*. London: Sage, pp. 338–51.

O'Reilly, K. (2005) *Ethnographic Methods*. London: Routledge.

Punch, M. (1994) 'Politics and ethics in qualitative research', in N. Denzin and Y. S. Lincoln (eds) *Handbook of Qualitative Research*. London: Sage.

Skeggs, B. (2001) 'Feminist ethnography', in P. Atkinson, A. Coffey, S. Delamont, J. Lofland, and L. Lofland (eds) *Handbook of Ethnography*. London: Sage, pp. 426–42.

ethics

Warwick, D. P. (1982) 'Tearoom trade: means and ends in social research', in M. Bulmer (ed.) *Social Research Ethics: An Examination of the Merits of Covert Participant Observation*. London: Macmillan.

Willis, P. and Trondman, M. (2000) 'Manifesto for ethnography', *Ethnography* 1(1): 5–16.

Examples

Adler, P. A. (1985) *Wheeling and Dealing: an Ethnography of an Upper-Level Drug Dealing and Smuggling Community*. New York: Columbia University Press.

Blee, K. M. (1993) 'Evidence, empathy and ethics: lessons from oral histories of the Klan', *Journal of American History*, September: 596–606.

Bolton, R. (1995) 'Tricks, friends and lovers: erotic encounters in the field', in D. Kulick and M. Wilson (eds) *Taboo: Sex, Identity and Erotic Subjectivity in Anthropological Fieldwork*. London: Routledge, pp. 140–67.

Estroff, S. E. (1981) *Making It Crazy. An Ethnography of Psychiatric Clients in an American Community*. Berkeley, CA and London: University of California Press.

Giulianotti, R. (1995) 'Participant observation and research into football hooliganism: reflections on the problems of entrée and everyday risks', *Sociology of Sport Journal*, 12: 1–20.

Gross, J. (2001) *Speaking in Other Voices. An Ethnography of Walloon Puppet Theatres*. Amsterdam/Philadelphia: John Benjamins.

Hobbs, D. (1988) *Doing the Business: Entrepreneurship, the Working Class and Detectives in the East End of London*. Oxford: Oxford University Press.

Monaghan, L. F. (2002) 'Regulating "unruly" bodies: work tasks, conflict and violence in Britain's night-time economy', *British Journal of Sociology* 53(3): 403–29.

Murphy, D. J. I. (1986) *Customers and Thieves: an Ethnography of Shoplifting*. Aldershot: Gower.

Scheper-Hughes, N. (2004) 'Parts unknown: undercover ethnography of the organs-trafficking underworld', *Ethnography*, 5(1): 29–73.

Feminist Ethnography

> *Feminist ethnography is informed by feminist epistemology, ontology, theory, and ethics. It therefore not only describes women's lives but also challenges how we might 'know' them.*

> *Outline: Feminist and critical research as critique of positivist and survey research. The focus on power, oppression, knowledge, and the traditional exclusion of women. A feminist epistemology and methodology, and their affinity with ethnographic approaches, empathy, relationship-building, rapport, and trust. Some feminist ethnographies.*

FEMINIST AND CRITICAL RESEARCH

Feminist ethnography has not just produced some of the most in-depth material about women's lives but also enabled significant challenges to what comes to be counted as knowledge. (Skeggs, 2001: 437)

Positivists (**positivism**) try to be value-neutral or objective. Interpretive researchers (**interpretivism**) accept that values are important and sometimes even that their own values cannot be avoided, but they usually believe social research should attempt to be value-free. For many interpretivists, there is often no attempt to try to change the world, just to describe it. Critical social researchers, on the other hand, argue that the purpose of research is to discover flaws and faults in society, and to find ways of dealing with these; to reveal their policy implications or suggest (or even take) action to implement change. Critical researchers tend to study the underdogs, the oppressed, and the powerless in society, and so ethnography has explored political and social minority groups, hospitalised ill, the victims of crime, migrant workers, and the handicapped. The idea is to give voice to the voiceless, the hushed. **Critical ethnography** tries to explain why certain people fail to reach their goals, or fail to get their feelings known, have their rights acknowledged, their achievements recognised.

Feminist ethnography is one variety of the critical approach; here the focus is on issues of dominance and oppression as they relate to women's lives. Their ontological position is that oppressed groups, structures of patriarchy and control, and dominance, all exist as phenomena. Epistemologically, feminist ethnography is to some extent premised on an attack on the basic tenets of positivism. While positivism pretends to be neutral and detached, so this argument goes, it is in fact very masculine and male focused. It is based on a distinction between male and female, men and women, which posits men as more detached, focused, and objective, and women as more subjective, warm, soft, and understanding (Harding, 1991). In positivist approaches, social researchers are advised not to engage with the interviewee, not to display emotions, to ask all questions in the same way and the same order, and not to affect the outcome (Oakley, 1981). Positivist approaches, feminist literature argues, assume that the researcher is intellectually superior and dominant, as is demonstrated in the language of research 'subjects', 'respondents', and 'informants'. Furthermore, survey interviews (which is considered the preferred method for positivists, see below) do not let the researcher talk, or the researched wander off the point, suggest new avenues, or digress. Positivist research seeks standardisation of interviews, as if interviewees as well as interviewers can be made to be interchangeable, looking for the common ground and ignoring individual differences. They insist on 'yes and no', answers, which can be intimidating or bullying in an interview. The approach strips away context, reducing the situation to general themes and calculable recurrences.

Ann Oakley (1981) described how when she studied childbirth, the women wanted to ask her questions, and a scientific approach meant she was not supposed to respond to them. She said this felt exploitative and uncomfortable, but more than that, she wonders how one can begin to understand someone and empathise with them with such detachment. And if we cannot empathise and understand, how can we explain their actions? Objectivity means detachment, but it is impossible to be detached when we are researching something we are involved in or have experienced ourselves. Furthermore, women have always found empathy and involvement a useful way to understand each other, so why should this not work in social research? This is how women understand each other.

She goes further. Positivists pretend to be neutral in their research design as well as their analysis, but what in fact they do is write their assumptions into the design of the work. The dominant culture gets written in, with women's roles belittled (survey research rarely asks about housework, friendships, informal work, and so on and it has been very difficult to get these topics on the research agenda as a result). The very vocabulary in questionnaires can make women defensive about their roles, or can simply exclude them and their interpretations. Furthermore, many early researchers completely ignored women from their research. Research has tended to focus on the public side of life (especially positivist research).

A FEMINIST METHODOLOGY

As a result of such debates, feminists worked out a new methodology that involved listening more, but allowed researchers to talk if they felt they needed to; empowering interviewees to set the agenda and the outcome while not withholding from them the researcher's own experiences and feelings. In this methodology questions should not be rigid; the agenda should not be fixed. It rests on an epistemological stance that says if you want to understand someone's world, you have to get inside it. This has resonances with many debates within ethnography, as covered under the concepts of **participant observation, insider ethnography**, and **going 'native'**.

Many anthropologists have argued for the need to get into the meaning world of the other, and to suspend attempts at objectivity (see various discussions in Ellen, 1984). Some talk of being socialised into a culture, learning to *do it*; or 'learning to behave according to the native's rules' (Bates, 1996: 24) in order to gain an insight into their world. Like ethnographers' debate about insiders and outsiders, some feminists go so far as to argue that there needs to be a shared culture between interviewer and interviewee. So, black women are needed to interview black women, a study of mothers should have a mother as interviewer, only a Kosovan refugee can understand a Kosovan refugee, and so on. Of course, there are difficulties with how far this can be taken and others argue that you need distance to be able to see clearly, or to be socialised into a culture and then leave it, in order to regain distance. Too much closeness, some believe, leads to a lack of clarity in the resulting study.

Nevertheless, all feminists agree that we can know much more, and much more honestly, if we give of ourselves a little, if we are warm, receptive, and accepting. Otherwise the dominant values are simply repeated, as the interviewee tells us what she thinks we want to hear. This suggests that the really interesting factors of social life are not always on the surface, and are not always easily discovered. Sometimes they even come as a surprise to the interviewee. With this kind of epistemology, the research is a conversation, a relationship, between two or more people, in which one learns about the other through interaction and experience, and then tries to interpret these findings for the academic (or whatever) audience.

FEMINIST ETHNOGRAPHY

It is easy to see why this sort of approach lends itself to the methods of contemporary ethnography. Ethnography uniquely, despite its positivist roots, permits a long-term view, gives participants a voice, is unobtrusive, gentle, almost passive, and emphasises lived experience. It also facilitates the discovery of how the everyday contributes to the maintenance of power (Skeggs, 2001).

Attending to gender issues is not necessarily a new trend in ethnography. Many of the earlier anthropologists (Margaret Mead, Hortense Powdermaker, Ruth Benedict) not only explored gender but also questioned power relations, including their own impact on the field (Skeggs, 2001). But it was the reflexive (or literary) turn (see **reflexivity**) that really awoke sensitivities to the role of the ethnographer in the construction of accounts and the politics of representation, and feminism has been implicated in this both in informing this critique and being affected by the outcome (Visweswaran, 1997). Feminist ethnographies also have their own traditions within sociology, education, and cultural studies. But contemporary feminist ethnographies do not simply look at women, they are informed by feminist politics, and acknowledge that gender cannot be separated from race, class, and sexual identity. Postmodernists, queer theorists, and feminists of colour have all had their impacts on 'gender essentialism'.

For some examples of feminist ethnography you might try Faye Ginsburg's (1989) sensitive study of both sides of the abortion debate in the US, Beverley Skeggs' (1997) study of women's working-class cultures, or Martin Mac an Ghaill's (1994) *The Making of Men*, which is a study of Asian men, deploying feminist analysis. I can also recommend the collection by Bell et al. (1993). You might also enjoy some of the chapters in Anthias and Lazaridis (2000), which explores the lives of women migrants in various sectors of European society. In my own chapter (O'Reilly, 2000) I describe the marginalisation and feelings of loneliness and isolation experienced by such an apparently privileged group as North to South migrants. The influence of **holism** on ethnographic methods has meant that even those who do not normally consider their work feminist can find themselves alerted to gendered experiences.

See also: critical ethnography; ethics; realism; reflexivity

REFERENCES
General

Bates, D. (1996) *Cultural Anthropology*. Boston and London: Allyn & Bacon.
Bell, D., Caplan, C., and Karim W. J. (eds) (1993) *Gendered Fields: Women, Men and Ethnography*. London: Routledge.
Ellen, R. F. (ed.) (1984) *Ethnographic Research. A Guide to General Conduct*. London: Academic Press.
Harding, S. (1991) *Whose Science? Whose Knowledge? Thinking about Women's Lives*. New York: Cornell University Press.
Oakley, A. (1981) 'Interviewing women: a contradiction in terms', in H. Roberts (ed.) *Doing Feminist Research*. London: Routledge & Kegan Paul, pp. 30–61.
Oakely, A. (1998) 'Gender, methodology and people's ways of knowing: some problems with feminism and the paradigm debate in social science', Sociology, 32(4): 707–32.
Skeggs, B. (2001) 'Feminist ethnography', in P. Atkinson, A. Coffey, S. Delamont, J. Lofland and L. Lofland (eds) *Handbook of Ethnography*. London: Sage, pp. 426–42.
Visweswaran, K. (1997) 'Histories of feminist ethnography', *Annual Review of Anthropology*, 26: 591–621.

Examples

Anthias, F. and Lazaridis, G. (2000) (eds) *Gender and Migration in Southern Europe*. Oxford: Berg.
Ginsburg, F. (1989) *Contested Lives: The Abortion Debate in an American Community*. Berkeley, CA: University of California Press.
Mac an Ghaill, M. (1994) *The Making of Men: Masculinities, Sexualities and Schooling*. Buckingham: Open University Press.
O'Reilly, K. (2000) 'Trading intimacy for liberty: British women on the Costa del Sol', in F. Anthias and G. Lazaridis, (eds) *Gender and Migration in Southern Europe*. Oxford: Berg, pp. 227–48.
Skeggs, B. (1997) *Formations of Class and Gender: Becoming Respectable*. London: Sage.

feminist ethnography

Fieldnotes

> Fieldnotes are the written record of the observations, jottings, full notes, intellectual ideas, and emotional reflections that are created during the fieldwork process.

> Outline: The importance of writing things down as quickly and elaborately as possible. Acknowledging fieldnotes will always remain somewhat partial and selective. What to write: from first impressions to insider sensitivities, and significant events. Distinguishing head notes, jottings, and full notes. Keeping a record of analytic and personal thoughts: personal and intellectual diaries. Producing an audit trail.

WRITING DOWN

Writing up fieldnotes immediately is one of the sacred obligations of fieldwork. (Lareau, 1996: 217)

For her research on parental involvement in children's education, Annette Lareau spent time in two elementary schools, helping children with stories and artwork, dictating, supervising tests, and even enforcing classroom rules. She enjoyed the work and the feeling of being an incorporated element in her surroundings, especially compared with how distant and passive she had felt at the early stages of her fieldwork. However, partly because she wanted to feel included and therefore to forget she was actually an outsider and ethnographer, she made a cardinal mistake: she fell behind in writing up her fieldnotes. Lareau said she would write up as soon as she could but had to acknowledge these were retrospective notes. But the longer she left it, the harder it got to remember things, and the more uncomfortable she felt about writing them at all. She says in comparison to the anxiety she felt when writing, simply 'being there' in the classroom was a relief. Lareau feels strongly, as a result of these experiences, that it is crucial to write frequently, regularly, and systematically, and to record, in calendar format, time spent where, when, and how, with as many details as possible.

Lareau's experiences highlight many of the problems associated with writing notes in the field. Few methodology textbooks actually tell us what to record or how. It is rare to ever see anyone's fieldnotes. Ethnographers have been notoriously reluctant to archive fieldnotes in the same way that interview transcripts can be archived for secondary analysis (Mauthner et al., 1998). This is possibly due to the impossibility of anonymising such detailed descriptions as much as epistemological concerns about the relationship between the researcher, researched, and co-constructed data (see **reflexivity**). But it does not make it any easier for novice researchers to know what they should be doing when they write things down.

Luckily, researchers are now using fieldnotes as well as interview quotations to illustrate their research findings; and authors like Emerson and colleagues (1995) are publishing in-depth analyses of the process of **writing**. The Economic and Social Data Service in the UK (ESDS) has a qualitative section that provides access to archived digital data collections. This is a marvellous resource for lecturers, academics, and students alike, to revisit the collected material (including fieldnotes, interview transcripts, photographs, and diaries) from a broad range of qualitative studies (readers may wish to explore the online collection at http://www.esds.ac.uk/qualidata/). What ethnographers actually write down is therefore finally becoming more transparent. This is especially fortunate given that it is incredibly difficult to know what steps to take in order to reach the point where the information eventually needed is available for recall when it is required. Being advised to write down everything that may be important (Becker, 1998; Rock, 2001), is not particularly helpful when writing takes longer than doing. You only have to write a few lines of fieldnotes to become aware that it is essential to be selective from the outset. It is impossible to write down everything, and it is unlikely you will know what will be relevant. However, do not despair. This is one of the reasons ethnographers spend so much time in the field. Fieldnotes, like observations, are cumulative.

MATERIALS

Let's start at a more simple starting point. Fieldnotes have to be written somewhere. Nowadays many people write onto a computer but since this is unlikely to go everywhere with you, you will first need to take brief notes in something more easily accessible. The most sensible option is to carry a pocket-sized notebook for scratch notes. Alternatively you may prefer to talk into a digital recorder (though this would depend on the setting. You may look ridiculous and draw attention to yourself in some places but I can imagine other settings where doing this regularly is considered quite normal). One of my students who was doing research in night clubs sent himself texts on his mobile phone as this was less conspicuous than writing in a notebook. Be careful to avoid James Spradley's (1979) problem where constantly trotting to the toilet led his research participants to conclude he was suffering with a bowel disorder!

Written up fieldnotes (or *full notes*) can be written onto a computer or kept in a larger notebook. I write more quickly on a computer now than I can by hand, but I still feel that fieldnotes should retain the mood they were written in, so I try to avoid the temptation to go back and correct mistakes or fill in gaps. If you are using **computer software**, you can always add memos or notes so that you can add information and still retain the purity of the original notes.

FROM FIRST IMPRESSIONS TO INSIDER SENSITIVITIES

Now let's think about what to write. Since ethnographic research is often iterative-inductive (**inductive and deductive**) it is not always clear from the outset what aspects of the group or setting will be relevant to the developing analysis, or what aspects of the culture and community will be interesting to focus on as time develops. However, it is likely you began with some foreshadowed problems, or some vague idea what it was you wanted to know, what puzzled you as a sociologist. The first forays into the field can be some of the most important moments, when you see things for the first time as a stranger (or with the stranger's eye). So it is important to note down in as much detail as you can your first impressions. I will share with you some of my own (which have had to be typed up as they were collected on a, now obsolete, word processor!):

> Went into Rusty's bar last night because they had a sign outside advertising Tuesday night as quiz night. This bar is where the British Legion meets so it will be useful to get our faces known there. Many of the customers seemed to know each other and were perhaps residents, others were perhaps tourists. Those that knew each other were seated along the middle of the seating area and at the bar on stools. There is a television which faces the bar and can be seen by those at the bar and in the middle of the room, but not by those at the edges. We sat by the door because these were the only remaining seats at 9pm. The quiz took the form of a list of questions on a sheet of paper – all written in English. The bar only had English-speaking people in it … Prizes were given out unceremoniously. I did not see what

they were or who they were given to. There was little interaction between groups although some clearly knew the bar staff. After the results all the people from the centre tables left quite quickly, saying goodnight to the couple behind the bar. (O'Reilly, fieldnotes, 1993)

As time progresses, it is likely that fieldnotes will be directed more precisely to those facets of social life you are taking an interest in at the given time (see Mackinem and Higgins, 2007). Research and note-taking become more reflexive and active as time goes on, so what you write may become both more specific and more detailed. On the other hand, the general, sweeping observations can now be left out as they are background impressions. It is important to begin with the maxim 'if in doubt, write it down' and to add dates, times, details, and background information to aid recall at a later date. You will always rely on your memory to some extent as you remember sounds, smells, emotions, and sights that were never recorded. Perhaps, also, it is possible to accept that fieldnotes are reflexive, creative, selective (even unruly and messy, Marcus 1994), and simply to enjoy writing them as you might enjoy other forms of creative writing. This does not mean to suggest you make them up as you go along, but try to paint a picture for yourself that is as faithful a representation as possible of what you have seen, heard, and felt.

SIGNIFICANT EVENTS

It is quite common for ethnographers to make very full and in-depth notes of key events or incidents (see **key informants and gatekeepers**); Clifford Geertz's (1973) description of the Balinese cockfight is a charming example. Such events may be interesting or revealing because they are representative or because they run counter to intuition, raise emotions, unite groups, or cause conflict. They can be useful in the feelings they arouse in the ethnographer as much as those generated within the members of the group. Other significant events are revealing because people talk about them a lot, or get animated by them. These should make you stop and ask: What is going on here? Why does this seem to be so important? What issues is it raising?

HEAD NOTES, JOTTINGS, AND FULL NOTES

Emerson and colleagues (2001) distinguish between head notes, scratch notes (or jottings), and full notes. This is a useful distinction in that it raises awareness of the need to observe critically, to make notes of observations as soon as possible, and to pad these notes out to full records on a daily basis.

Head notes are notes held in the memory, observed and mentally recorded. Immersion is not the same as merging, or becoming one with a setting, group, or culture; and writing (or thinking about writing) is one of the things that enables that distance to be maintained. Some people do get so involved with some individuals in the field they decide not to write about them. Others decide all relationships in the field are more important than anything they might write and so abandon their work! Mostly, ethnographers retain the perspective of the stranger as they observe, make mental notes, and then write. In some ways this involves balancing *present-oriented* immersion with the *future-oriented* desire to write an ethnographic account. So head notes are about noticing and thinking about writing as one participates (see **the participant observer oxymoron**). If we are participating specifically in order to write at some stage about what we have observed, then we must be aware that we seek observations in order to write, that what we observe affects what we write but also that what we write (and aim to write-up) will affect what we observe.

Scratch notes are brief jottings that inform fuller notes and act as aide-mémoire. Some people write their scratch notes, or jottings, in short-hand; others record lists of words to act as triggers, or even diagrams and pictures. Whatever is used remember these are actually aides-mémoire, to be written up more fully later. Jottings should include both things that will trigger memory (which may even include smells and sounds) and details one is likely to forget (names, quotations, dates).

Full notes contain all details that might be required at a later stage. Full notes are the first stage of **writing** up. Full notes should include running descriptions of anything and everything thought relevant, and record the when, where, who, and how of events. They should make sense to someone who has never been there, and thus will provide a wealth of material on which to base, and validate, analyses. Full notes, however, are not simply facts but are implicitly theorised. They have an imposed order or structure, they are selective, purposeful, and angled. Full notes reflect developing theories or theoretical and epistemological frameworks.

INTELLECTUAL DIARY

Analysis of ethnographic data begins as early as the first set of fieldnotes. As soon as you collect data, you begin thinking about what you have seen and heard. You start asking yourself how this relates to your research questions, and what its implications are for who you should talk to or what you should take part in next (**sampling**). As you go about your daily business, even as you do routine tasks, ideas impinge on your brain, making connections between observations, starting to make sense of things you experienced. William Foote Whyte (1984) calls these flashes of insight that come to you when you were not even consciously thinking of a research problem, and they must be recorded just as your observations are recorded.

Some people write them as memos, padded out collections of thoughts and reflections, or sketched pieces of analysis. I prefer to think of the entire process as the intellectual process involved in ongoing ethnographic fieldwork, and so record these things in an intellectual diary. This, for me, is a hardback book I keep on my coffee table (and hide when we have visitors). But I admit if ideas come as I am transcribing an interview or writing fieldnotes on the computer, I cannot be bothered to go and get the intellectual diary so I simply add my thoughts there and then to what I am writing and change the font. Later I cut and paste them to my alternative, computerised, intellectual diary. Over time these ideas become consolidated, linked, incorporated into other plans and sketches, so the fact that they are in different places rarely matters. Some people argue that the attempt to keep analytical ideas and records of events separate is futile since all records are an attempt to sort and analyse (Jackson, 1990). I still prefer to distinguish them as best I can, recognising that it all gets a bit blurred at times. Emerson et al. (2001) go even further, distinguishing 'asides' , commentaries, and 'in-process memos', all of which contribute to the historical record of the emergent analysis.

PERSONAL DIARY

When I am doing fieldwork, I also keep a personal diary which I write in each night before I go to sleep. It serves as a useful record of my own feelings, thoughts, and reflections as I adapt to the fieldwork setting, cope with feeling strange and bewildered, and then become more settled. Perhaps it even helps retain the perspective of the stranger, guarding against merging instead of immersion (see **going 'native'**). It also has an analytic function, alerting us to feelings and emotions that participants in the field may well share (Lofland and Lofland, 1995), and providing a space for creative integration of the objective and subjective.

fieldnotes

75

Malinowski's diary, which was published by his wife after his death, is often used to demonstrate his ambivalence towards his 'natives', but I appreciate the sentiments many of us can share when he expresses:

> [t]he feeling of confinement, the obsessional longing to be back even if for the briefest while in one's own cultural surroundings, the dejection and doubts about the validity of what one is doing, the desire to escape to a fantasy world of novels or daydreams, the moral compulsion to drag oneself back to the task of field observation. (Firth's Introduction in Malinowski, 1967: xv)

FIELDNOTES AS AN AUDIT TRAIL

Despite what has been said above about the selectivity and essential bias inherent in the act of fieldnote construction, good fieldnotes can illuminate the interconnected process of observation, data collection, theorising, and analysis. Arturo Álvarez Roldán (2002) analyses Malinowski's fieldnotes (which are available in the British Library of Political and Economic Science, at the London School of Economics) in order to produce some kind of audit trail, demonstrating how his notes were used in conjunction with explicit theorising to construct a valid and internally consistent text. This goes some way to counter critiques, associated with the reflexive turn (**reflexivity**), that ethnographic texts are mere literary fictions. The notes demonstrate careful and rigorous data collection, and give evidence of Malinowski's techniques in checking for inconsistencies in accounts, and verification by triangulation. Furthermore, the written-up fieldnotes (in this case the text, *Baloma* 1916), explicate his methodological considerations in order that the reader can assess the validity of the 'tale'. The point of good notes then is that ethnographers base their descriptions, interpretations, and explanations on continuous references to fieldwork, fieldnotes, and theories. Roldán concludes, having compared the fieldnotes with the written *Baloma*, 'It is hard to imagine Malinowski writing a different essay with the materials that he had collected and analysed in a particular way'(2002: 379). Nevertheless, as Jackson (1990) observes, no matter how full the notes, they will never be sufficient to fully explain the intellectual work that went into determining what to do and write, when and how.

See also: analysis; coding; computer software; reflexivity; writing

REFERENCES

General

Becker, H. (1998) *Tricks of the Trade: How To Think About Your Research While You're Doing It*. Chicago: University of Chicago Press.

Emerson, R. M., Fretz, R. I. and Shaw, L. L. (2001) 'Participant observation and field-notes', in P. Atkinson, A. Coffey, S. Delamont, J. Lofland and L. Lofland (eds) *Handbook of Ethnography*. London: Sage, pp. 352–68.

Jackson, J. E. (1990) '"I am a fieldnote": fieldnotes as a symbol of professional identity', in R. Sanjek (ed.) *Fieldnotes: the Making of Anthropology*. Ithaca, NY: Cornell University Press.

Lofland, J. and Lofland, L. H. (1995) *Analyzing Social Settings: A Guide to Qualitative Observation and Analysis*, 3rd edn. Belmont, CA: Wadsworth.

Marcus, G. E. (1994) 'What comes (just) after the "post"? The case of ethnography', in N. K. Denzin and Y. S. Lincoln (eds) *Handbook of Qualitative Research*. Thousand Oaks, CA: Sage.

Mauthner, N., Parry, O. and Backett-Milburn, K. (1998) 'The data are out there. Or are they? Implications for archiving and revisiting qualitative data', *Sociology*, 32(4): 733–46.

Rock, P. (2001) 'Symbolic interactionism and ethnography', in P. Atkinson, A. Coffey, S. Delamont, J. Lofland and L. Lofland (eds) *Handbook of Ethnography*. London: Sage, pp. 26–38.

Spradley, J. P. (1979) *The Ethnographic Interview*. London: Holt Rinehart & Winston.

Examples

Emerson, R. M., Fretz, R. I. and Shaw, L. L. (1995) *Writing Ethnographic Fieldnotes*. Chicago: University of Chicago Press.

Geertz, C. (1973) *The Interpretation of Cultures*. New York: Fontana.

Lareau, A. (1996) 'Common problems in field work: a personal essay', in A. Lareau and J. Shultz (eds) *Journeys through Ethnography*. Boulder, CO: Westview, pp. 195–236.

Mackinem M. B. and Higgins, P. (2007) 'Tell me about the test: the construction of truth and lies in drug court', *Journal of Contemporary Ethnography*, 36(3): 223–51.

Malinowski, B. (1916) 'Baloma: The spirits of the dead in the Trobriand Islands', *Journal of the Royal Anthropological Institute*, 46: 353–430.

Malinowski, B. (1967) *A Diary in the Strict Sense of the Term*. London: Athlone Press.

Roldán, A. (2002) 'Writing ethnography. Malinowski's fieldnotes on Baloma', *Social Anthropology*, 10(3): 377–93.

Whyte, W. F. (1984) *Learning from the Field: a Guide from Experience*. Newbury Park: Sage.

fieldnotes

77

Focus Groups and Group Discussion

> *Here we distinguish between the sorts of group discussions that take part in ethnographic research and what social scientists have called focus groups.*

> *Outline: The difference between focus groups and group discussions. The role of naturally occurring and planned discussions, within ethnographic research, for revealing culture and internal structures. Bringing the conversation around to your topic to generate an opportunistic group discussion. The creativity and dynamism of group discussions. Conducting a planned group discussion without being restricted by focus group prescriptions. Managing group discussions and combining with other methods.*

INTRODUCTION

Ethnography not only involves observing and participating but also listening, talking, asking questions, taking part in debates and discussions, and sometimes leading them. Social groups are usually based on talk as much as action and an ethnographer's task is to participate (join in with conversations) and observe (think about what is being said, reflect on it, and even write about it). The role can be passive (e.g., taking part in conversations as a full participant) or more active (directing conversations or asking questions). The language of interviewing and focus groups makes little sense in these contexts. 'Interviews' imply power relationships, conjuring up the imagery of job interviews, police interviews, or confessions. 'Focus groups' imply market and, increasingly, government research. They sound purposeful, directed, and unequal. For these reasons I suggest ethnographers employ the language of **asking questions**, sharing conversations (see **interviews and conversations**) and, here, engaging in group discussions.

OPPORTUNISTIC DISCUSSIONS

Many of the discussions we have within **participant observation** take place in groups or at least with more than one person. These discussions can be incredibly dynamic and creative and revealing of all sorts of shared meanings, underlying structures, and implicit norms. I observed in Spain many times that when in a group anyone voiced negative feelings about life in Spain, it was never very long before someone reminded the group of the positive aspects, others joined in and eventually the tone of the discussion had swung back to the positive. I interpreted this as being one way in which the migrants coped with the uncertainties and ambivalences that marked their daily lives as migrants (O'Reilly, 2000). Such discussions, governed by rules and norms of interaction, take place over coffee, in restaurants, as people walk together, while watching television and in any number of settings (Alasuutari, 1995; Kamberelis and Dimitriadis, 2005). They provide rich material for ethnographers for their content as well as the patterns they reveal. They are often more bountiful than focus groups, where the researcher has to try so hard not to direct the conversation too much. Discussions that occur naturally like this are an opportunity to see how ideas are shared or generated, how thoughts are shaped in interaction, how norms are reproduced, and how power relations are managed.

In such naturally occurring discussions, our own presence can either become immaterial or we can take a more active role, saying things to test responses or subtly bringing the topic around to something we are puzzling over in our ethnographic analysis. We might then consider this is becoming something inbetween a naturally occurring discussion and a focus group, and we could call it an *opportunistic discussion* (O'Reilly, 2005). This acknowledges, reflexively, the ethnographer's role in the discussion; that it was taken advantage of opportunistically but that she intentionally took part with research goals in mind. The same thing can happen when (as so often occurs) you turn up to interview someone in depth and all their neighbours and friends have been invited around to join in. Take advantage of such situations to observe group dynamics, generate creative debates, let participants bounce ideas off each other, and go off in tangents you had not previously considered relevant. Of course, it is then necessary to accept that some voices or opinions may not manage to be heard, but an ethnographer can create space and time for this later. Subordinate or shy people can be encouraged to join you another time in an in-depth conversation, and unpopular ideas can be raised in sensitive settings in unthreatening ways.

PLANNED DISCUSSIONS

An ethnographer may want, more intentionally and purposefully, to make use of the techniques employed in what are commonly known as focus groups. But textbooks can be overly prescriptive about the size, nature, management, and purpose of focus groups. I would recommend a much more flexible approach. Although the recommended number of individuals in a group is between 4 and 12 (Gibbs, 1997; Morgan, 1998), I have had a discussion with over 30 school pupils all aged around 14. I cannot say it was very fruitful as a stand-alone method, but it was very creative and dynamic, generating some fascinating themes for me to pursue through participation, observation, and one-to-one conversations. I think of this approach as a *planned discussion*. It can involve any number and any mix of participants that suit the purpose. It can involve simply gathering together a group of friends or asking an existing group (such as a school class) to discuss a topic you suggest. The advantages of such planned discussions are that they generate conflicting ideas, cause people to think about things they may not have considered alone (and you may not have thought relevant), cause participants to question assumptions, and perhaps to change their minds. They can also generate material on rule-following, power relations, norms, and interaction. They are faithful to the belief that people make sense of their worlds through interaction with others rather than as individuals.

Planned discussions can be difficult to manage at times. They can get very heated and you may find you need to pour oil on troubled waters. Participants can become emotional or angry and you will need to think about how to deal with this if it is the result of your intervention. It is important to consider the implications of encouraging quiet or reticent people to speak or of raising topics that might not otherwise have been raised. You will need to think about how you treat material, emotions, or attitudes which would not have emerged naturally and to think very reflexively about your own role (see **reflexivity**). However, it is naïve to think that you had no role to play in the more opportunistic or natural discussions above.

Unlike traditional focus groups, planned discussions undertaken by an ethnographer are likely to use already existing groups of people who know each other and have some relation to the topic you are pursuing. They may take place more than once, building up relationships over time, in settings with which the participants are familiar. They work particularly well in the early stages of a project, since they generate a range of topics, approaches, and responses. Finally, planned discussions may provide an opportunity to talk with people you would not be able to talk to alone, and about topics that would be inappropriate one to one. For example, Fiona Hutton (2004) combined group interviews with ethnography to research how women view their participation in the contemporary club scene in New Zealand. The study yields several important insights about the ways women avoid sexual harassment, the use of alcohol to aid self-esteem, and the role of pleasure in risk-taking behaviour. Here group interviews are empowering, creating the space for sharing of confidences. Or for a further example, within a context of long-term ethnographic fieldwork in Thailand, Andrea Whittaker (2002) was able to encourage open and detailed group discussions about how decisions about abortion are made and reconciled with social norms. She did this using the technique of vignettes, where participants discuss imaginary or proffered stories rather than their own personal circumstances.

See also: asking questions; interviews and conversations; participant observation

REFERENCES

General

Gibbs, A. (1997) 'Focus groups', Social Research Update, 19: 1–7.
Kamberelis, G. and Dimitriadis, G. (2005) 'Focus groups. Strategic articulations of pedagogy, politics and inquiry', in N. Denzin and Y. Lincoln (eds) The Sage Handbook of Qualitative Research, 3rd edn. London: Sage, pp. 887–907.
Morgan, D. (1998) Focus Groups as Qualitative Research. London: Sage.
O'Reilly, K. (2005) Ethnographic Methods. London: Routledge.

Examples

Alasuutari, P. (1995) Researching Culture. Qualitative Method and Cultural Studies. London: Sage.
Hutton, F. C. (2004) 'Up for it, mad for it? Women, drug use and participation in club scenes', Health, Risk & Society, 6(3): 223–37.
O'Reilly, K. (2000) 'Trading intimacy for liberty: British women on the Costa del Sol', in F. Anthias and G. Lazaridis (eds) Gender and Migration in Southern Europe. Oxford: Berg, pp. 227–48.
Whittaker, A. (2002) 'The truth of our day by day lives: abortion decision making in rural Thailand', Culture, Health & Sexuality, 4(1): 1–20.

focus groups and group discussion

Generalisation

> Generalisation in ethnography involves (implicitly or explicitly) taking the findings from one group or setting and making a claim that they are relevant to other groups at other times and places.

> Outline: Ethnography often claims it offers depth rather than breadth. There is a need to be explicit about what is being generalised to where or whom. Representing ethnographic accounts as if they are of societies in miniature. 'Banal' generalisation which leads from experience to expectation. Issues of representativeness, inference and transferability of findings. The call for a reflexive analysis of rich data that leads to modest, sceptical, empirical, and theoretical generalisations.

INTRODUCTION

To generalize is to claim that what is the case in one place or time, will be so elsewhere or in another time. (Payne and Williams, 2005)

Ethnographers have tended to argue that, rather than attempt to meet the rigid standards set for evaluating quantitative research, their research should be viewed as an entirely distinct endeavour. Like other qualitative research, ethnography is depicted as exploring the messy nature of the social world in depth and in all its complexity rather than seeking broad generalisations or predictable patterns. Depth, then, is sought over and above breadth, and entire groups have been studied in all their intricacy with no consideration as to whether or where they represent anything wider. And this is very admirable and worthwhile. However, I do not see this as sufficient reason to entirely dismiss any attempt to make broader inferences, draw comparisons, or make generalisations. Furthermore, I think that in practice ethnographers often generalise without being explicit about how or to what extent they are able to do so. This is often achieved by sleight of hand, by studying one group but having a title and introductory chapter that refer to a broader population, or simply by using general language in the description of a broader group than was actually studied (e.g. Fechter, 2007; Okely, 1983). Roger Gomm and colleagues (2000) have recognised two such techniques ethnographers use: the Jonesville-in-the-USA approach and what I will call 'banal' generalisation. I argue (following Williams, 2000) that it would be far better to think systematically about the extent to which ethnographers might be able to make confident and overt, but *modest* generalisations.

JONESVILLE-IN-THE-USA

In *The Interpretation of Cultures*, Clifford Geertz (1973) drew critical attention to an approach to generalisation in which a case or an instance of something (such as a town, organisation, or person) is used as if they were a simple miniature and therefore directly representative of something bigger, just like the imaginary Jonesville is supposed to be able to represent the USA. Here, the ethnographic study is seen as a microcosm or a 'universal singular'. Gomm and colleagues (2000: 99) say this is like using a synecdoche: 'the use of a part of something to stand for the whole'. The approach has a long history but is not really justified empirically and is certainly problematic for a methodology that emphasises richness and complexity.

BANAL GENERALISATION

Geoff Payne and Malcolm Williams (2005) believe that everyday social life depends on actors generalising from their experiences and basing future actions on what they have seen happen so far. We might call this *banal generalisation*. I notice that every day just after 9am, the traffic volume in my town reduces and I can get to work more quickly. So I plan future journeys expecting this to be the case. Generally this sort of inductive (**inductive and deductive**) reasoning works. However, I am also drawing on other information – what I understand about the rhythms of the working day in the UK, traffic in cities as opposed to country areas – to enable me to determine the extent to which this is transferable to other times and other places.

Robert Stake (2003) says this natural form of generalisation develops within a person as a product of experience and rather than leading to prediction as such, it nevertheless does lead to expectation. We can transfer this sort of thinking to ethnographic methods of research. However, in ethnography, such banal generalisations may guide our actions but tend not to take the form of formal generalisations. Nor are they turned into predictions or

generalisation

hypotheses. Furthermore, Stake argues, neither should they. Guided by the pragmatic approach typical of the **Chicago School**, he says 'the aim of the practical arts is to get things done' (2003: 23) and such naturalistic generalisations are better at guiding actions than abstract statements of law which social science increasingly seeks. The result is that based on previous experiences (or systematic ethnographic research), we can expect to find similar events/outcomes/experiences in other similar situations.

TRANSFERABILITY

This is similar to Clive Seale's (1999) argument that qualitative researchers, rather than using the language of representativeness or generalisation, can consider the extent to which their research is transferable. In other words, it is possible that what has been learned in depth and richness, after a long time immersed in the field, can be transferred to some extent to other situations or settings that are similar enough to warrant it. Of course, in order to be able to do this it is crucial that we know enough of relevance about both situations in order to be able to decide if they are similar enough, in *relevant* ways, in the second place. We might do this ourselves by directly comparing places, groups, or people. Alternatively, we might let our readers do this having ensured that we give enough information in our ethnographies to allow the reader to really 'know' the setting and be able to judge for themselves. This is somewhat problematic since we cannot be sure what information might be relevant in the future. It is also somewhat defeatist and cannot be used to actually justify doing research in the first place. Are we conducting it just in case someone wants to transfer and, if so, what background information should we give with what comparisons in mind? Gomm and colleagues (2000) ask why we cannot draw general conclusions without being deterministic or reductionist. In other words, is it possible to generalise while leaving space for creativity, action, free will, and difference? This is what Malcolm Williams (2000) has tried to achieve with his concept of *moderatum* generalisation.

INTENTIONAL MODEST GENERALISATION

Banal generalisation is all very well for practitioners of daily life, but as social researchers we are aiming to do more than this. In the natural sciences, and then later in the social sciences, attempts to improve on the predictability of inductive reasoning were developed by calculating the probability of outcomes and the application of deductive (or axiomatic) reasoning. The problem of this for the social world is that individual actors impute various meanings to behaviours, interpret the meanings of others, and act unpredictably on the basis of free will (of course, the extent to which this is true remains a matter for ongoing debate). Some interpretivists (**interpretivism**) have therefore concluded that it is impossible to generalise; that each event, organisation, or situation, should be studied on its own terms, understood within its own frame of reference, and can even be represented in multiple ways (see Denzin, 1989).

Williams (2000) and Payne and Williams (2005), on the other hand, contend that we are able make *moderatum* generalisations (I prefer to think of these as *modest*). These resemble everyday, banal generalisations but can be expressed formally and remain moderate in scope and open to development and modification. Rob Stones (1996) would say we should remain sceptical about them. Modest generalisations can also generate hypotheses that can be tested for their applicability to other settings. The important requirement is that ethnographers do this generalisation intentionally, honestly, openly, and modestly. For a generalisation to be valid, it cannot be seen as a natural outcome of qualitative research, but should be explicitly considered, should impact on the research design and **sampling**, and then be discussed fully in the conclusions. The research then needs to be evidently competent and the generalisation claims clearly linked to the data on which they are based. Readers need to be given the evidence with which to evaluate the generalisations, and the assumptions on which arguments about transferability of findings are based need to be explicit. Ethnographic research is particularly suited to this as it yields such thick descriptions. The researchers should also consider alternative possible general statements and demonstrate why they were dismissed, and outline what constraints there are to any generalisations that could be made. Finally, general statements should be expressed modestly. That is to say, depending on the ethnographer's ontological position (or the kinds of phenomena generalised about), he/she may limit claims of generalisability to basic patterns or tendencies in given times or contexts and as only applicable to certain other settings, groups, or institutions.

THEORETICAL GENERALISATIONS

Most textbooks distinguish theoretical and empirical generalisation. The discussion above relates to empirical generalisations, in which observed tendencies or patterns are generalised out beyond the given case. This often involves treating people or situations as categories or classes of phenomena, for example by talking about teachers and pupils and schools rather than John, Mary, and Granchester High. Theoretical generalisation is when a theoretical statement is used to explain relationships between phenomena, or to summarise and make sense of disparate observations. I believe that theorising is a crucial part of ethnographic research and is what makes the data collected on a given case have relevance beyond that situation.

Theoretical generalisation can be inductive or deductive or a combination of both. Theories explain, or offer abstract propositions about, an entire society or limited aspects of social life and can be adopted, applied to the ethnographic data and adapted accordingly as a result, or can be generated from the ethnographic data as in grounded theory (see Snow et al., 2003, for example). Gary Alan Fine (2003a and 2003b) is doing this when he uses his study of one mushrooming organisation to discuss, theoretically, the inter-relationship between nature and community. The theories that ethnographic research produces and/or refines are stories about connections between things that may have relevance beyond the ethnographic situation in which they were produced, but, of course, remain open to revision and refinement in the light of new empirical data. In other words, like more empirical generalisations, they remain modest and we remain sceptical of them. This involves acknowledging, reflexively (**reflexivity**), that though we have rich and complex data, we are always working with fragments of the real that have come to us through various means of translation, interpretation, and critique (Stones, 1996). However, for now they are the best we can do.

See also: analysis; case study; coding; sampling

REFERENCES

General

Denzin, N. (1989) *Interpretive Interactionism*. London and Newbury Park: Sage.

Gomm, R., Hammersley, M., and Foster, P. (eds) (2000) *Case Study Method: Key Issues, Key Texts*. London: Sage.

Payne, G. and Williams, M. (2005) 'Generalization in qualitative research', *Sociology*, 39(2): 295–314.

Seale, C. (1999) *The Quality of Qualitative Research*. London: Sage.

Stake, R. E. (2003) 'Case studies' in N. K. Denzin and Y. S. Lincoln (eds) *Strategies of Qualitative Inquiry*. Thousand Oaks, CA, and London: Sage, pp. 134–64.

Stones, R. (1996) *Sociological Reasoning. Towards a Past-modern Sociology*. London: Macmillan.

Williams, M. (2000) 'Interpretivism and generalization', *Sociology*, 34(2): 209–24.

Examples

Fechter, A. -M. (2007) *Transnational Lives. Expatriates in Indonesia.* Hampshire: Ashgate.

Fine, G. A. (2003a) *Morel Tales: the Culture of Mushrooming.* Urbana and Chicago: University of Illinois Press.

Fine, G. A. (2003b) 'Towards a peopled ethnography: developing theory from group life', *Ethnography*, 4(1): 41–60.

Geertz, C. (1973) *The Interpretation of Cultures.* New York: Fontana.

Okely, J. (1983) *The Traveller-Gypsies.* Cambridge: Cambridge University Press.

Snow, D. A., Morrill, C. and Anderson, L. (2003) 'Elaborating analytic ethnography: linking fieldwork and theory', *Ethnography*, 4(2): 181–200.

Going 'Native'

> **The term 'going native' refers to the danger for ethnographers to become too involved in the community under study, thus losing objectivity and distance.**

> *Outline: Going 'native' as a derogatory term associated with the rhetoric of colonialism. The continuing problem of what is now termed 'over-rapport'. The lure of acceptance and its implications for lack of distance. 'All but the dissertation': the problem of never getting enough distance to be able to write it all up. Balancing distance and empathy, and the role of reflexivity in the participant observation oxymoron.*

GOING 'NATIVE' AND THE RHETORIC OF COLONIALISM

The term 'going native' refers to the tendency for some ethnographers to forget they are conducting research, to become fully fledged members of the community under study, and perhaps never 'go home'. It implies the loss of all objectivity, complete socialisation or immersion into the culture, and probably abandonment of the project. As John Johnson (1975) points out, it was considered a serious problem in the earlier days of fieldwork and even through to the 1960s. Johnson cites several authors who discuss the problem, including Colin Turnbull (1961) in *The Forest People*, who is clearly devastated to have to say goodbye to 'his' pygmies, 'his' forest, and what became his home for several years.

However, 'going native' is now seen as a derogatory or offensive term, associated with the language and attitudes of colonial ethnography. In fact, these early ethnographers could more easily be accused of suffering the problem of too much distance, of creating some sort of chasm between the researcher and researched. The very language of 'native', subject, respondent, or informant implies the 'othering' of the anthropological gaze (hence the title of books such as *Other Cultures*, by Beattie, 1966). Perhaps going a little bit 'native' would not have been a bad thing if it were used to counteract their often complex involvement in external structures of domination and control. The relationship between social anthropology and colonialism has been revealed and we now know that in some cases, anthropologists were directly funded by the colonial administrators (for example, Evans Pritchard's work with the Nuer was government-sponsored). Anthropologists often relied on the reports of missionaries, explorers, and government officials rather than gathering first-hand information. Some sort of bias was an inevitable result of such involvement and detachment. At best this merely meant turning a blind eye to some of the exploitation that went on under their noses, at worst there was pressure to get involved in the project of 'civilising the savages' (Asad, 1973; Burgess, 1984).

OVER-RAPPORT CAN STILL BE AN ISSUE

Now that ethnography is as likely to be undertaken in societies and communities where the ethnographer is already to some extent an insider (**insider ethnographies**), the problem of 'going native' is discussed less frequently. Furthermore, it is increasingly recognised that complete physical and emotional distance is neither possible nor even desirable. Nevertheless, some textbooks, though they might not use the language of 'going native', continue to concern themselves with its implications.

Martyn Hammersley and Paul Atkinson (1995) accuse Paul Willis (1977) of over-rapport. In his celebrated ethnographic study, *Learning to Labour*, Paul Willis followed 20 working-class boys through the last 18 months of school and beyond into the world of work. These 'lads' as they called themselves, accepted that they could not expect middle-class jobs, and as a result shunned schooling by constructing a disruptive counter-culture, oppositional to the norms and values of the school. Willis argues that this is indeed what capitalist society expects of them and their attitude merely demonstrates their easy and fatalistic acceptance of their inevitable futures. Through their own actions, the lads unwittingly contribute to class reproduction. But Hammersley and Atkinson suggest that Willis became too involved, that he identifies with the lads so completely he is unable to distance himself from their views. The ethnography then becomes essentially a celebration of their culture. Crucially, Willis explains the behaviour and attitudes of the 'lads' with reference to their working-class background but he fails to address the fact that other working-class boys are not the same. This is severe criticism indeed and appears to be evidence that Willis was too involved, but I am not at all sure that Willis's problem was actually one of over-rapport. In fact, his study is a **critical ethnography**, and it is this philosophical and epistemological position that impacts on his analysis more distinctly than his level of involvement. Indeed it could be argued, conversely, that it is his critical reading of the material that enables him to analyse his data with distance.

Nevertheless, the terms 'going native' and 'over rapport' remain useful for causing us to consider the extent to which we become involved and the implications of that involvement for our participants, ourselves, and our studies. It is still important to think about the delicate balancing act of empathy and distance that is such an essential component of the participant observer oxymoron.

THE LURE OF ACCEPTANCE

Because the ethnographic position falls somewhere between distance and empathy, insider and stranger, it can often feel uncomfortable and the pull to be accepted can become very strong. As a graduate student, Annette Lareau (1989) undertook ethnographic fieldwork exploring social class differences in parental involvement in schools. Her ethnography is rich and she proposes some insightful analyses, one of which is that an explanation for the apparent disinterest of working-class parents in their child's education is that in their minds, they have handed over this task to skilled and educated people to whom they feel they have nothing to offer. Middle-class parents, on the other hand, feel much better equipped to interfere, evaluate, and even criticise the competence of the professionals. However, such interpretations came as a result of considerable angst, emotional distancing, and painstaking, retrospective note-taking and writing. Lareau was disappointed with the lack of reflection on the fieldwork experience, revealing this process, in most publications. She therefore wrote an impassioned appendix (in the style of William Foote Whyte, 1993) describing her doubts, insecurities, and difficulties, which is reprinted in the wonderful collection by Lareau and Schultz (1996). Here, Lareau admits that a great deal of what she noticed and observed was never written down. She did not take field-notes as systematically and carefully as textbooks advise, and she puts this down to a tendency to 'go native'. She says:

> I liked being in the classrooms; I liked the teachers, the children, and the activities – making pictures of clovers for St Patrick's day, eggs for Easter, and flower baskets for May. I liked being there the most when I felt accepted by the teachers and children. Thinking about taking notes reminded me that I was a stranger, forced me to observe the situation as an outsider, and prevented me from feeling accepted and integrated into the classroom. (Lareau, 1996: 218–19)

Lareau thus reminds us how difficult ethnography can be at times; how uncomfortable the role of stranger can become and how the pull to be accepted, both for our own sake and for the sake of the research, can so easily lead to a tendency to go 'native', or to over-rapport. However, Lareau does not give us all this information in order that we can simply feel better. She concludes that researchers should never go into the field unless they have time to write up their **fieldnotes** afterwards. 'Field work without notes is destructive and useless' (1996: 219); it detracts from the validity and competence of the project. Here Lareau is reminding us, intentionally or not, that it is in fact this balancing of stranger and insider, of taking part and writing about it, that is the essential nature of ethnography.

ALL BUT THE DISSERTATION

Even in these days of electronic text, computer-aided analyses, insider ethnographies, and PhD completion rate records, it is still common for ethnographers to endlessly delay the final act of writing it all up; to achieve what Johnson (1975) has called the phenomenon of ABD (doing All But the Dissertation). But as Johnson goes on to explain, the problem is so much more complex than a simple label can encompass. Ethnographic field research is more intense and absorbing than any other data collection method, and always and inevitably results in some transforma-tion of the researcher in the process. 'That we make and are made up of the phenomena we seek to understand is the irremediable paradox of our enterprise' (Johnson, 1975: 160). Our relationship to the field that we attempt to understand through long-term engagement is therefore undeniable and endurable. It is no surprise then that the final acts of going home and writing it all down, the final acts that distance ourselves possibly irretrievably from the field, are so difficult to confront.

DISTANCE OVER EMPATHY

The debate about **rapport** and objectivity is really one about the extent to which we might get involved and how this impacts on our work and our participants. I think we do have to worry a little about getting too involved, whether we call that over-rapport or going 'native', or whatever. On the one hand, the goal is empathy, insider understandings, and perhaps learning about things as others experience them. On the other hand, as Sue Estroff (1981: 21) so eloquently puts it, 'The proposition that one must become or be mentally ill oneself (for example) in order to reach the desired quality of understanding may hold some logical or intellectual merit, but it is patently absurd and dangerously impractical at the personal level' and not only that, it would destroy any value the work may have had. However, this is clearly a matter of where you position yourself between extremes. Many people would consider that Estroff did go too far anyway, when she spent a period of time actually taking the drugs prescribed to her research participants. We have reached a point where it is crucial to think reflexively about our role as ethnographers.

See also: insider ethnographies; participant observation; participant observer oxymoron; reflexivity

REFERENCES

General

Asad, T. (ed.) (1973) *Anthropology and the Colonial Encounter*. London: Ithaca Press.
Beattie, J. (1966) *Other Cultures: Aims, Methods and Achievements in Social Anthropology*. London: Routledge & Kegan Paul.
Burgess, R. G. (1984) *In the Field. An Introduction to Field Research*. London: Routledge.
Hammersley, M. and Atkinson, P. (1995) *Ethnography. Principles in Practice*, 2nd edn. London: Routledge.
Johnson, J. M. (1975) *Doing Field Research*. London and New York: Free Press.

going 'native'

Examples

Estroff, S. E. (1981) *Making It Crazy. An Ethnography of Psychiatric Clients in an American Community*. Berkeley, CA and London: University of California Press.

Lareau, A. (1989) *Home Advantage: Social Class and Parental Intervention in Elementary Education*, London and Philadelphia: Falmer Press.

Lareau, A. (1996) 'Common problems in field work: a personal essay', in A. Lareau and J. Shultz (eds) *Journeys through Ethnography*.Boulder, CO: Westview, pp. 195–236.

Turnbull, C. (1961) *The Forest People*. London: Cape.

Whyte, W. F. (1993) *Street Corner Society: the Social Structure of an Italian Slum*, 4th edn. Chicago: University of Chicago Press.

Willis, P. (1977) *Learning to Labour. How Working Class Kids Get Working Class Jobs*. Farnborough: Saxon House.

Grounded Theory

> Grounded theory is both a methodology and a product. As a methodology it consists of techniques and guidelines for data collection and analysis in order to produce theory grounded in data.

> Outline: Glaser and Strauss and the discovery of grounded theory. An inductive approach to theorising and the influence of both positivism and interpretivism. The key, ground-breaking ideas. Interpretivist and constructivist developments of grounded theory methodology. The overlapping stages in the development of a grounded theory. Some of the techniques: coding, memo-writing, theoretical sampling. Writing grounded theory. Some grounded theory ethnographies.

GLASER AND STRAUSS AND GROUNDED THEORY

Grounded theory began in 1967 with the publication of the book *The Discovery of Grounded Theory*, by Barney Glaser and Anselm Strauss.

Glaser and Strauss had been exploring the process of dying in hospitals, especially the way such a difficult and often taboo subject is experienced and managed. This was joint work between two academics of quite different backgrounds. Glaser had been trained in quantitative methods and was influenced by many of the canons of the positivist approach (**positivism**), and its appeal to natural science, detachment, and the collection of sense data. Strauss had been a student at the University of Chicago (**Chicago School**). He understood people as actors in the social world and saw social life as a process: the outcome of interactions between people in given contexts. Glaser was also interested in social and socio-psychological processes in particular settings and in the experiences of actors. But he wanted to retain the rigour and objectivity of a scientific approach. They both saw the appeal and advantage of a qualitative approach but aimed to address some of the current criticisms aimed towards these methodologies: that they were subjective, unreliable, unsystematic, and invalid.

Glaser and Straus thus worked very closely together, sharing their notes and emergent ideas, and jointly conducted overt, systematic, and methodical analyses which led to what they refer to as the *discovery of theories*. What they achieved above all was to make explicit what had actually been done many times in practice, which is the process of qualitative analysis. They favoured an inductive approach (**inductive and deductive**). They believed in a world that exists independently of how it is perceived or understood (see **realism**), and that this pure reality is what social science should capture. And they sought theories, grounded in (rather than imposed on) data, which would explain observed processes. Their key ground-breaking ideas (Charmaz, 2006: 5) are as follows:

- Data collection and analysis go hand in hand.
- Codes, concepts, and categories to sort the data come from the data not from hypotheses.
- Analysis proceeds in stages with constant comparisons between data and ideas.
- Theory is developed in stages.
- Memos are used to elaborate (discuss, compare, limit, link) codes.
- Sampling is for theory construction not representativeness.
- The literature review comes later, after the independent analysis.

Grounded theories tend to be substantive. They address given problems in specific situations, but they can be generalised to broader situations.

Grounded theory is commonly used in medical and criminological settings, perhaps because of the demand in these fields especially to proffer theories that can be acted upon to effect change.

INTERPRETIVIST AND CONSTRUCTIVIST GROUNDED THEORY

Glaser and Strauss diverged over the years. Glaser has been at pains to defend the empiricist elements of the approach, which meant staying close to data and seeking the discovery of middle-range theories. Glaser now defends classical grounded theory and runs the Grounded Theory Institute. Strauss, who went on to work with Juliet Corbin, has been content to view the approach as more of a methodology: 'a way of thinking about and studying social reality' that sees theory as being grounded in data but rejects a simplistic adoption of inductive reasoning. For Strauss and Corbin, the discovery of grounded theory results from an interplay between researchers and the data, where the researcher is not afraid to draw on his or her own experiences. The theories that are produced are seen as modifiable, qualifiable, and open (in part) to negotiation, but because these theories are grounded in data, researchers are confident about their validity. Strauss and Corbin believe grounded theory is successfully achieved by teams because they are better at generating creativity and flexibility. For these researchers, it is possible to begin with some preconceived ideas or even hypotheses, but the researcher must remain sceptical of them until they have earned their way into the theory. Finally, they do believe grounded theories can have relevance beyond the specific case, can be generalised and acted upon.

This methodology thus shares a considerable amount in common with what I have described as ethnographic **analysis** and is compatible with the description of ethnography outlined in my introduction. The techniques that the grounded theory approach offers are merely methods for putting this methodology into practice. However, a key difference may be the express goal not simply to describe but to 'create new and theoretically expressed understandings' (Strauss and Corbin, 1998: 8).

CONSTRUCTIVIST GROUNDED THEORY

To continue the genealogy, a student of Strauss and Corbin, Kathy Charmaz, has now written extensively in the field, yet distinguishes herself in turn from her tutors by labelling her own approach constructivist.

For Charmaz, grounded theories are *constructed* through the researcher's engagement with the world, rather than simply discovered. Grounded theory, then, can be adapted for a range of philosophical approaches and theoretical and substantive interests. Like ethnography, it is affected but not determined by its roots. And it is possible to see all grounded theories as in some way realist, whilst in turn they are influenced by constructivist, positivist, or interpretivist ideas.

METHODS: THE PROCESS OF DISCOVERING OR CONSTRUCTING GROUNDED THEORIES

Grounded theory discovery or construction is not a linear process. Nor is it unitary – different researchers do it in different ways, and Charmaz often cites, as examples of grounded theory, ethnographic research which does not recognise itself as such. For this reason I invite readers to compare what I have called ethnographic analysis with grounded theory in practice (see O'Reilly, 2005). I think you will notice many similarities. The overlapping phases in the discovery or construction of grounded theory are as follows:

- defining research problems and opening questions
- data collection and initial coding
- writing memos and raising codes to categories
- data collection and focused coding
- writing advanced memos and refining categories
- theoretical sampling and directed data collection
- adopting categories as theoretical concepts, elaborating further memos
- sorting and linking memos
- integrating memos, constructing diagrams of concepts
- writing.

These phases rely on a set of systematic techniques and key concepts which would enable those ethnographers who prefer concrete guidelines for analysis to proceed with the messy business of sorting, analyzing, and making sense of data. I will outline some of the techniques and concepts that help to make grounded theory somewhat more transparent, but I recommend those who want to teach themselves the approach to read the relevant texts, especially Charmaz (2006) and Strauss and Corbin (1998).

Coding: labelling segments of texts with short phrases

A key and initial stage in analysis is **coding**. Grounded theorists begin with *open coding*, which is used to delve into the material to look for patterns, surprises, meanings, and intentions. Open coding generates the bare bones of analysis, is open to refinement and change, is open and free, yet remains very close to the data. Open coding works well in teams as it then becomes more creative, and it leads to more data collection and analysis. Try using gerunds for labelling text; it has an interesting impact. Try some coding word by word, and line by line. Try using *in-vivo* codes, which come from the research participants themselves.

Later coding will become more focused. *Focused coding* is more directive. It sees if codes used in one place work well elsewhere, so it is comparative. It refines, defines, and unpacks codes using memos. It leads to clusters of codes, which fit together into categories. You may want to use *axial coding*, which formally links categories together into a broader framework. Some grounded theorists also use theoretical coding. This involves applying labels and concepts from existing theory where they are useful for linking or associating codes and categories that emerged through open coding. Theoretical codes must be used carefully, explicitly, and reflexively. They must earn their way as codes rather than be imported as preconceived ideas. Coding can and should be creative and fun.

Memo-writing

Memo writing is simply writing out developing analytic ideas, explaining what codes mean, comparing data with ideas, and working through emergent theories on paper (see **fieldnotes**). They can be jottings, ramblings, or more systematically worked through arguments and schemata. *Memos* are the pivotal intermediate step between coding and writing (Charmaz, 2006). They often lead to more data collection. Memos can be sketched out quickly as they are for your own (or your team's) consumption only. They should help those who are intimidated by the idea of writing up, because they reflect work in progress, and are open to adaptation and change. Memo-writing can include sorting, diagramming, and integrating the emergent theoretical insights. These are all further tools in the construction of grounded theory.

Theoretical sampling

In grounded theory, sampling is not undertaken once and for all at the beginning of research, but as I have described under the concept of **sampling**, is ongoing and continuous as ideas develop and theories emerge. However, a key difference between what I have described elsewhere in this book and grounded theory's *theoretical sampling* is that the latter involves 'seeking and collecting pertinent data to elaborate and refine categories in the emerging theory' (Charmaz, 2006: 96). When you begin a grounded theory project, it is impossible to know what categories will be important or what will emerge as relevant processes to pursue and elaborate. I did not know, for example, when I began my work in Spain, that I would be interested in the relationship between concepts of tourism, yet it has become crucial to understand the articulation of migration and tourism in migrants' everyday lives and the way these can lead to exclusion and marginalisation (O'Reilly, 2003 and 2007).

As these theoretical explanations are developed, it becomes important to collect more data in order to refine and elaborate the developing (or constructed) theory. Theoretical sampling is iterative; it moves between data collection and analysis, collecting data to ensure that the developing categories (or clusters of ideas) are fully robust. That is to say, to ensure it is clear where they explain and where they do not apply; what they cover and what they do not. Theoretical sampling is only complete when categories are saturated. That is to say, that no new theoretical insights or properties are revealed when new data are gathered. *Saturation* means being able to talk abstractly and generally about the data in a way that is inclusive, subtle, and complete.

Writing

Finally, grounded theory involves **writing**. However, writing should not be seen as a final stage but as part of the process of analysis. Grounded theorists write memos, drafts, re-drafts, and then eventually begin to shape something up for dissemination and publication. Writing provides the opportunity to share ideas with others, to elaborate the theory that has been developed. It can critically examine the grounded theory, provide the context needed to outline it, make links with other theories, and provide the data to support it. Writing should emerge out of memos that have been continually elaborated as time went on. Interestingly, many grounded theory projects continue to result in quite descriptive

grounded theory

written pieces rather than in the elaboration of a new grounded theory. Charmaz believes that 'theory generation continues to be the unfilled promise and potential of grounded theory' (2006: 135). I would argue that a further continuing lack of grounded theory is its overt linking of substantive theories (and description) to existing literature and to broader structural conditions and processes, that is to history, power, and institutional constraint. However, grounded theory is an evolving method and I would recommend an open mind when deciding whether or not to employ some of its techniques and methodology.

SOME ETHNOGRAPHIES

Since reading more about grounded theory, I believe my own work to be sufficiently close to be able to label it grounded theory in practice. As I have said above, ethnographic analysis and grounded theory methodology share a lot in common. Strauss and Corbin (1997) have prepared an edited collection of grounded theory research projects which is worth consulting for examples.

See also: analysis; coding; computer software; inductive and deductive; writing

REFERENCES
General

Charmaz, K. (2006) *Constructing Grounded Theory: a Practical Guide through Qualitative Analysis*. London: Sage.

Glaser, B. G. and Strauss, A. (1967) *The Discovery of Grounded Theory: Strategies for Qualitative Research*. Chicago: Aldine de Gruyter.

O'Reilly, K. (2005) *Ethnographic Methods*. London: Routledge.

Strauss, A. L. and Corbin, J. (1998) *Basics of Qualitative Research: Techniques and Procedures for Developing Grounded Theory*, 2nd edn. Thousand Oaks, CA: Sage.

Examples

O'Reilly, K. (2003) 'When is a tourist? The articulation of tourism and migration in Spain's Costa del Sol', *Tourist Studies*, 3(3): 301–17.

O'Reilly, K. (2007) 'Intra-European migration and the mobility – enclosure dialectic', *Sociology*, 41(2): 277–93.

Strauss, A. L. and Corbin, J. (1997) *Grounded Theory in Practice*. Thousand Oaks, CA: Sage.

key concepts in
ethnography

Holism

Ethnographic research has often taken a holistic approach, linked to functionalism. This perspective views societies as discrete and coherent entities, or as organisms. Holism also acknowledges the interconnectedness of elements of a society.

Outline: Classical ethnography and the influence of Durkheimian sociology. The critique of holism and functionalism as ahistoric, static, and consensual. Contemporary ethnography's focus on both the global and local, within and beyond boundaries, as well as on the continuing salience of place and locality. The contribution of holism to an integrated and interdisciplinary methodology.

CLASSICAL ETHNOGRAPHY

Classical ethnographies often attempted to portray a whole way of life of a given society at a given time without necessarily acknowledging that it was just at that given time. Indeed, an ethnography was defined as 'a whole description of a way of life' (Asad, 1973). This became known as holism. Holism implied a coherence of discrete cultures, a timeless 'ethnographic present', a synthesis of place and culture (Faubion, 2001).

Many early ethnographers in the field of anthropology were influenced by the work of Émile Durkheim (1982). Durkheim argued that all societies are bounded units, held together by shared values, with clear boundaries between insiders and outsiders, and which must be understood on their own terms rather than as the sum of the individual parts that constitute them. Furthermore, for Durkheim, social life is external to the individual, exerts its influence on actions, and shapes cultures. Cultures, in turn, serve to integrate individuals into the harmonious functioning of the *whole* society. These ideas fed into the functionalist school of thought which viewed societies as complex systems whose parts each served its own function for the whole society.

Bronislaw **Malinowski** was one of the founders of the functionalist school of anthropology, and he used a holistic approach in his ethnography. One of the clearest ways this can be seen is in his admonition that ethnography should study all aspects of a society, from religion and sex, to kinship and political institutions. Malinowski's holism is also apparent when he draws an analogy between the body and the study of society. Survey work, he says, is all very well for providing a skeleton or for describing the framework of a society, but this kind of work lacks flesh and blood, or the intimate details of daily life. From surveys: 'we cannot perceive or imagine the realities of human life, the even flow of everyday events, the occasional ripple of excitement over a feast or ceremony, or some singular occurrence' (1992 [1922]: 17).

Malinowski's studies are excellent examples of the holistic approach. Holism continues to have an influence in anthropological ethnography today, with Daniel Bates arguing (in 1996) for example, that holism involves looking beyond the particular to wider issues and contexts in a given society.

CRITIQUE

Since the 1960s, functionalism has become discredited for being ahistoric and static, unable to account for social change or for conflict. It is sometimes described as consensus theory because of its focus on how things work rather than on the conditions leading to societies not working. Functionalism has also been linked to colonial attitudes which saw 'native' societies as different and exotic, and criticised because functionalists neglected the role of outside influences, especially their own.

With the critique of functionalism came a critique of holism and the assumption that a society can be studied as if it were an isolated island divorced from history and wider influences (Macdonald, 2001). At the same time, doubts were raised about the implications of the anthropologist's role in the colonial encounter, given that many had been funded by colonial administrators or informed colonial attitudes. However, there remains this sense of researching something exotic and 'other' even for those doing ethnography 'at home' (see **insider ethnographies**). And even as they began to undermine holism, still it was common for ethnographers to choose a setting and a people and just turn up and look for a topic. It is also important to note that the tradition of holism is what has inspired the ethnographer's desire to understand the aspects of a society in the context of other aspects of that society, even if it did not then look beyond the bounded confines of the given group or culture.

For Sue Estroff (1981), holism is broad rather than narrow. It involves acknowledging that what you are interested in sociologically might be linked or associated with other aspects of the society. In her study of psychiatric outpatients, holism urges a more integrated view of the person and therefore the inclusion of medicine and other illness experiences. Holism also implied the need to understand a society on its own terms and is therefore part of an important ethnographic tradition (Faubion, 2001). For Daniel Bates (1996), holism continues to encourage ethnographers to collect data on things that may seem peripheral or only tangentially related to the focus of a research project, and it encourages us to look beyond the particular to a more generalist viewpoint. In my own research in Spain, this has meant that I was always interested in migration more broadly defined than the 'retirement migration' label some researchers had already attached to this group, and has led me to explore broader sociological issues not often associated with migration studies (O'Reilly, 2003).

CONTEMPORARY ETHNOGRAPHY AND HOLISM

Contemporary ethnography attempts to take more account of history, geography, and power relations than was common in the classical tradition. Ethnographers are now as likely to study their own societies as those of others. They explore the interconnectedness of societies in the context of globalisation. They acknowledge the role of history, their own role as researchers, as well as the interrelatedness of people and institutions within and beyond the given setting and group. We therefore have **multi-sited**, historical, transnational, and global ethnographies as well as more local and small-scale studies that address outside influences and processes. Ethnographers still often want to understand how different people in discrete locales experience their everyday lives; the sense of a group and a locality has not gone, but there is an argument that people can no longer be understood simply in their local context, that the regional or global context must be addressed, as well as political, economic, social, and cultural relations.

Marwan Kraidy's (2002) study of Maronite youth in Lebanon directly challenges a holistic view of discrete societal units, where society has been taken to equal culture. Maronites are members of a Christian community living in a country composed entirely of ethnic minorities, with a predominance of Arabic identities in the wider culture. They are caught between West and East, Christianity and Islam, and attempt to articulate their own identities through these opposing discourses. Generally, they staunchly oppose belonging exclusively to one or other community but this is all the more difficult given the preponderance of wider, global representations that dialogically oppose 'the West' and 'the Arabs'.

holism

More recently still, ethnographers have begun to question the increased attention given to processes between and across societies and have drawn attention back to the persistent salience of place and space in people's daily lives. Some of these explore the process of boundary maintenance and construction. This is especially important in the context of migration studies (Cunningham and Heyman, 2004). In my own work on British migration to Spain, I have argued that even in Europe, with its open internal borders, intra-European migrants can end up socially excluded as a result of ambiguous rules of residence, taxation, rights, and responsibilities (O'Reilly, 2007). Some British migrants creatively live in a transnational third space, between Britain and Spain, with homes in both countries, and able to move betwixt and between at will. Others, however, are not so fortunate. These have moved to Spain to escape high crime rates, unemployment, divorce, insecurity, and risk. They have sold everything they once owned in the UK to fund their search for a better quality of life for themselves and their families. However, they end up living on the margins of society, not able to speak the language or to integrate, with no political representation and little in the way of future prospects. This happens because the borders between Britain and Spain still exist in the form of cultural, linguistic, political, and social phenomena. These can be invisible borders but are still very real in the context of people's daily lives. This sort of analysis can only be achieved by combining a holistic approach that explores an entire group or society and its interrelated parts, but also looks beyond the group to the wider society and to historical and other external factors.

It is because of the holism of ethnography both in anthropology, and the **Chicago School**, that it has developed an open mind to disciplinary boundaries, and to combining qualitative and quantitative methods. Ethnographic holism can be as much about inclusiveness as boundaries.

See also: Chicago School; Malinowski; multi-sited and mobile ethnographies; virtual ethnography

REFERENCES

General

Asad, T. (ed.) (1973) *Anthropology and the Colonial Encounter.* London: Ithaca Press.

Bates, D. (1996) *Cultural Anthropology.* Boston and London: Allyn & Bacon.

Durkheim, E. (1982) *The Rules of Sociological Method and Selected Texts on Sociology and its Method.* Edited with an introduction by Steven Lukes. Hampshire: Macmillan.

Faubion, J. D. (2001) 'Currents of cultural fieldwork', in P. Atkinson, A. Coffey, S. Delamont, J. Lofland and L. Lofland (eds) *Handbook of Ethnography*. London: Sage, pp. 39–59.

MacDonald, S. (2001) 'British social anthropology', in P. Atkinson, A. Coffey, S. Delamont, J. Lofland and L. Lofland (eds) *Handbook of Ethnography*. London: Sage, pp. 60–79.

Malinowski, B. (1992 [1922]) *Argonauts of the Western Pacific: An Account of Native Enterprise and Adventure in the Archipelagoes of Melanesian New Guinea*. London: Routledge.

Examples

Estroff, S. E. (1981) *Making It Crazy. An Ethnography of Psychiatric Clients in an American Community*. Berkeley, CA, and London: University of California Press.

Cunningham, H. and Heyman, J. M. (2004) 'Introduction: mobilities and enclosures at borders', *Identities: Global Studies in Culture and Power*, 11(3): 289–302.

Kraidy, M. M. (2002) 'The global, the local and the hybrid: a native ethnography of glocalization', in S. Taylor (ed.) *Ethnographic Research: A Reader*. London: Sage, pp. 187–210.

O'Reilly, K. (2003) 'When is a tourist? The articulation of tourism and migration in Spain's Costa del Sol', *Tourist Studies*, 3(3): 301–17.

O'Reilly, K. (2007) 'Intra-European migration and the mobility – enclosure dialectic', *Sociology*, 41(2): 277–93.

holism

Inductive and Deductive

In deductive *research a hypothesis is derived from existing theory and the empirical world is then explored, and data are collected, in order to test the hypothesis. An* inductive *approach is where the researcher begins with as few preconceptions as possible, allowing theory to emerge from the data.*

Outline: Qualitative research and the emphasis on induction. The problems with a naïve inductivism that ignores the role of the researcher. The contemporary use of a more sophisticated inductivism. The role of sensitising concepts, which are inspired by theory but which have to earn their way into iterative-inductive explanations. Abductive reasoning and feeling your way. Theory as the outcome of the interaction of experience and logic.

QUALITATIVE RESEARCH AND THE EMPHASIS ON INDUCTION

It has been common to claim that qualitative research suits a more inductive approach to reasoning and theorising. In *deductive* research a hypothesis is derived from existing theory and the empirical world is then explored, and data are collected, in order to test the truth or falsity of the hypothesis. Thus a deductive approach can be used to test existing theories but not to develop new perspectives that might challenge existing ideas. One wonders where the theories to be tested come from in the first place if not from the real world. An *inductive* approach to research is one where the researcher begins with as open a mind and as few preconceptions as possible, allowing theory to emerge from the data (see Znaniecki, 1934).

Qualitative researchers often explicitly reject a deductive approach, arguing that the social world is too complex and messy for patterns, laws, and regularities to make any sense. Furthermore, they have reasoned, when data are collected with theories in mind that have already been formed into working hypotheses, the focus of the research is restricted and perceptions distorted. Researchers tend to force data into preconceived categories or relations. As Michael Agar (1980) says, a hypothesis-testing social scientist cannot think outside of the framework imposed from the outset, and so all research participants get to do is offer up a bit of themselves for the framework.

However, the alternative emphasis on *induction* is also now seen as simplistic and problematic. It has been associated with naturalism or a naïve form of *realism* in the philosophy of science; the notion that there is a real world waiting to be captured by the ethnographer in all its complexity if he or she only hangs around long enough and unobtrusively enough. Since the publication of such work as Thomas Kuhn's (1970) *The Structure of Scientific Revolutions*, and especially since the series of debates in the reflexive turn, ethnographers are now much less naïve about their own (and wider society's) subtle influence on what gets researched, how, with what focus, and with what reporting. Indeed some forms of social constructionism and critical theory believe the researcher's task is actually to challenge and question received wisdom, or culturally accepted ways of seeing and categorising the social world. Here, inductive theorising is seen to have an inherently conservative bias.

In other words, while contemporary ethnographers do not want to be restricted by the testing of rigid hypotheses, they nevertheless acknowledge the impossibility of complete objectivity and openness in practice. Everyone starts out with some preconceived ideas, and some (even lay) theories about how the world works. All ethnography needs a focus of some sort, a boundary, a discipline, a loose framework. Most of us will begin with a research design, a title, and some indefinite objectives. Usually we will conduct a review of the literature before we begin. The point is to acknowledge their role in the research.

Consultation of extant theory, reviewing and revising grounded theory, analysis, and writing, are all now seen as integral overlapping parts of an ongoing research process, rather than stages in a linear progression. Ethnographers seek a sophisticated inductivism, or what I have called an iterative-inductive approach (O'Reilly, 2005). That is to say, ethnography moves back and forth iteratively between theory and analysis, data and interpretation. It emphasises the strengths and advantages of inductivism, but also takes the opportunity to test theoretical insights deductively, shining a brilliant light on problems and issues while simultaneously retaining a soft focus that enables inclusions and relations not previously considered (Peacock, 1986). As Douglas Ezzy contends:

> all data are theory driven. The point is not to pretend they are not, or to force the data into theory. Rather, the researcher should enter into an ongoing simultaneous process of deduction and induction, of theory building, testing and rebuilding. (Fzzy, 2002: 10)

inductive and deductive

Here, theory is precursor, medium, and outcome of ethnographic research and writing (Willis and Trondman, 2000) and research design is a reflexive process that operates throughout the study.

FORESHADOWED PROBLEMS AND SENSITISING CONCEPTS

Bronislaw **Malinowski** (1935) tended to speak as if the social world were made up of facts waiting for him to simply collect and chart. He saw himself as the chronicler and spokesman of the Trobriand Islanders and saw the task of anthropology to be one of letting the facts speak for themselves. An ethnographer must be prepared to change his views, and to cast off his theories, under the pressure of evidence. But he was not suggesting the ethnographer is some sort of blank page; rather he distinguished *foreshadowed problems*, which are inspired and stimulated by theory, and can be adapted or discarded in the field, from *preconceived ideas*, which cannot. Foreshadowed problems now tend to take the form of concepts, ideas, theoretical perspectives, and even common-sense notions ethnographers take into the field with them to help them focus but not to foreclose the research.

As Sara Delamont argues, 'The ethnography is only as good as the ideas the researcher deploys' (2004: 212). At the outset of an ethnographic study of opera tourism in Central Europe, her foreshadowed problems included a whole host of ideas about opera-goers, gleaned from opera magazines and tour brochures, that might or might not be confirmed in practice. When I began my research in Spain, I started by exploring media representations and common-sense knowledge on the British in Spain. This was not simply to judge if these were true, but to lend some direction to my research to begin with. As time went on, I discovered the concepts of tourism and escape were also useful. Kathy Charmaz (2006) says that grounded theorists (**grounded theory**) tend to use *sensitising concepts*, which give ethnographers ideas to pursue or sensitise them to look at certain angles or ask certain questions. Whatever shape they take, sensitising concepts and foreshadowed problems must be revised, revisited, and supplemented as the research progresses. They must remain questions until they have earned the status of answers.

ABDUCTION

Some readers may find the work by Gary Shank (2006), on abduction and praxical logic, a useful way to think about the role of induction and deduction and the development of explanations in ethnography. Deductive reasoning, Shank says, begins with a rule. For example: 'All dogs bark'. It then looks at the specific case, and so perhaps makes an observation that 'Fido is a dog' and concludes therefore that 'Fido barks'. This takes the shape of Rule, Observation, Result. Inductive reasoning begins with the observation, for example: 'Fido is a dog', followed by a further observation: 'Fido barks'. It then makes a tentative suggestion that is open to being tested further, that 'All dogs bark'. This follows the pattern: Observation, Observation, Rule.

Shank claims ethnographic research uses *abductive* reasoning. Ethnographic data are not clear signs of things such as dogs barking, but are more subtle and open phenomena. When we work inductively, we observe one thing and wonder if it is a sign of something else, broader and more general. Then we gather more evidence that leads us towards a family of things that all seem to point in one direction. Finally, a lot of evidence looks to be factual so we can start to generate formal looking, empirically based laws to account for them. But these remain open to revision. Abductively, rather than search for evidence, we follow hunches and omens, reading signs and playing with possible explanations that draw on the things we know, and looking for clearer signs or clues. We gather evidence towards a pattern, but not in a linear way. Shank says we must try to remain sensitive to the most subtle nuances in the field in case we overlook something of importance or foreclose the emerging theoretical understanding. It is crucial to move forward slowly and, as described in **analysis**, iteratively in order to avoid tuning out important data simply because they do not seem relevant to the concepts we have latched onto or theories we are using as a framework.

Abductive reasoning helps us to understand the meaning of settings for those involved in this research. But we can try to look for overall, coherent pictures to describe individual acts and their meanings. It is possible we may even pull together this 'rich, complex, meaningful, and coherent picture of the people, places and things in our field setting' (Shank, 2006: 33) into a theory of sorts, with which we may make predictions about future events or other settings.

FEELING YOUR WAY

Abductive reasoning is a scientific-sounding label for something that is inherently messy and uncertain. When we read other accounts of the analytic process of ethnography, one thing that comes out loud and clear is that it is more a matter of feeling your way than an overt process of logic. Susan Krieger (1996) researched a lesbian community in the US in the 1970s, where she had previously been a participant. She eventually left the community armed with 400 pages of 'rich data' and sat down to write. But she found she could not do it. For a year she moved, sorted, and copied notes. Then she tried writing a novel, then a personal account of her fieldwork experience. The problem, she eventually realised, was that she had been trying to distance herself from her data. Analysis for her meant revisiting the experience of data gathering, recalling the year of participation, 'to feel it as fully and deeply as possible and to analyze my feelings' (1996: 183). She needed to remember why certain things had moved her, why she had felt estranged, what had unfolded over the year. In the end the process was so personal that when reviewers said *The Mirror Dance* (Krieger, 1983) seemed a valid portrayal of the community, she was uncomfortably surprised.

William Foote Whyte (1996) believes **analysis** does not proceed in a neat linear fashion but emerges subconsciously out of the interplay of logic and experience. Ethnographers find themselves immersed in and living amongst a mass of confusing data which they attempt, often unsatisfactorily, to logically consider while simultaneously trying to live. Just when they seem able to detect some patterns or consistencies, something happens to cast doubt on it all. At other times an occurrence shines like a flash of light onto a mass of inconsistencies with the potential to explain them away. Still, we cannot trust such insights, because logic must play its part as well as experience, and notes must be re-examined, new data collected, as the explanation is tested for robustness. For this reason, Whyte believes the best way to explain the process of analysis is through an autobiographical account of 'living in the community', conceding that ethnographic research is inextricably mixed up with the researcher's personal and social life.

See also: analysis; coding; generalisation; grounded theory; Malinowski; sampling; time

REFERENCES

General

Agar, M. H. (1980) *The Professional Stranger*, 2nd edn. New York: Academic Press.

Charmaz, K. (2006) *Constructing Grounded Theory. A Practical Guide through Qualitative Analysis*. London: Sage.

Delamont, S. (2004) 'Ethnography and participant observation', in C. Seale, G. Gobo, J.F. Gubrium and D. Silverman (eds) *Qualitative Research Practice*. London: Sage, pp. 205–17.

key concepts in ethnography

Ezzy, D. (2002) *Qualitative Analysis: Practice and Innovation*. London: Routledge.

Kuhn, T. S. (1970) *The Structure of Scientific Revolutions*. Chicago: University of Chicago Press.

O'Reilly, K. (2005) *Ethnographic Methods*. London: Routledge.

Peacock, J. (1986) *The Anthropological Lens: Harsh Light, Soft Focus*. Cambridge: Cambridge University Press.

Shank, G. (2006) 'Praxical reasoning and the logic of field research', in D. Hobbs and R. Wright (eds) *The Sage Handbook of Fieldwork*. London and Thousand Oaks, CA: Sage.

Willis, P. and Trondman, M. (2000) 'Manifesto for ethnography', *Ethnography*, 1(1): 5–16.

Znaniecki, F. (1934) *The Method of Sociology*. New York: Farrar & Rinehart.

Examples

Krieger, S. (1983) *The Mirror Dance: Identity in a Woman's Community*. Philadelphia: Temple University Press.

Krieger, S. (1996) 'Beyond subjectivity', in A. Lareau and J. Shultz (eds) *Journeys through Ethnography*. Boulder, CO: Westview Press, pp. 177–94.

Malinowski, B. (1935) *Coral Gardens and Their Magic*. London: Allen & Unwin.

Whyte, W. F. (1996) 'On the evolution of street corner society', in A. Lareau and J. Shultz (eds) *Journeys through Ethnography*. Boulder, CO: Westview Press, pp. 9–74.

Insider Ethnographies

ethnographies insider

The goal of ethnography, to gain the perspective of the insider and to render it meaningful, raises special issues for ethnographers who are also members of the group they study.

Outline: The insider/outsider distinction. The development of ethnography 'at home' and explanations for more 'insider' ethnographies. Challenging the insider/outsider distinction. Criticisms of and problems with insider ethnography: accusations of over-involvement and bias. Advantages of being an insider: finding strangeness on your own doorstep. The ethnographer as key informant. Degrees of difference and the mirror of ethnography.

INSIDERS AND OUTSIDERS

The more or less explicit goal of thorough ethnographic research is to gain an insider perspective and to collect insider accounts. In order to achieve this insider perspective, it is considered best to adopt (if you do not already have one) an insider role within the community. The distinction between insiders and outsiders is based on the traditional conception of fieldwork as conducted by the lone ethnographer in some kind of exotic outpost. Here the goal was to become gradually socialised into the group, thereby gaining insider knowledge and understandings (see Ellen, 1984). However, such texts also acknowledge the importance of the initial outsider perspective, the initial culture shock or surprise that draws our attention to the unusual and strange that over time we will neglect to see. Several ethnographers have thus written about the experience and process of becoming an insider, about the process of merging self with other (Coffey, 1999). However, ethnographers also do research in settings in which they are already insiders, and this is becoming more common. This has led to discussion and debate about the implications of doing ethnography 'at home'.

ETHNOGRAPHY AT HOME

It was so taken for granted that ethnographic research within anthropology was undertaken away from home that, as it became more usual for it to take place in one's own country or community, the implications needed thinking about. Two books on doing anthropology at home, one centring mainly on Europe (Jackson, 1987) and one from North America (Messerschmidt, 1981), were compiled in recognition of the debates and the assumption that ethnography was traditionally done in distant lands, alone, as some kind of *rite de passage*. However, although the history of ethnography in anthropology is to some extent also the history of the colonial encounter, in sociology this has always been less the case. The Chicago sociologists (**Chicago School**) not only got out into the streets in their own cities and communities, but they were in many cases also personally involved in the lives or lifestyles of those they studied (Deegan, 2001).

But why did ethnography come home, as it were? Jackson wonders if one of the reason was that sociologists began to realise that ethnographic methods were needed to understand their own societies since other methods, such as survey work, were failing so badly. But other key reasons include: changes to funding opportunities; realising the exotic can be found just down the street; objections to intellectual imperialism; and changing international relations. Wars, civil unrest, governments who are unwilling to admit foreign researchers, can all make it difficult or inadvisable to go to some places. There was also an increase in the number of minority group and indigenous anthropologists working in the areas over which white, male, Euro-Americans thought they had a monopoly (Messerschmidt, 1981). In the US, American Indian and Hispanic anthropologists worked in their own communities, while female feminists researched the women's movement. Meanwhile, anthropologists who would previously have gone abroad started to focus on issues at home, specialising in fields such as medicine, urban studies, criminology, business, housing, or education.

But perhaps more important was the development of ideas that has led to the recognition of our own role in research and writing (see **interpretivism** and **reflexivity**) and the impact this must have on the naïve distinction between insider and outsider. Anthropologists and sociologists are now less wedded to the idea of a *science* of society; they have more or less accepted that research is complicated, messy, personal, and subjective, and so are less concerned with achieving distance. Or at least they are aware of the problematic nature of trying to achieve it.

CRITICISMS OF INSIDER ETHNOGRAPHY

However, when anthropology and ethnography did turn their gaze upon western and 'advanced' societies, they still tended to seek the 'primitive within' (along with ethnologists and folklorists) in peasant or rural communities, or focus on the exotic outsiders that could be found in strip joints, cocktail bars, retirement homes, and subcultures (Löfgren, 1987). Exploring one's own society and culture simply seemed too problematic.

Ethnography of what were termed 'contemporary' societies (as if more distant cultures were somehow also more distant in time) was seen to be too complex, or the insider was seen as too close, too involved, and lacking detachment. The anthropologist in a foreign culture has to struggle to gain insights; the anthropologist in her own culture must struggle to withdraw from it (Hennigh, 1981: 125). Some describe the knowledge gained, John Aguilar notes, as no more than subjective involvement, 'a deterrent to objective perception and analysis' (1981: 15). A widely held view is that outsiders can more easily read a society's 'unconscious grammar', implying that what ethnographers *infer* from behaviour is more fruitful than what they *derive* from locals' statements. The insider is seen as too familiar with the setting for the unfamiliar and exotic to arouse curiosity. Critics argue that outsider ethnography is essentially comparative because the ethnographer has been socialised into a different culture. They argue that the culture shock and subsequent adaptation which an ethnographer experiences in a foreign culture aid understanding of that way of life. Insider ethnography is seen as biased and as beginning with political aims. The non-involved outsider can be more scientific and more likely to question what others see as familiar. Critics invoke the advantages of the position of the stranger in Simmel's work. The stranger 'surveys conditions with less prejudice: his criteria for them are more general and more objective ideals; he is not tied down in his action by habit, piety, and precedent' (quoted in Aguilar, 1981: 17).

The advantage of a cross-cultural context

Kirsten Hastrup (1987) prefers to make a distinction not between insiders and outsiders, or home and away, but between cross-cultural and parallel-cultural contexts. And while she concedes there may be advantages in doing ethnography in a parallel culture to our own, she also recognises the advantage of strangeness and difference. For example, she says, it has been common for female anthropologists doing research in 'strange' cultures to be able to take advantage of their own difference and strangeness and to gain access to people and insights from which they would have been excluded, by being granted some sort of honorary male status. In research in a culture similar to one's own, participants are more likely to treat the ethnographer according to pre-conceived categories associated with class, education, gender, and so on. Outsiders are thus more likely to be told things insiders would not; and respondents are less partisan in their relations with them. Adopting the pose of naïve ethnographer who needs to be taught how to behave in the culture and can ask difficult questions is not so easy 'at home'.

DIFFICULTIES OF DOING ETHNOGRAPHY ON YOUR DOORSTEP

Ethnographers at home do not just research at home but also write and publish at home and they do not go home (thus achieving detachment and distance) at the end of the fieldwork period. They cannot so easily duck their moral or ethical obligations or ignore the implications of their work as stranger ethnographers. To the researched, the ethnographer is 'one of us'. Angela Cheater (1987) says this is not so much ethnography in your own backyard as in your own front room! I see it as not so much 'living amongst' another culture as weaving your way in and out of other people's worlds. It is thus crucial to confront your own role, and your impact on the topic, the research, the subjects. The problem for ethnographers in their own milieu is not so much how to gain access as how to stand back and see ourselves as others see us. However, Maryon McDonald believes it is possible to discover symbolic boundaries – the strange, exotic, and different – anywhere, even right on our own doorstep and 'they are none the less real for that' (1987: 122). Sue Estroff talks about this eloquently in her research on people labelled mentally ill:

> Instead of arranging for passage, visas, fearsome injections, getting out my hiking boots, and packing my trunk, I got in my car, drove for ten minutes to the downtown area of a city where I had lived for five years, and thus began fieldwork. Despite the geographic proximity and lack of exotic contingencies, I am convinced that the experiences of the two years that followed constituted as long, arduous, exciting and frightening a journey into differentness and newness as that of any anthropologist on her first vision quest. (Estroff, 1981: 3)

One problem when doing ethnography in a group with whom you are very familiar or in a parallel culture is that people tend to think they cannot be an object of interest because they are not *interesting* enough. In France, McDonald found herself constantly directed towards the Breton-speaking peasant communities, as if they were who she really wanted to learn about. In my own research in Spain, British people would tell me to talk to others who spoke more Spanish or had been there longer, or whatever else they considered more valuable than what they themselves had to offer.

But doing ethnography at home is not just about Europeans researching Europeans (or westerners, westerners) but also non-westerners engaging in research in their own communities. Indigenous anthropologists in Brazil, India, and North America, and later in other parts of the world, have increasingly explored their own societies. Cheater (1987) thinks that with such research opportunities on their doorstep, they have little inclination or need to go elsewhere. Third world or indigenous anthropologists (or what we might call ethnographers of and in the majority world) have their own particular problems: contexts are more likely to be overtly political and politicised, and perhaps dangerous and violent. And in some settings the independent ideas we seek or bring may be considered more dangerous than physical violence (Cheater, 1987).

ADVANTAGES OF AN INSIDER PERSPECTIVE

To counter to these criticisms of doing ethnography at home, insider ethnographers either find fault with the outsider perspective or demonstrate the advantage of their own. Defendants of insider research may see outsiders as less trustworthy, less discerning, lacking commitment to the group, or having no political axe to grind. Insider ethnographers argue that the experience of culture shock is a negative rather than positive reaction more likely to cause the ethnographer to recoil than open up. Insiders believe they blend in more, gain more **rapport**, participate more easily, have more linguistic competence with which to ask more subtle questions on more complex issues, and are better at reading nonverbal communications. Where they are politically engaged, research participants are more likely to open up to them, whereas a stranger is always to some extent strange and alien. Insider ethnographers argue that they are less likely to construct stereotypes or to caricature communities, and are more likely to present complex interpretations of events. They get beyond the ideal to the real, daily, lived, and back-stage experiences. Rather than *describing* the unconscious grammar of the community, their ethnographies are *expressions* of it, the result of a superior insider knowledge gained through primary socialisation.

Even ascribed status roles, though more severe in parallel cultures, can be an advantage to insider ethnographers. The ethnographer is never seen as no one. Aguilar in his research in Chiapas, was categorised according to his Spanish surname and non-Indian appearance. In Spain I was seen as a woman, of a certain age, and treated accordingly. Respondents wondered if I represented a government agency: the department for social security perhaps, or the tax office. It was assumed as a female academic I was feminist, left-wing, and middle class. Ethnographers learn about the unwritten codes and rules, assumptions, and categorisations of their community from such ascription. And **access** can be aided as well as impeded. In Hastrup's (1987) research in Iceland, she found that being Danish meant that her access and experiences were very much circumscribed by the gendered role in which she was cast. However, in this role she perceived things she might have missed if she had been cast in the role of honorary male.

The ethnographer as key informant

Many deal with the problem of being an insider by trying to make the familiar appear strange or looking for the symbolic boundaries. Alternatively, Lawrence Hennigh (1981) contends that we can use ourselves as **key informants**. He did long-term ethnographic research in a school and local community in Oregon in the 1970s in an area affected by economic slump, rapid population growth, and mass migrations. During his time in the field he became so involved in community affairs that eventually newcomers were directed to him for information about local matters; he was seen as an expert and activist in a variety of areas. The more he got involved in school–community relations, the more he realised these became his research 'problem'. Although he was being guided into this by the community, to resist would have seemed unnatural to him. There was an expectation to be civic-minded and an emphasis on community spirit, which he learned about through being cast in the role.

The ethnographer as key informant, he argues, has greater access, has negotiated entry to a range of settings and people, knows who to ask, can interpret responses more subtly, can more easily gain knowledge that interviews might never reveal. Furthermore, the research is more ethical, contributing real investment of time and energy as opposed to the token membership so typical of traditional ethnography. In such long-term fieldwork it becomes very difficult or even uncomfortable to remain objective or detached and to constantly solicit other people's opinions while suppressing our own (Hennigh, 1981). One's approach therefore tends towards the active and participant, but this can be seen as a positive thing if interpreted sensitively and used to full advantage.

Criticisms of outsider perspective

Jackson (1987) notes the tendency for traditional ethnography to search for novelty in their work and says this is much more difficult to find at home. As Maryon McDonald (1987) points out so articulately, French reality is not captured by bringing home croissants and wine any more than the French might capture British reality by taking home lamb chops. There has also been a tendency for anthropologists to see culture as static and as something to be preserved. It is far less easy to think like this in one's own country with extensive records of past events to contend with. Furthermore, those who studied what we might think of as the strange exotic 'other' often ended up being so involved that the distinction between insider and outsider became blurred. Consequently, ethnographers practically adopted 'their' communities, engaged in activism or advocacy, or ended up **going 'native'**.

CONCLUSIONS: DEGREES OF DIFFERENCE

Both insider and outsider ethnographies have their own problems and advantages. But these are more a matter of degree than a simple distinction between one or other perspective. Human societies have as much in common as they do that is unique, and generally ethnographers are only more or less insiders or outsiders. Most societies are characterised by difference and internal variation, so neither insiders nor outsiders are status-free. Neither can gain access everywhere. The insider lives in a culture and so thinks they understand it. The outsider remains outside the culture but perhaps can thereby describe it more easily. Both can be biased for or against their own primary socialisation; either can have implicit or explicit goals. Both can lose objectivity. Both must acknowledge their own impact, by being reflexive (**reflexivity**). Both must attempt to synthesise emic (insider) and etic (the ethnographer's own) representations. 'Thus, the outsider must to some extent get into the natives' heads, skins, or shoes, whereas the insider must get out of his or her own' (Aguilar, 1981: 24). Ethnographers in any situation can select settings and events that alter the extent of social and cultural immersion in order to enjoy and benefit from both insider and outsider status, when either at home or away. Or they can engage in team work, using team members to provide distance or constituting the team from insiders and outsiders (Mackinem and Higgins, 2007).

It is undeniable that humans tend to notice the unfamiliar and unexpected more than the familiar. But Aguilar argues that it is theory that directs our gaze as ethnographers, not personal curiosity:

> In terms of the goals of science, the difference between the existentially familiar and unfamiliar is of little significance … the 'scientific perspective' differs from the ordinary view of life in that scientists, like philosophers, marvel at the familiar, or the theoretical implications of normal events. (Aguilar, 1981: 19–20)

The ethnographer takes his or her informal and formal training and theoretical perspectives into the field. During and after the fieldwork, he/she will write and thereby gain emotional and mental distance. Even

key concepts in ethnography

physical distancing may occur at the end of the fieldwork period, as the researcher returns to university or work.

The mirror of fieldwork

Kirsten Hastrup (1987) says fieldwork is like looking in a mirror at what is going on around you. In the mirror of fieldwork you see yourself at the same time as you see others. You are both subject and object. The ethnographer, like the mirror, she argues is a third-person character, neither you nor I. He or she lives in the third person, and is a friend to the locals and a stranger to herself.

> This is the truly privileged position for ethnographic fieldwork. It is not solely a matter of both participating (assuming the role of *you*) and observing (keeping *my* professional aims intact), but also, and more importantly, to let go of both and live, feel, and experience from the position of the third person. Here the silences of both you and I are heard, and the blank banners are readable. (Hastrup, 1987: 105)

This is why when we leave the field we tend to feel such sorrow. We are leaving behind this third person with whom we have become so familiar: 'the mirror-image of noone … who will forever exist as a language-shadow in the discourse upon our friends' (1987: 105).

See also: going 'native'; interpretivism; participant observation; participant observer oxymoron; reflexivity

REFERENCES

General

Aguilar, J. (1981) 'Insider research: an ethnography of a debate', in D. A. Messerschmidt (ed.) *Anthropologists at Home in North America: Methods and Issues in the Study of One's Own Society*. Cambridge and New York: Cambridge University Press, pp.15–28.

Coffey, A. (1999) *The Ethnographic Self: Fieldwork and the Representation of Identity*. London: Sage.

Deegan, M. J. (2001) 'The Chicago School of ethnography', in P. Atkinson, A. Coffey, S. Delamont, J. Lofland and L. Lofland (eds) *Handbook of Ethnography*. London: Sage, pp. 11–25.

Ellen, R. F. (ed.) (1984) *Ethnographic Research. A Guide to General Conduct*. London: Academic Press.

insider
ethnographies

117

Jackson, A. (ed.) (1987) *Anthropology at Home, ASA Monographs 25*. London and New York: Tavistock Publications.

Messerschmidt, D. A. (ed.) (1981) *Anthropologists at Home in North America. Methods and Issues in the Study of One's Own Society*. Cambridge and New York: Cambridge University Press.

Examples

Cheater, A. P. (1987) 'The anthropologist as citizen: the diffracted self?', in A. Jackson (ed.) *Anthropology at Home, ASA Monographs 25*. London and New York: Tavistock Publications, pp. 164–80.

Estroff, S. E. (1981) *Making It Crazy. An Ethnography of Psychiatric Clients in an American Community*. Berkeley, CA, and London: University of California Press.

Hastrup, K. (1987) 'Fieldwork among friends: ethnographic exchange within the Northern civilization', in A. Jackson (ed.) *Anthropology at Home, ASA Monographs 25*. London and New York: Tavistock Publications, pp. 94–108.

Hennigh, L. (1981) 'The anthropologist as key informant', in D. A. Messerschmidt (ed.) *Anthropologists at Home in North America: Methods and Issues in the Study of One's Own Society*. Cambridge and New York: Cambridge University Press, pp. 121–32.

Löfgren, O. (1987) 'Deconstructing Swedishness: culture and class in modern Sweden', in A. Jackson (ed.) *Anthropology at Home, ASA Monographs 25*. London and New York: Tavistock Publications, pp. 74–93.

McDonald, M. (1987) 'The politics of fieldwork in Brittany', in A. Jackson (ed.) *Anthropology at Home, ASA Monographs 25*. London and New York: Tavistock Publications, pp. 120–38.

Mackinem, M. B. and Higgins, P. (2007) 'Tell me about the test: the construction of truth and lies in drug court', *Journal of Contemporary Ethnography*, 36(3): 223–51.

Interpretivism

The term interpretivism refers to epistemologies, or theories about how we can gain knowledge of the world, which loosely rely on interpreting or understanding the meanings that humans attach to their actions.

ETHNOGRAPHY AND POSITIVISM

Ethnography is often described as interpretivist, or at least as anti-positivist. However, since Bronislaw Malinowski is considered one of the founders of contemporary fieldwork methods, then ethnography clearly has at least some roots firmly in the positivist tradition (**positivism**). Many early British anthropologists, including Malinowski, were influenced by the work of Émile Durkheim and sought a science of society that could emulate the achievements and influence of the natural sciences. Durkheim proposed that *social facts* could be compared to other, natural phenomena, and thereby studied as things that are external to the individual in their ability to influence actions and behaviours, ideas, and beliefs. A **participant observation** with such an intellectual heritage was one in which the role of participation was actually quite minimal, and any interest in individuals was secondary to the study of the 'forms of life' (Radcliffe-Brown, 1952). However, as time went on, philosoph-ical reflection in various forms led to a critique of positivist assumptions, especially the assumption that social life can be studied using the same principles and ideas as natural science. These philosophical reflections and critiques can be grouped under the umbrella term of *interpretivism* because of their emphasis on understanding and interpreting the mean-ings humans attribute to actions.

INTERPRETIVIST CRITIQUE AND *VERSTEHEN*

Interpretivism views individuals as actors in the social world rather than focusing on the way they are acted upon by social structures and exter-nal factors. An early critique of positivism came from the sociologist Max Weber (1864–1920), who has been described as a methodological (or ontological) individualist. This is to say, he believed that in order to understand human societies, we must begin with the individual actor, with the meanings attached to individual actions, with what was intended when choices were made, possible reactions reviewed, and an eventual action selected. For Weber people do not (always) simply respond to external stimuli but often think and then choose how to react. In other words they tend to attach meaning to what they do. The task of the sociologist is to try to understand, or interpret (Weber used the word *verstehen* for the work sociologists need to do), what individuals intend when they do certain things. However, Weber also believed (following Kant) that it was impossible to gain objective knowledge of the world simply using the senses. The sociologist had to make sense of, or interpret, what was observed, and inevitably he or she would do this by drawing on his or her own cultural values. This did not mean being subjective and allowing values to affect the work, but rather being sensitive to cultural values and the relevance of meaning for action.

Weber did not seek causal laws of human society but instead tried to construct meaningful stories that tried to explain historical links between series of events. He used *ideal types*, or plausible models of societies' features, in order to talk abstractly about relations between phenomena. He saw social life as complex and unpredictable because people's actions can have unintended consequences, but nevertheless he thought it possible to identify contributory factors that, if removed, might mean an outcome was impossible. Weber's methodology implied that in order to understand why people do things, it is essential to get close enough to them to begin to empathise or to understand from their point of view why they made certain choices.

PHENOMENOLOGY

Another contribution to the complex of ideas clustered under the term interpretivism was the development of phenomenology. The term is used with various meanings and interpretations and has been developed in diverse ways in different social science disciplines. It owes a huge debt to the work of Alfred Schutz (1972) who argued that, rather than simply receive external stimuli as disordered chaotic reality, humans order and categorise information as it is received by the senses. In other words, we immediately try to make sense of, and typify, what we see and hear, and to associate sets of typified things with others, into categories and sub-categories. In the social world, this leads humans (including sociologists) to organise people into types of people, to distinguish them from other types of people, and to expect certain types of behaviour from each. These typifications and understandings then affect subsequent behaviour. Schutz's ideas have informed later work in ethnomethodology (Garfinkel, 1967) and the work of social constructionists such as Peter Berger and Thomas Luckmann (1967). Methodologically, the implications are the focus on everyday social experiences, on the way social reality is produced through interaction, on the daily meanings people attach to actions, and on the individual in society rather than on external structures. Phenomenologists also explore the way categorisations and typifications are taken-for-granted and seen as natural and inevitable. It is easy to see how these approaches lend themselves to ethnographic methods.

Other interpretive approaches include symbolic interactionism, which explores the way meanings are constructed between individuals through the process of interaction (see **Chicago School**), and idealism. Idealism is influenced by the work of Peter Winch, who argued that the way a group or society views the world in which they live will to some extent define their experience of that world, or the reality in which they live. A society's language, for example, will frame what can be experienced and how, as will sets of ideas, cultural attitudes, and concepts. If we are to understand a society, therefore, we need to understand its language, its culture, its rules, and norms, and other basic ideas groups share about their world. Only when fully immersed in a culture can we understand it as an insider does and therefore share their view of reality. Taken to extremes, this can imply an extreme relativism, in which no culture or society can be understood outside of its context, no comparisons made because each group needs to be understood on its own terms, and no judgements can be made to settle ethical or truth claims (see **postmodernism**). For ethnography, on the one hand, the methodology is suited to the interpretation of cultures within their own worlds of meaning, but there remains a problem with translating what has been observed for other, or academic, audiences. Of course, Winch's ideas do not necessarily lead ethnographers to abandon all attempts to make value judgements, or comparisons; indeed they can be used to critique contemporary society (see Benton and Craib, 2001).

HERMENEUTICS

A further thread in the fabric of interpretivism is hermeneutic understanding, which for ethnography can be translated as the interpretation of cultures. Influenced by Hans-Georg Gadamer (1976), hermeneutics has its roots in the interpretation of biblical texts and hence critiques all notions of objective knowledge in favour of understanding through a merging of horizons with the producers of knowledge in order to begin to think like them. This knowledge can then be translated for other systems of meaning, such as social science, by a sort of double interpretation. Knowledge production here is seen as a historical process of moving between parts and wholes, cultures and individuals, history and texts. A hermeneutic understanding involves understanding the other's point of view, from their perspective, and in the context of the social world within which it was produced.

INTERPRETIVE ETHNOGRAPHIES

There is no direct line between these ideas and ethnographic methods; researchers use the terms interpretivism, phenomenology, and hermeneutics in different ways with different implications for methods. Indeed, contrary to what is often supposed, there is no essential link between interpretivism and qualitative methods; many people use interpretive methods to understand statistical correlations, by trying to understand the shared meanings, cultures, and individual motives that led to action. Similarly, ethnography can be (and has been) influenced by ideas we might label positivist. However, those influenced by philosophies of interpretivism aim to understand individual human action either in terms of their daily interactions and common-sense ideas or in the context of the wider culture. This is achieved more easily by participation in those daily lives and contexts, and may even lead to full immersion and empathy which, in turn, yield an even better understanding through experience or even co-construction of the social world (Holy, 1984; Charmaz, 2006).

Ethnographic methods do lend themselves well to an interpretivist stance and the methods have systematically and persistently been adapted in relation to philosophical arguments about the way social life can be known. Nevertheless, the extent to which we can ever achieve understanding of a group in which we are not fully an insider, or understandings can then be translated for another audience, or the extent to which causal mechanisms or explanations can be found, or society acted on to effect change, all remain debatable. Fortunately it is now not essential to make a simple choice between a positivist and an anti-positivist (hermeneutic, phenomenological, or interpretivist) approach, because there are non-empiricist accounts of science, generally accepting that scientific practice is socially and historically located, that can inform contemporary ethnography (see **realism**).

SOME EXAMPLES

I am not personally in favour of labelling a piece of work as interpre- tivist, realist, postmodern, or whatever. There is much overlapping, for example some contemporary ethnographies clearly owe a debt to both postmodernism's interest in multiple realities *and* to some of the posi- tivist's desire to emulate the natural sciences (see Barry, 2002). Instead I find it useful to note the *influence* of these philosophical reflections on the way ethnography is now being conducted.

The influence of varieties of interpretivism, such as hermeneutics, can be recognised in many ethnographies. An interesting piece of work on drug courts in the US, for example, engages in something of a triple interpretation. Drug-courts are court-supervised drug treat- ment programmes that have sprung up in several states in the US in response to a dramatic increase in arrests related to cannabis and crack use during the 1980s. Through long-term participant observa- tion in three courts, Mitchell Mackinem and Paul Higgins (2007) investigated how drug-court staff interpret whether clients are telling the truth or lying when they respond to accusations they have tested positively for drugs. In other words, they interpreted the inter- pretations and then re-framed them in scientific language for a social science audience. Whether or not the clients are lying becomes irrel- evant, in as much as the outcomes are produced by the interpreta- tions within the interaction.

A phenomenological approach has led to some meticulous ethno- graphies that offer no more than 'folk explanations' or rich descrip- tion. Others have dared to stand back and look critically at what they have observed in such depth (see **critical ethnography**). Annette Lareau says that while she enjoys reading phenomenological studies that are rich in the flesh and blood of vivid detail, she does not believe the researcher's descriptions must *only* reflect actors' subjective expe- riences. She argues, in relation to her study of parental involvement in schools:

> It does not trouble me if my interpretations of the factors influencing their behaviour is different from their interpretation of their lives. Parents at Prescott and Colton schools cannot be expected to be aware of the class structure of which they are a part, nor of the influence of class on behav- iour. (Lareau, 1996: 225)

Interpretivism

It is often possible to see the influence of many philosophical ideas together in one piece of work and, again, possible to interpret practice in various ways. Philosophy in ethnography should be used in an under-labourer role. That is to say, it is most useful when used to untangle the reasoning that is going on when we attempt to acquire knowledge in practice.

See also: analysis; critical ethnography; positivism; postmodern ethnographies; realism

REFERENCES

General

Benton, T. and Craib, I. (2001) *Philosophy of Social Science: the Philosophical Foundations of Social Thought*. Basingstoke: Palgrave.

Berger, P. and Luckmann, T. (1967) *The Social Construction of Reality*. London: Allen Lane.

Charmaz, K. (2006) *Constructing Grounded Theory. A Practical Guide through Qualitative Analysis*. London: Sage.

Gadamer, H-G. (1976) *Truth and Method*. Berkeley, CA: University of California Press.

Garfinkel, H. (1967) *Studies in Ethnomethodology*. Englewood Cliffs NJ: Prentice Hall.

Holy, L. (1984) 'Theory, methodology and the research process', in R. Ellen (ed.) *Ethnographic Research. A Guide to General Conduct*. London: Academic Press, pp. 13–34.

Radcliffe-Brown, A. R. (1952) *Structure and Function in Primitive Society*. New York: The Free Press.

Schutz, A. (1972) *Phenomenology of the Social World*. London: Heinemann.

Examples

Barry, C. (2002) 'Multiple realities in a study of medical consultations', *Qualitative Health Research*, 12(8): 1093–111.

Lareau, A. (1996) 'Common problems in field work: a personal essay', in A. Lareau and J. Shultz (eds) *Journeys through Ethnography*. Boulder, CO; Westview Press, pp. 195–236.

Mackinem, M. B. and Higgins, P. (2007) 'Tell me about the test: the construction of truth and lies in drug court', *Journal of Contemporary Ethnography*, 36(3): 223–51.

key concepts in
ethnography

Interviews and Conversations

> An ethnographic interview is like an in-depth conversation that takes place within the context of reciprocal relationships, established over time, based on familiarity and trust.

> Outline: Creating space for in-depth conversations. Structured, unstructured, and semi-structured interview styles and their role in ethnography. In-depth conversations as an interconnection of views. Flexibility in style and approach. Distinguishing an ethnographic interview from other approaches. Some practical issues and some examples.

CREATING SPACE FOR IN-DEPTH CONVERSATIONS

All sorts of social research uses interviewing. In fact it is now the most popular method in social science in the UK (US social scientists rely on it a little less heavily). Ethnographic research employs interviewing tools but always in the context of the ethnographic perspective discussed in the introduction. Under the concept of **asking questions**, I have already demonstrated the way ethnography consists of talking and listening and asking questions as much as it does participating and observing (**participant observation**). In daily life people talk, listen, debate, explain, discuss, and ask questions. Social life is heavily dependent (in most contexts) on conversation and talk. The task of the ethnographer is to tune in to such talk, engage in it, and to ask questions pertinent to her own research as and when she can. However, there are also times when taking someone aside or making a little time out of the hustle and bustle of everyday life to have an in-depth conversation is really worthwhile. In-depth conversations (or interviews) give the ethnographer and respondent time to delve more deeply, to express their feelings, to reflect on events and beliefs, and to even expose their ambivalences. In-depth interviews also create space for the participants to focus on intimate details, to remember historical events, and to discuss things that would not be discussed in normal circumstances. In-depth interviews, then, are an important tool in the ethnographer's toolkit.

INTERVIEW STYLES

There are different interview styles ethnographers can draw on depending on the demands of the research, the expectations of the participant, and external circumstances. Most qualitative methods textbooks distinguish structured, semi-structured, and unstructured interviews (see May, 2001). It is a useful starting point as it provides some of the language through which we might understand what we are doing when we plan an interview.

- A *structured* interview is where a set of questions is predetermined and fixed. The researcher does not add or delete questions during the interview. The wording and ordering of the questions are preserved, usually in order to ensure standardisation across interviews.
- An *unstructured* interview is much more free-flowing and formless. The interviewer is likely to have no more than a list of topics to cover or a guide to themes. The interview is more like a conversation than an interview, with the researcher able to insert questions as and when it feels right, and the respondent able to answer at leisure and in ways that suit her.
- A *semi-structured* interview contains elements of both styles. Some questions will demand fixed responses while others are presented as themes to explore in depth.

Ethnography relies much more heavily on unstructured conversations than on structured interviews. This is why Steiner Kvale (1996) prefers to talk of InterViews, which provide the context for an exchange or *interconnection* of views rather than a one-way flow of information. Conversations encourage reflexivity on both parts, enable the time it takes for participants to explore their own beliefs, and to express contradictory opinions, doubts, fears, hopes, and dreams. They also provide space for the interviewer to adapt her own perspective. We usually begin with an outline, guide or plan, but are content to let the interviewee wander off what we think is the point. An ethnographer is usually attempting to learn about participants from their own perspective, to hermeneutically understand the other's view, and this will not be achieved by imposing one's own line of questioning on people. As William Foote Whyte (1981: 35) contends, 'the whole point of not fixing an interview structure with pre-determined questions is that it permits freedom to introduce materials and questions previously unanticipated'. This new material can be introduced by the ethnographer or (more likely) the participant.

An ethnographic interview is usually informal and relaxed; they take time, and are usually enjoyable for all parties. However, other interview styles may be drawn on for different circumstances. Do not be afraid to find out what you want to find out using any techniques and tools at your disposal. Only remain clear as to your overall purpose as an ethno-grapher. Ethnographers often require, for example, some standard infor-mation from everyone in a given group (their ages, how many sheep they have, whether or not they have health insurance, for example). This demands direct questioning. There may be times when a respondent demands to see a more structured interview schedule before agreeing to discuss a topic in depth. A lawyer who had happily agreed to an in-depth interview asked me, just as we began, to show him the list of questions I would ask. I showed him my interview guide and he was happy with that. A British Consul official, on the other hand, requested a printed list of questions in advance and insisted I stick to those. However, once the interview was over and I had turned off the tape recorder he was content to talk freely and at length about any number of topics I had not thought to include. He then agreed to my including this material in my research! Similarly, some participants respond better to a more formal approach than a very relaxed one.

It is useful to distinguish interviewing people in their private role and interviewing people in their work role. Often when we talk to someone in their work role, for example, as a teacher, policewoman, doctor, or bank manager, they are much more formal and guarded than when we talk to them as a mother, son, migrant, or whatever. They work harder to maintain a front-stage persona (Rubin and Rubin, 1995). Treating someone more formally, showing them an interview guide, explaining our purposes and intentions, are all ways of showing due respect to any research participant. Informality should result from **rapport** rather than be imposed.

WHAT MAKES AN INTERVIEW ETHNOGRAPHIC?

Some ethnographers use interviewing as their main data collection technique, or rely on it quite heavily alongside the use of other methods and tools (Hobbs, 2001). This leaves us wondering where we might draw the line between interviewing and ethnography. In other words: what makes an interview ethnographic? I think Barbara Sherman Heyl (2001) has some of the answer in a very useful and informative discussion of ethnographic interviewing. For Heyl, a key distinction between ethnographic and other forms of interviewing is that ethnographic interviewing is conducted in the context of an established relationship with a research partner. Here ethnographic fieldwork provides a context for building relationships with people that can improve and inform qualitative interviews. The relationship must be respectful of each other, as equal as possible, ethical, and sensitive. This can only occur where the ethnographer and participant have got to know each other over time, through several conversations where an exchange of views was enabled. The interview itself must be unstructured, perhaps only having a list of vague topics the ethnographer hopes to cover. Here, the respondent is able to offer her own insights, to guide the research in directions he or she thinks appropriate, and to wander off the subject when and where it suits. The interviews should be relaxed and enjoyable, not forced into a framework determined by the interviewer.

Life history, narrative, and biographical interviewing provide us with some good examples of ethnographic interviewing at their best. Life history interviews explore a specific topic in the context of a whole life story. The approach has a long heritage beginning with such **Chicago School** classics as Nels Anderson's *The Hobo* (1961) and *The Polish Peasant in Europe and America* (Thomas and Znaniecki, 1927). For his famous study of *The Jack Roller*, Clifford Shaw (1966) established an eight-year relationship with Stanley (the mugger whose story is being told in his own words) and they became such close friends that the relationship did not end once the research was finished. For more up-to-date examples, see Rosie (1993) for an interesting combination of life story with other techniques in the construction of a narrative account, and Humphrey (1993) for a series of life stories conducted within a single community.

However, Heyl's attention is more focused on the interview than on the ethnography. One gets the sense that the ultimate goal is to extract verbal information. I believe ethnographic interviews are also about building relationships in order to enhance ethnography. Both the chats and the in-depth conversations are valuable; as are the participation and observation. Just as when you meet a new colleague or potential friend (or even partner), ethnographic relationships begin with casual, brief conversations. But for a friendship or relationship to develop, you need to make time to walk together, have coffee or dinner together, to provide an opportunity to get to know each other better. You then ask about each other in more depth and reciprocally. Ethnographic interviewing uses this model; it is just a little more one-sided.

WHERE, WHEN, AND HOW? INTERVIEWS AS CONVERSATIONS

For the reasons above, I think it is far better to think of ethnographic interviews as conversations. Participants should be asked 'Can I talk with you about this?' rather than 'Can I interview you?' They should be allowed to choose time and place, as long as you indicate the sort of conversation you are seeking. It works best if there is time and space somewhere relaxed and comfortable for a frank exchange, where the participants can reflect on the meanings they place on actions, and can bring back to mind historical events as they are remembered, and the accompanying emotions.

I am often asked by students how long an interview should last and how many one should do. There is no definitive answer to this question; it really depends on where the interview/conversation fits within the overall research project and what form the conversation takes. I would recommend at least an hour is required if a topic is to be explored in depth; however, more than three hours tends to get tiring for both (or all) participants. But this is a guide not a rule. Some intimate confidences and crucial insights can be revealed in seconds (within the context of relationships that are gradually built as part of an ongoing ethnographic project). Alternatively, some people take a long while to get going yet can talk for hours without needing a break.

I would also recommend that in-depth conversations take place somewhere both ethnographer and participant feel relaxed, without pressures from others or demands on time. The ideal seating arrangement is where you are sitting at a 90 degree angle from each other; not quite facing each other full on but easily facing each other with a slight turn of the head. This is less confrontational than head on. Again these are mere guides and you must do what feels right for you and the conversational partner in the given circumstances. I have had some in-depth conversations in a noisy bar with a television blaring, in someone's dining room with three children playing around our feet, sitting around a swimming pool sipping sangria, and even in a police sergeant's office with an interior window facing massive queues for residence permits. In most cases I was not given the opportunity to decide where and how to sit or how long I could take.

Finally, in-depth conversations may take place just once or may occur several times as a long historical or in-depth perspective are constructed. Life history and biographical interviews normally take place over several interviews.

SOME EXAMPLES

To conclude, an ethnographer may use semi-structured interviews, and even some structured ones. But these would be secondary tools used in the context of long-term participant observation, the establishment of relationships based on trust, where rapport has been built over time. For a research project that relies solely on interviewing to be considered ethnographic, there must have been time, quality, trust, **rapport**, openness, and a focus on meanings (O'Reilly, 2005). Gavin Smith's (2007) work is undoubtedly ethnographic but some of his conversations lasted a few seconds while others lasted for hours.

In my own research I have asked people for details about their lives at every opportunity, using these bits of information to gradually build up a more complex picture of the entire culture (O'Reilly, 2007). But I have also asked people to sit down with me for a while to really talk in depth about their reasons for moving to Spain, their experiences of learning the language, their hopes and dreams for the future, and their experiences in light of the dreams they set out with. These conversations would last for anything from one to three hours.

Patricia and Peter Adler spent a number of years collecting the stories of people who self-harm. They conducted 80 in-depth interviews with people aged 16 to mid-fifties. They also joined self-injury Internet groups and collected hundreds of emails and Internet communications of 'cutters, burners, branders and bone breakers' (Adler and Adler, 2007: 540). However, these were not fleeting encounters in order to collect the buried treasure of interview transcripts (see Kvale, 1996). Many of the conversations and interviews took part within the formation of deep and enduring friendships that lasted years (and some that continue still).

See also: asking questions; focus groups and group discussions; participant observation, participant observer oxymoron; rapport

REFERENCES

General

Heyl, B. S. (2001) 'Ethnographic interviewing', in P. Atkinson, A. Coffey, S. Delamont, J. Lofland and L. Lofland (eds) *Handbook of Ethnography*. London: Sage, pp. 369–83.

Hobbs, D. (2001) 'Ethnography and the study of deviance', in P. Atkinson, A. Coffey, S. Delamont, J. Lofland and L. Lofland (eds) *Handbook of Ethnography*. London: Sage, pp. 204–19.

Kvale, S. (1996) *InterViews: An Introduction to Qualitative Research Interviewing*. Thousand Oaks, CA: Sage.

May, T. (2001) *Social Research. Issues, Methods and Process*, 3rd edn. Maidenhead: Open University Press.

O'Reilly, K. (2005) *Ethnographic Methods*. London: Routledge.

Rubin, H. J. and Rubin, I. S. (1995) *Qualitative Interviewing. The Art of Hearing Data*. London: Sage.

Spradley, J. (1979) *The Ethnographic Interview*. Orlando, FL: Harcourt Brace Jovanovich.

Examples

Adler, P. and Adler, P. (2007) 'The demedicalization of self-injury: from psychopathology to sociological deviance', *Journal of Contemporary Ethnography*, 36(5): 537–70.

Anderson, N. (1961) *The Hobo*. Chicago: University of Chicago Press.

Humphrey, R. (1993) 'Life stories and social careers: ageing and social life in an ex-mining town', *Sociology* 27(1): 166–78.

O'Reilly, K. (2007) 'Intra-European migration and the mobility – enclosure dialectic', *Sociology*, 41(2): 277–93.

Rosie, A. (1993) 'He's a liar, I'm afraid: truth and lies in a narrative account', *Sociology*, 27(1): 144–52.

Shaw, C. (1966 [1930]) *The Jack Roller. A Delinquent Boy's Own Story*. Chicago: University of Chicago Press.

Smith, G. J. D. (2007) 'Exploring relations between watchers and watched in control(led) systems: strategies and tactics', *Surveillance and Society*, 4(4): 280–313.

Thomas, W. I. and Znaniecki, F. (1927) *The Polish Peasant in Europe and America*. New York: Dover.

Whyte, W. F. (1981) *Street Corner Society: the Social Structure of an Italian Slum*, 3rd edn. Chicago: University of Chicago Press.

Key Informants and Gatekeepers

A key informant is an individual who becomes central to the ethnography for one of a number of possible reasons.

Outline: Using gatekeepers and key informants to gain access to a group. 'Encultured' informants and key members of a community. The role of informants (or participants) who are central, high status, and less easily available than other members of the community. Key events or incidents for revealing insights, illuminating analyses, altering the direction of the research, or challenging assumptions. Distinguishing the 'traveller' ethnographer from the 'miner', and therefore distinguishing participants from informants.

key concepts in ethnography

132

GAINING ACCESS AND GATEKEEPERS

The history of ethnography is replete with the stories of key informants and gatekeepers. Gatekeepers are sponsors or individuals who smooth access to the group. They are the key people who let us in, give us permission, or grant **access**. Sometimes, problematically, this is provided on behalf of the other participants, who may not even be aware of the research (Brewer, 2000). Gatekeepers may be official or unofficial leaders, managers, organisers, or simply busybodies. They may be in a position to grant permission themselves or able to persuade others (see Smith, 2007). I have used several gatekeepers at different times. It has occurred to me more recently that a lot of them have been men, but this may reflect the fact that men are more likely than women to have power and influence. They included: the African man who introduced me to a social club, the field club, and the English theatre; the English army Major who introduced me to the Anglican church community and obtained membership for me of the Royal British Legion; the American woman who introduced me to the foreign resident's department at Mijas and came with me on trips to Gibraltar and to the International Day fair; the English woman who was glad of a companion on coach trips and introduced me to all her friends; and the Irish man who had spent some time in a Spanish prison and who accompanied me to some 'seedy joints'.

Annette Lareau (1996) notes that though informal contacts usually work best in the field, it is crucial to get the permission of the most high-ranking officials as early as possible to pre-empt any difficulties later on. Powerful people can close down access in an instant if they choose to. However, the person through whom access is gained will have important impacts on the research itself. John Brewer's (1990, 1991) work with the Royal Ulster Constabulary was enhanced by access via the Chief Constable but the topic itself had to be presented (and therefore researched) in such a way that it would appeal to the Chief Constable rather than the police officers themselves. As a result, many police officers wondered just who the research was really for, and how it might benefit them.

THE ROLE OF THE KEY INFORMANT

It is not easy to distinguish gatekeepers from key informants; one often blurs into another. A gatekeeper may be key in that it is their approbation which enables access to the group, or someone may be a key informant because of who and what they know. James Spradley (1979) talks of 'encultured informants' who are consciously reflexive about their culture, and either enjoy sharing local knowledge or are in a status position where this is expected of them. Loughborough University has its own key informant in the shape of a retired academic who not only worked for the university for many years but has made a hobby of learning the university's history and sharing this information, most engagingly, to visitors and newcomers. Mary, who came on coach trips with me also went shopping with me, gave me advice about what to buy and how, and told me lots of stories about her experiences and funny tales about her friends and family. I like to think every participant is in some ways an informant and in some ways key, but a *key informant*, as the term has been widely used, is someone who becomes particularly central. They enjoy sharing the ethnographic enterprise with us and relationships with them can lead to long-lasting friendships. William Foote Whyte's friend Doc is a perfect example of this kind of key person. Doc famously told Whyte

You tell me what you want to see, and we'll arrange it. When you want some information, I'll ask for it, and you listen. When you want to find out their philosophy of life, I'll start an argument and get it for you. If there's something else you want to get, I'll stage an act for you. (Whyte, 1993: 292)

Doc clearly thought the research would be more reliable if he himself sought the answers rather than if Whyte did the questioning. Indeed, he once warned him off asking too many questions himself. Gary Armstrong's (1993) research with 'The Blades', Sheffield United Football Club supporters, was made much easier because key informants would ring him up and tell him where the action was. These examples illustrate how helpful key informants can be but also serve to warn ethnographers that findings can be skewed if we rely too heavily on just a few individuals who may be so keen to help that they stage events. A further warning is that gatekeepers can restrict as well as aid access, especially if they are members of gangs or cliques and seek commitment from the ethnographer.

BUSY INFORMANTS

It is worth spending some time thinking about the role of a particularly busy informant in the ethnographic account. While some individuals can be easily located and will join you on coach trips or shopping trips or can be chatted with over a beer at the drop of a hat, others are more difficult to locate and to obtain time with. Examples in my own research include the Chief of Police, the British Consul, the editor of an English-language magazine, and the Anglican vicar. These people were simply not to be found hanging around in public spaces and so had to be sought out especially for their view of things. Interviewing (**interviews and conversations**) such people often requires much more careful planning than is required for other informal chats, since there may be just the one opportunity. I recommend leaving such interviews until later in the fieldwork, when you have a clearer idea what it is you want to know than you might at the outset. However, sometimes these key people will raise exactly the range of issues you discover are central to the topic. The Anglican vicar spoke so authoritatively about death, marriage, national identity, going home, the informal economy, and the establishment of community that I wondered he had not written his own ethnography! Talk to such people as and when you can, but if you just have one opportunity then plan for it carefully.

KEY EVENTS

It is also worth considering the role of key events. A key event or 'key incident' (Emerson, 2004) is where something happens during fieldwork that is likely to be revealing for the research as a whole. A key event can act as a trigger for discussion and reflection because people are brought together that might not usually be, or emotions are aroused in novel ways, such as at wedding ceremonies, funerals, or festivals. They can be instances when all those themes you are interested in are played out, such as the International Day Fair which is held in Mijas (Southern Spain) each year and brings together all sorts of migrant groups as well as Spanish clubs and associations (O'Reilly, 2000). A key incident can be something that opens up new lines of inquiry, directs analysis in new ways, or confirms all sorts of emergent hypotheses. Key incidents tend to appeal specifically to a **grounded theory** or inductive approach since they 'provoke movement from description to analysis' (Emerson, 2004). They are often out of the ordinary, dramatic, exciting, or emotional events, but a mundane occurrence may just as easily turn out to be a key incident because of the way it was perceived by the ethnographer. Emerson distinguishes 'extreme cases' and 'interactional disjunctures'.

Extreme cases are rare occurrences that serve to exaggerate, accentuate, or make visible qualities that are normally implicit. My own example would be the Fiesta del Carmen ceremony in Fuengirola. During this ceremony a huge float bearing the statue of Carmen, the patron saint of fishermen and sailors, is slowly carried by 100 men in sailor's uniforms through the town and out to sea to bless the sea and the fisherman, before returning through the town followed by a long procession of townsfolk bearing candles. When I saw this ceremony during my first fieldwork period in Spain, I was absolutely enchanted to witness the float and procession stop at a small town house while from the first balcony a young woman sang a beautiful unaccompanied aria. However, just underneath the balcony was a British pub, the Queen Vic. The pub doors remained open as the woman sang, the clientele continued chatting, and the juke box was playing English pop songs. The contrast between the beautiful, peaceful clear voice of the woman listened to in silence by the enchanted crowd and the noisy bustle of the pub-goers, entirely oblivious to their surroundings could not have been more profound (O'Reilly, 2000).

Interactional disjuntures are awkward encounters, unexpected interactions, or situations that do not turn out as might be expected. These may be subtle incidents which raise all sorts of questions for analysis. For example, when trailing a psychiatric emergency team conducting its duties, Emerson (2004: 436) witnessed the way one patient 'quietly but effectively refused to assume the role of patient', thus challenging fundamental taken-for-granted aspects of the psychiatrist–patient interaction.

Finally, some ethnographers use a key event to frame subsequent analyses; Geertz's (1973) study of a *Balinese Cockfight* is a perfect (and amusing) example. Having found it quite difficult initially to settle and be accepted in Balinese life, Clifford Geertz and his wife one night decided to go along to an illegal cockfight. However, as luck would have it, the police decided that very night it was time they conducted a raid. Everyone ran for it, including Geertz and his wife. This turned out to be a key event because from that moment on the villagers accepted them much more warmly, joking with them about how they had run, and the looks on their faces. It was also a key event because it served as a useful way to discuss, often through analogy, many aspects of Balinese culture.

KEY 'PARTICIPANTS'

Notwithstanding all of the above, it is probably better to think in terms of key participants, than informants. The language of key *informants* reflects the 'miner' approach to social research that Steiner Kvale (1996) has identified, where the data are considered to be out there, simply waiting like nuggets of gold to be unearthed by the ethnographer. Since the reflexive turn (**reflexivity**) and related debates about the role of the researcher in data collection, about power, exploitation, and ontological debates about the nature of reality (see **interpretivism**), Kvale's metaphor of the 'traveller' who seeks knowledge by travelling through the social world simultaneously affecting and affected by encounters with other cultures, is more appropriate. The language of informants has thus tended to give way to that of *participants* in order to reflect the more equal relationship we attain between researcher and researched and the way that ethnography is a means of learning together. Participants and events can still be *key*, in the ways discussed above, but the naturalistic approach has generally given way to a more reflexive one.

See also: access; case study; participant observation

REFERENCES

General

Brewer, J. (2000) *Ethnography.* Buckingham: Open University Press.

Brewer, J. D. (1990) 'Sensitivity as a problem in field research', *American Behavioural Scientist,* 33: 578–593.

Emerson, R. M. (2004) 'Working with "key incidents"', in C. Seale, G. Gobo, J.F. Gubrium and D. Silverman (eds) *Qualitative Research Practice.* London: Sage, pp. 427–42.

Kvale, S. (1996) *InterViews: An Introduction to Qualitative Research Interviewing.* Thousand Oaks, CA: Sage.

Spradley, J. P. (1979) *The Ethnographic Interview.* London: Holt Rinehart & Winston.

Examples

Armstrong, G. (1993) 'Like that Desmond Morris?', in D. Hobbs and T. May (eds) *Interpreting the Field: Accounts of Ethnography.* Oxford: Oxford University Press.

Brewer, J. D. (1991) *Inside the RUC: Routine Policing in a Divided Society.* Oxford: The Clarendon Press.

Geertz, C. (1973) *The Interpretation of Cultures.* New York: Fontana.

Lareau, A. (1996) 'Common problems in field work: a personal essay' in A. Lareau and J. Shultz (eds) *Journeys Through Ethnography.* Boulder, CO: Westview Press, pp. 195–236.

O'Reilly, K. (2000) *The British on the Costa del Sol: Transnational Communities and Local Identities.* London: Routledge.

Smith, G. J. D. (2007) 'Exploring relations between watchers and watched in control(led) systems: strategies and tactics', *Surveillance and Society,* 4(4): 280–313.

Whyte, W. F. (1993) *Street Corner Society: the Social Structure of an Italian Slum,* 4th edn. Chicago: University of Chicago Press.

Malinowski

Bronislaw Malinowski (1884–1942), author of numerous monographs, especially of the Trobriand Islanders, is often considered the founder of ethnographic fieldwork methods in anthropology.

Outline: Malinowski: from Poland, to London, to Australia and the Trobriand Islands. Malinowski's holistic methodology and the influence of positivism and functionalism. The importance given to time, context, participation, and observation. Criticisms of Malinowski's work, from the publication of his diary to his theoretical framework. A lasting influence.

HISTORY

Bronislaw Malinowski is often considered to be the founder of contemporary ethnographic fieldwork, especially within anthropology, establishing many of the principles adhered to today and outlined in this book. He was born into an aristocratic family in 1884, in Poland, and studied maths, physics, and philosophy at the Jagiellonian University, in Cracow. But, having read Fraser's *The Golden Bough*, he was inspired to move to England in 1910 to study anthropology at the London School of Economics and Political Science. However, having gained support for his studies in Australia, he found himself legally an 'enemy' there when war broke out. Fortunately the Australian government allowed him to continue his research in the Pacific islands as long as he regularly reported his movements.

Most ethnographic information at this time had been collected unsystematically by what Malinowski referred to as amateurs – missionaries, colonial administrators, and travellers – who brought back from the field artefacts and stories of the strange and exotic peoples they had encountered. Some nineteenth-century human scientists conducted survey-style research on these travellers' growing collections, measuring skulls and charting physical traits (see Banton, 1977), but for the most part analysis and theoretical work were conducted from the armchair. However, by the early 1900s, academics had begun to consider the

key concepts in ethnography

scientific merits of travelling to meet, experience, and learn about these new peoples and cultures first hand. Malinowski did not, then, invent fieldwork all alone, but he was the first systematically to record and later to teach his students the canons of the method (Urry, 1984).

MALINOWSKI'S METHODOLOGY

Malinowski's most famous research was carried out in the Trobriand Islands in Melanesia, off the north-east coast of Australia. He was a founder member of the functionalist school of anthropology and his holistic (**holism**) perspective frames his research focus. As a result his monographs include the description of the Kula, a trading system between New Guinea islands involving shell jewellery, which is of central importance to the lives of the 'natives' it binds. He also made studies of Trobriand courtship, marriage, and domestic life; of gardening and magic; and studies of crime, the spirit world, and social control (Malinowski, 1926, 1932, 1935, 1960). But, above all Malinowski writes passionately about the methods he employed in his research.

First, he insisted that all ethnographers should give a full and detailed account of their research methods and the conditions and experiences by which they have reached their conclusions. He recognised the considerable distance, in time, space, and intellectual labour, between the information as collected (the brute material or 'native' statements) and the author's own account. He then proceeded, in the first chapter of *Argonauts of the Western Pacific* (Malinowski, 1922) to spell out, rather polemically, his own methodology. Influenced by current debates about the nature of scientific enquiry and how the methods of natural science can inform social inquiry, Malinowski insists that scientific fieldwork has three aims:

1 To describe the customs and traditions, the institutions, the structure, the skeleton of the tribe
2 To give this flesh and blood by describing how daily life is actually carried out, the imponderabilia of actual life
3 To record typical ways of thinking and feeling associated with the institutions and culture.

DESCRIBE THE SKELETON

At first, a new culture or society seems to an outsider unruly, disordered or chaotic. But when we look closely and carefully, we begin to see that things are more structured and organised than we first thought. We begin to see that many actions are controlled by rules and laws, customs and traditions, that help to make sense of the activities that at first seemed so strange. In order to become aware of and learn these customs and rules and their role in the given society, the ethnographer spends time watching events and asking the participants about what is expected of them and how they should behave in different circumstances. For Malinowski, this involved survey work: collecting detailed information on how things work and on rules and behaviours, norms and customs, as witnessed and described. This survey work then gives the ethnographer a descriptive framework of the society. He says it provides the *skeleton* of information. However, this skeleton lacks flesh and blood. Hence the second aim: to describe the actualities of daily life.

GIVE THIS FLESH AND BLOOD

Malinowski was aware that ethnography at his time was being undertaken with what were seen as exotic, strange, and wonderful tribal peoples whose cultures, lifestyles, and appearances were very different to those of the ethnographer. He recognised the temptation to simply describe the strange and peculiar aspects of the culture and to ignore the more mundane aspects that would really begin to help understand the people and their way of life from their own perspective. In order to overcome this temptation (what we now refer to as ethnocentricity), Malinowski advocated a truly scientific endeavour that involved the close, deliberate, and sustained exploration of daily habits and routines; what he referred to as the imponderabilia of actual life. Nowadays we think of this approach as making the strange look familiar. The adverse effect is that when it is undertaken with people with whom we are very familiar it ends up making the familiar look rather strange and exotic.

RECORD WAYS OF THINKING AND FEELING

Finally, Malinowski argued that it is important to understand how the members of the society perceive and think about their actions, or 'to grasp the native's point of view, his relation to life, *his* vision of *his* world' (1992: 25). (Please note that the sexist language Malinowski uses is his not mine.) Here Malinowski is not arguing that we need to understand *individuals* but is saying that a *group* shares a mentality, a perspective on life, and this helps us understand them. He contends that the way a society is organised will affect what feelings can be experienced. For example, 'a man who lives in a polyandrous community cannot experience the same feelings of jealousy as a strict monogynist' (1922: 23). Similarly, the way people behave in a given society is dictated by their ideas about how the world works and so to understand them we need also to understand their beliefs and ideas.

In addition to these main aims, there are a few key elements to Malinowski's ethnography. These are that data are collected in context, over a period of time, using participant observation as well as other data collection techniques. These are discussed in more depth within the various concepts in this book; here we simply introduce them from Malinowski's point of view.

CONTEXT

First of all, Malinowski was adamant that an ethnographer should not engage in armchair theorising but should spend time with people in their natural surroundings, learning from them as they go about their daily business and witnessing events as they unfold. This is far more scientific, he thought, than trusting the reports of others (the colonial administrators or travellers who brought home wonderful tales and exotic artefacts to study). It is also more trustworthy than taking someone aside and interrogating (or interviewing) them. It is worth noting here that much survey data, interviews, life histories, and other sociological data are collected out of context and should always be analysed as such. What people say they do is not always the same as what they actually do. What they do varies with circumstance and setting. Research undertaken in context offers the unique opportunity to ask about events as they occur, and to witness and discuss all manner of daily occurrences that an interview participant might think too insignificant to mention.

TIME

Second, Malinowski believed that an ethnography takes **time**. Indeed, what made Malinowski's ethnography so unique compared with his contemporaries was the length of time he devoted to it (Ball and Smith, 2001). There are three key reasons for this. First, time limits the effects of an outsider, so that people will feel comfortable in the ethnographer's presence:

> It must be remembered that as the natives saw me constantly every day, they ceased to be interested or alarmed, or made self-conscious by my

presence, and I ceased to be a disturbing element in the tribal life which I was to study. (Malinowski, 1992: 8)

Second, time is necessary to become something of an insider and, as Malinowski puts it, to learn how to behave, to acquire the 'feeling' for good and bad manners, to feel in touch with the 'natives' (1992: 8). Finally, time is necessary for the ethnographer to gradually build an explanation that is based on both fieldwork and the application of theory. Malinowski admits he often thought he had sufficient information to be able to write up his results only to find he needed more time to gather material. He calls this approach a 'cross-fertilisation of constructive work and observation'.

PARTICIPATION AND OBSERVATION

Finally, but crucially, an ethnographer should not only watch but join in the activities going on around. Malinowski wanted to capture 'native' life in all its naturalness and to avoid upsetting it by his presence. By living amongst the villagers and taking part in daily activities, he ensured that life went on around him as it had before, that he was already there when important events occurred, and that he witnessed the banal as well as the exotic. However, Malinowski sought a scientific understanding of tribal life and this demanded an element of objective detachment that could only be achieved through mentally standing back, seeing, and noting events. Thus participation is balanced with, or even secondary to, observation and the systematic collecting and recording of minute and intimate details. Malinowski was a prolific collector and documenter, using charts, statistical summaries, photographs, lists, and maps to log the minutiae of daily life. For him everything was data: habits, customs, speeches, myths, magic formulae, genealogies, relationships, and rituals.

CRITICISMS OF MALINOWSKI

In 1967 Malinowski's wife released for publication the personal diaries he had kept during his fieldwork. The diary proved to be a disturbing read, revealing an obsession with sex, an often frustrated and negative view of the 'natives', and a distinct lack of empathy deemed essential if participation is to enable a 'feeling' for the culture. The diary to some extent contributed to the crisis of anthropology that took part during the 1980s, since it so clearly challenged the notion of 'impartial observer'. However, debate has raged over whether or not it should ever have been released and I think it apt to note Firth's comment in the introduction, that anyone wishing to criticise should first consider what they themselves might have written had they assumed no one would ever read it.

Malinowski's work is also problematic for its functionalism and **positivism**. He sought a scientific understanding of a discrete society in all its uniqueness at the cost of any interest in outside influences, process, or change. His functionalism is apparent in almost everything he writes. This has had a heavy influence on anthropology and its tendency to holism, which is now being challenged through the development of **multi-sited and mobile ethnography**. Functionalism has been discredited as ahistoric and static, ignoring the role of the researcher as well as colonial and religious intrusions. Positivism is challenged for the very notion that methods suitable for study of the natural world can be simply transferred to social life. Indeed, both British and American traditions in social and cultural anthropology have faced crises as a result of postmodern and poststructuralist critiques (see Faubion, 2001; MacDonald, 2001). Contemporary ethnography attempts to be reflexive. That is to say it is conducted in full awareness of the myriad limitations associated with humans studying other human lives. Nevertheless, Malinowski established many of the fieldwork principles outlined in this book, whether they are religiously adhered to or vigorously challenged (O'Reilly, 2005).

See also: holism; participant observation; participant observer oxymoron; time; visual ethnography

REFERENCES

General

Ball, M. and Smith, G. (2001) 'Technologies of realism? Ethnographic uses of photography and film', in P. Atkinson, A. Coffey, S. Delamont, J. Lofland and L. Lofland (eds) *Handbook of Ethnography*. London: Sage, pp. 302–20.

Banton, M. (1977) *The Idea of Race*. London: Tavistock.

Faubion, J. D. (2001) 'Currents of cultural fieldwork', in P. Atkinson, A. Coffey, S. Delamont, J. Lofland and L. Lofland (eds) *Handbook of Ethnography*. London: Sage, pp. 39–59.

MacDonald, S. (2001) 'British social anthropology', in P. Atkinson, A. Coffey, S. Delamont, J. Lofland and L. Lofland (eds) *Handbook of Ethnography*. London: Sage, pp. 60–79.

O'Reilly, K. (2005) *Ethnographic Methods*. London: Routledge.

Urry, J. (1984) 'A history of field methods', in R. F. Ellen (ed.) *Ethnographic Research. A Guide to General Conduct*. New York: Academic Press, pp. 35–61.

malinowski

Examples

Malinowski, B. (1992 [1922]) *Argonauts of the Western Pacific: an Account of Native Enterprise and Adventure in the Archipelagoes of Melanesian New Guinea*. London: Routledge.

Malinowski, B. (1926) *Crime and Custom in Savage Society*. London: Kegan Paul, Trench, Trubner.

Malinowski, B. (1932) *The Sexual Life of Savages in North Western Melanesia*. London: Routledge.

Malinowski, B. (1935) *Coral Gardens and Their Magic*. London: Allen & Unwin.

Malinowski, B. (1960) *Sex and Repression in Savage Society*. London: Routledge.

Malinowski, B. (1967) *A Diary in the Strict Sense of the Term*. London: Athlone.

Multi-sited and Mobile Ethnography

In the context of increased global interconnectivity, and mobility of people, objects and ideas, ethnographers are taking their methodology to multiple and mobile places and spaces.

Outline: Immobile ethnography and the traditional notion of a bounded social group and culture. Mobile ethnography and the developing focus on pathways, interconnections, and transnational spaces. Comparative, global, and virtual perspectives, and the emphasis on processes and change. The challenges a multi-sited ethnography poses for traditional ethnographic practice, especially for becoming an 'insider'.

IMMOBILE ETHNOGRAPHY

Traditionally ethnography, as espoused by **Malinowski,** was seen to engage the lone researcher travelling to distant lands to study a whole community at a given time. It was therefore (arguably) holistic, functionalist, positivist, and naïve. The language early ethnographers used such as the native, the tribe, and the culture/site/field all attest to this position. Traditional ethnography has therefore been criticised for ignoring ethical issues, the impact of the researcher, wider social issues and structures, history, process, and, above all, its relationship to colonialism.

Sociological ethnography was always slightly less guilty of taking the idea of the bounded social group as its entity or focus. The **Chicago School** studies, for example, may have focused on *The Hobo* (Anderson, 1961) or *The Gang* (Thrasher, 1963) but nevertheless did not treat these groups in isolation, at least from the rest of Chicago, nor from wider social processes. Nevertheless, sociological and anthropological textbooks alike invariably discuss choice of location as a first step in ethnography. Even where the global, the system, or wider social processes were acknowledged, the focus has been on the local, the daily life-world, in places (and usually only one place). Links to the macro level have tended to take place by adopting macro theory or doing archival work and literature searches to extend the case beyond the local (Marcus, 1995).

However, we should be wary of judging past endeavours in the light of contemporary knowledge, ideals, practices, and configurations. Not only have our ideas about what constitutes a social science changed since ethnography's early days, but so too has the world around us. A growing body of literature on the phenomenon of globalisation now describes an increased awareness of the world as a single place; a world characterised by complex mobilities and interconnections; a world where boundaries and borders are increasingly porous. In the globalised world, the authority of the nation state is supposedly attenuated in the face of supranational, transnational, and global institutions. Rather than focus on places and societies, nations and borders, theorists of contemporary global society increasingly rely on metaphors of mobility, fluidity, flux, and flow (Bauman, 2000; Urry, 2000). As a result, ethnographers have had to rethink basic ideas about locality, place, space, and time and are 'groping their way' (Marcus, 1995) to try to understand fragmentation, time–space compression, globalisation, and its multiple interconnections.

MOBILE AND MULTI-SITED ETHNOGRAPHY

Multi-sited ethnographic research is therefore mobile. The approach pursues links, relationships and connections, follows unpredictable trajectories, and traces cultural formations in its pursuit of explanations beyond borders. Multi-sited or mobile ethnography invokes a sense of voyage, where the ethnographer traces clues by travelling along pathways, spatially, temporally, virtually, or bodily (Ina Maria, 2002). To some extent this approach, in its postmodern form (**postmodern ethnographies**), has arisen out of interdisciplinary work in the fields of media studies, feminist studies, science and technology, and cultural studies. Postmodern multi-sited ethnography 'moves out from the single sites and local situations of conventional ethnographic research designs to examine the circulation of cultural meanings, objects and identities in diffuse time-space' (Marcus, 1995: 1). However, we do not have to accept that nations are disappearing or borders becoming irrelevant to want to broaden ethnography beyond the local, or to appreciate the need to understand the connections and interconnections between things and people. Even those who do not buy into the argument that the influence of the nation state is being undermined may still want to consider global, macro, historical, and mobile ethnography, as in my recent exploration of the impact of ambiguous border controls on poverty and exclusion (O'Reilly, 2007).

Nancy Scheper-Hughes's multi-sited project explored the global traffic in human body parts. Her basic method was 'follow the bodies' as she mapped circuits of trade and illicit trafficking that brought powerful and powerless strangers together in intimate contact for the procurement of tissues and organs. Surprisingly, this mobile ethnography took her to 'some of the more privileged and technologically sophisticated transplant units, research institutes, biotechnology forms, organ banks and public and private hospitals in the world' (2004: 32). Following new paths in the global economy, she snowballed from one patient, one surgeon, one mortuary to the next, and a string of clues led her (among other places) to Brazil, Argentina, Cuba, Israel, South Africa, Baltimore, and New York City. But rather than focus on novel intersections in time and space of previously unconnected powerless and powerful groups, Scheper-Hughes notes the profound continuities between the contemporary human organs market and the Atlantic slave trade.

COMPARATIVE, GLOBAL AND VIRTUAL ETHNOGRAPHY

Multi-sited ethnographies may simply compare sites rather than be as mobile as described above. Nevertheless, this amounts to something more than conducting a series of case studies. Multi-sited ethnography tends to follow an object or idea as it travels through networks of global capital. Or it pursues cultural artefacts, stories, ideas, or people who emerge or travel across time and/or space. A fascinating study of *Médecins sans Frontières* by Julie Laplante (2003) compares indigenous Brazilian perspectives on health and medicine with the rhetoric of medical humanitarianism. Her ethnography thus shifts focus from the local to the international, and within and through changing relations of power and influence in varying contexts, to explore how indigenous remedies and health knowledge can be reconciled with the biomedical model of those offering aid.

Multi-sited ethnographies also acknowledge global connections and so could include those such as Sheba George (2000), whose fieldwork took place with an immigrant population of Kerala origin in Central City, USA and also in Kerala, India. This ethnography examines an unusual migration pattern where women go first, taking up posts as nurses, and men follow later on, often taking menial jobs even when professionally trained or highly qualified. George explores the migratory process across time and space and the ongoing connections to the native country that shape migrants' discourses and practices, and she observes how the migrants' experiences, identity, and status continue to be tied to social change and developments in Kerala even after migration.

Virtual ethnography could also be seen to challenge the idea of a single site or even be described as 'unsited'. Similarly, ethnographies are pursuing the journeys of discourses, ideas, and texts as much as people and things. Millie Thayer wanted to study globalisation, particularly 'the construction of a transnational social movement and the complex network of relationships that sustained it' (2000: 203). She chose a feminist NGO in Recife, Brazil, which was influential inside and outside Brazil, but found pinning down the global to study it rather elusive. Emails, international conferences, researchers visiting from abroad, faxes, and news publications all followed global connections but Thayer did not feel she was doing the same. She decided to delimit the field and traced the paths of the travelling discourses instead, which sometimes met, sometimes left a trace, and sometimes passed each other by entirely. For example, some of the Brazilian women's ideas had originated from Boston, in a book on women's health, and as a result Brazilian discourses had become linked to those of gender and citizenship. But on travelling back to Boston to see if the flow of ideas had been reciprocal, Thayer found the Boston women surprisingly uninformed about debates in Brazil.

DIFFICULTIES FOR ETHNOGRAPHY

George Marcus identifies three difficulties that ethnography has to think through as the result of these developments in the methodology. First, the limits of ethnography are tested. Here the question is how far an ethnography that is predicated on the everyday knowledge of face-to-face communication can be stretched and still be considered ethnography. We are already witnessing a severe stretching of the definition as it comes to be applied indiscriminately to a multitude of approaches. The challenge now is for ethnographers to continue to work through what is unique and distinctive about the methodology. Second, it becomes essential to ask if multi-sited ethnography is actually practical in terms of being able to go out into the many fields for sustained periods. Although Marcus argues that most ethnography already does take place in a variety of locations and involve a range of methods, there is a danger that its very strength becomes attenuated as the definition is stretched. To what extent is it still ethnography? Finally, Marcus is concerned about the 'loss of the subaltern'. The focus for ethnography has traditionally been dominated groups, the dispossessed, the people. But in multi-sited ethnography, the focus tends to be on the powerful, privileged, controlling, or dominating. Some may worry that ethnography thus is letting go of its roots too much.

These difficulties cannot be resolved just now, as the field continues to emerge and develop, but they are leading to tensions or contradictory commitments that ethnographers will need to reflect on. Marcus argues that ethnographers may have to change their position or role as they encounter changing sets of subjects in the mobile fields, sometimes being for and sometimes against given stances, even in apparently apolitical fieldwork. In such mobile fieldwork, as you work with one group you are also always aware of the other, who is also your research subject or participant. Marcus suggests that you often find yourself affiliating with activists who represent 'the people' in traditional research and this can replace the sense of 'being there' in that field. But that may not be the case. Nevertheless, a multi-sited ethnography is doing its best to embrace global social change, incorporating it into its methodology and thereby dealing with some of its own inherent problems as discussed at the beginning. By looking for general processes that go beyond natural boundaries and narrowly defined social entities (tribes, communities, ethnic groups) and examining long-term interrelationships among people who seem to have no connection with one another, we see the truth of the common-place observation that we occupy one world (Bates, 1996: 21).

See also: *holism; insider ethnographies; postmodern ethnographies; virtual ethnography*

REFERENCES

Key text

Marcus, G. (1995) 'Ethnography in/of the world system: the emergence of multi-sited ethnography', *Annual Review of Anthropology*, 24: 95–117.

General

Bates, D. (1996) *Cultural Anthropology*. Boston and London: Allyn & Bacon.
Bauman, Z. (2000) *Liquid Modernity*. Cambridge: Polity Press.
Urry, J. (2000) *Sociology beyond Societies. Mobilities for the Twenty-First Century*. London: Routledge.

Examples

Anderson, N. (1961) *The Hobo*. Chicago: University of Chicago Press.
George, S. (2000) '"Dirty Nurses" and "Men who Play": Gender and class in transnational migration', in M. Burawoy, J.A. Blum, S. George and Z. Gille (eds) *Global Ethnography: Forces, Connections and Imaginations in a Postmodern World*. Berkeley, CA: University of California Press, pp. 144–74.
Ina Maria, G. (2002) 'Anthropological voyage. Of serendipity and deep clues', *Anthropological Journal on European Cultures*, 11: 9–50.
Laplante, J. (2003) 'Pharmaceuticals at the borders of humanitarian and indigenous knowledge', *Anthropologie et Sociétés*, 27(2): 59–75 (in French).
O'Reilly, K. (2007) 'Intra-European migration and the mobility–enclosure dialectic', *Sociology*, 41(2): 277–93.
Scheper-Hughes, N. (2004) 'Parts unknown: undercover ethnography of the organs-trafficking underworld', *Ethnography*, 5(1): 29–73.
Thayer, M. (2000) 'Travelling feminisms: from embodied women to gendered citizenship', in M. Burawoy, J.A. Blum,, S. George and Z. Gille (eds) *Global Ethnography: Forces, Connections and Imaginations in a Postmodern World*. Berkeley, CA: University of California Press, pp. 203–34.
Thrasher, F. (1963) *The Gang. A Study of 1,313 Gangs in Chicago*. Chicago: The University of Chicago Press.

mobile ethnography

multi-sited and

149

Participant Observation

> *Participant observation is the main method of ethnography and involves taking part as a member of a community while making mental and then written, theoretically informed observations.*

> *Outline: Learning through first-hand experience. Initial stages of awkwardness and strangeness, and living a 'multiplex life'. Becoming a more active seeker of knowledge. From distance to immersion, and how far to take participation. Participant-observer positions: being covert or overt; gaining an insider role; asking what you aim to achieve; and practical considerations.*

PARTICIPATING AND OBSERVING

Ethnographic research is driven by a methodology (or theory about research) which dictates that researchers learn about the lives of the people they are interested in through first-hand experience in their daily lives. While ethnography can include the collection of documents, **interviews and conversations,** survey methods, the analysis of statistics, and even the collection and creation of visual and audio data, the main method of ethnography is participant observation. Of course, the two key elements of participant observation are participating and observing. But what does this actually mean in practice? Once one has gained **access** to a group or setting what does one actually do? For **Malinowski,** the purpose of participation was twofold: to understand things from the 'native's' point of view and to blend into the setting so as to disturb it as little as possible. For the **Chicago School** sociologists, making sense of the world involved understanding what works in practice, in everyday experience. Also, they viewed the social world as the outcome of interaction between the various actors in a setting. This implied a practical and grounded methodology that took place in everyday settings.

But both participating in and observing a setting or group can be difficult to achieve in practice. A participant is a member of a group, joining in activities, sharing experiences and emotions, contributing to debates, and taking part in the very interactions on which social life is built. An observer is an outsider, watching and listening, not always fully taking part, and rarely being a fully-fledged member of the community. An observer intentionally joined the group and will leave at some time; her participation is instrumental. Even the insider ethnographer (**insider ethnographies**) has taken time to mentally stand back from the group and observe and take notes in order to write something. From a personal point of view this can feel uncomfortable. Ethnographers may have to cope with being a long way from home, in a strange place, among people they do not immediately understand, yet still be an ethnographer, an outsider, an academic, one of us but not one of us. As Clifford Geertz (1988: 77) rather poetically puts it: 'It is a question of living a multiplex life: sailing at once in several seas'. From a practical point of view, this tension can be difficult to manage. From a theoretical point of view, it needs careful consideration.

BECOMING A PARTICIPANT AND OBSERVER

The initial stages of participant observation are often the most difficult. However, the tension and awkwardness can remain throughout, and it is becoming common to read ethnographers' own stories about false starts, misunderstandings, and crucial errors (see Ellen, 1984; Lareau and Shultz, 1996). However, as long as you remain humble, you are usually forgiven for making silly mistakes, and you can find ways to cope with strangeness and difference. Hortense Powdermaker (1966) notes that she used to read novels and poetry to help her cope, allowing her to mentally escape for a while from her surroundings. She also reassures us that she was eventually forgiven for arranging for a sick child to go to hospital, where the people she was living amongst believed people only went to die (luckily the child returned home, well). However, mistakes in the field can often be very revealing. In Spain I certainly learned about the struggles to achieve status in a community of migrants stripped of history and continuity when I failed to realise that the role of tea-lady I had been granted was only meant as a backstage role and I was expected to serve the staff in the backroom not customers in the bazaar (O'Reilly, 2000).

Arguably, observation is the more objective part of participant observation. A participant is simply a member, joining in, gaining access to some interesting discussions, sharing experiences, and witnessing some fascinating and some mundane events. Without observation, a

participant observation

151

participant is no more than a participant. The participant observer, on the other hand, is participating in order to observe, notice, record, and try to make sense of actions and events. This involves an element of standing back intellectually and reflecting on things, writing them down and thus objectifying them, asking directed questions in order to address research questions, and seeking access to groups and situations that another participant might not access. A participant observer has to sample people, settings, and times and be increasingly directed in the way she collects observations and asks questions (**sampling**). The observation element of the participant observation dichotomy, then, often becomes more crucial and evident as time goes on and as the researcher becomes more active in her pursuit of answers to questions that emerge in the field. At the same time, participation and asking questions both also become more active, focused, and directed as time progresses.

THE EXTENT OF PARTICIPATION

A key issue is the extent to which one takes the participation role. In contemporary studies the extent of participation ranges from spending some small time in the community in order to obtain access (to then conduct interviews or other means of data collection) to full immersion in the culture of the group. For example, although Daniel Murphy (1986) interviewed hundreds of individuals in a range of outlets for his influential ethnography of shoplifting, he only spent up to a week in most stores. He defends such brief visits against arguments of superficiality by describing his ethnography as 'summative'. In other words, he began with longer visits and then saw subsequent visits as building on the earlier ones. Similarly, Bronislaw **Malinowski** has been criticised for his claim to have camped right in the village in contrast to his actual distance from, and even contempt for, his 'natives'.

How far to take participation becomes a real issue for ethnographers in the field of crime. Should one go so far as to take part in a criminal activity? If not, then how does one deal with the need to withdraw from the community at crucial periods? Patricia Adler (1985) undertook partly covert research in a community of drug dealers. She and her husband actually made friends with the neighbour before realising what his 'occupation' was and then deciding to make this their research interest. So, they had already made friends in this community and continued to do so, going to parties and social gatherings, travelling with them, and watching them execute business activities (deal drugs). They only stopped short of actually dealing drugs themselves. Of course, the extent of participation also raises all sorts of ethical issues (**ethics**).

Some researchers participate fully in order to empathise more effectively. Sue Estroff (1981), for example, for her ethnographic study of psychic disorder among clinical outpatients, went so far as to take, for a period of six weeks, the antipsychotic medication that most of the clients in her study were taking. She says:

> The decision to take the medication was a difficult one, and caused much consternation among my family, friends, and colleagues. Those staff members whose opinions I sought strongly advised against it. However, because these medications represented such a substantial and meaning-laden part of the clients' world and experience, anthropologically it seemed logical and worthwhile. (1981: 30)

I would not recommend such extreme participation, but Estroff was driven by the desire to discover the worlds and individual lives, to share and thereby understand the experiences, of some of those who suffer psychic disorder. Her participation was therefore so full as to reveal some important insights. She says:

> I have acutely experienced the urge and propensity to flee to psychic dis-organization and disability – have felt the lure of craziness in ways that further sensitize me to the worlds of my friends. (1981: 4)

However, even here Estroff was not merely a participant: her research participants realised she was different and she was acutely aware of needing to balance the needs of her friends with the requirements of her research.

Most participant observation takes place between the two extremes outlined above. In Spain I have joined societies and clubs, made friends, been to parties and gatherings, and even spent Christmas day and birthdays with the migrant community. I found myself irresistibly drawn by the constant rhetoric of good Britain and bad Spain, but remained overtly a researcher and made it plain I was going home one day to write up (O'Reilly, 2000).

PARTICIPANT OBSERVER POSITIONS

Textbook discussions of fieldwork roles usually cite Gold's (1958) four positions: the complete participant; participant as observer; observer as participant; and complete observer. The complete participant is covert and runs the risk of **going 'native'** and therefore losing any sense of objectivity, while the complete observer is overt and detached. I believe, however, that all ethnographic observation involves at least a minimum of participation. Even trying to act as if we are not there would have effects. On the other hand, a complete participant is not an ethnographer; he or she is a participant. If she decides to research the group or culture in which she participates, she becomes a participant observer.

The distinction between the middle two positions is far more interesting and is more of an attempt to disentangle the various ways an ethnographer approaches the extent to which he or she participates and observes. It is more useful to consider the aims and the extent of participation. Daniel Murphy (1986) describes his role as one of 'limited interaction', while Patricia Adler (1985:18) describes hers as 'peripheral', noting that she and her husband were granted a kind of 'courtesy membership' of the group. Lee Monaghan (2002) calls his an 'active membership' role, since in his study of violence in Britain's night-time economy, he adopted the role of pub and club doorman, or bouncer. Indeed, for Monaghan, employing and analysing his embodiment in research was a crucial aspect of his sociology. Gavin Smith (2007), on the other hand, in his ethnography in CCTV control rooms, adopted the role of 'sociological voyeur', watching both the watchers and the watched. Such typologies as Gold's (1958) and Junker's (1960) confound several discrete themes, as follows (see O'Reilly, 2005):

- being covert or overt
- the participant role
- the aims of participant observation
- practical considerations.

COVERT OR OVERT

The concept of **covert** research is discussed under that concept. Briefly, ethnographers need to consider the extent to which to be open about, and gain full consent for, the research, and this will affect and be affected by the extent to which he or she is a participant. The decision to be covert might be a purely practical one, or it may reflect an attempt to become immersed in a setting. Some ethnographers conduct undercover research and yet retain such a sense of objective distance that they fail to be reflexive about the ethnographer's own part in the data collection and analysis.

Alternatively, an overt researcher might adopt an insider role and use participation in order to learn through experience and empathy, and as a result may become quite involved in the community. So it is just as possible for an overt researcher to 'go native' as it is for a covert researcher to retain distance. Covertness is more likely to occur on a continuum between openness and concealment (Lugosi, 2006).

A PARTICIPANT ROLE

Acquiring an insider role is discussed more in **insider ethnographies** and **access**. But for a moment we need to think about organisational or institutional roles which are recognised within the community, and which we may be able to adopt, such as Humphreys' (1970) famous role of the 'watchqueen'. Such roles can be more or less engaged within the community, and so more or less participant. Some people are already members when they begin, such as Jason Ditton (1977) and so already have a role. I took on a variety of accepted roles in Spain, such as club secretary, doctor's receptionist, teaching assistant, and wife and mother. However, when Arlie Hochschild (1989) did her research on how parents balance work and home life, she spent time with families in their homes, but there was no clear role she could adopt. She participated fully in the lives of the family, making breakfast, washing up, going on outings, and even baby-sitting, but she did not adopt a participant role. Similarly, for Gavin Smith's (2007) work on CCTV watchers, there was no suitable participant role he could adopt.

THE AIMS OF PARTICIPATION

The aims (purpose, role, or intention) of participation are discussed under the concept of the **participant observer oxymoron**. Briefly, the point is to ask what participation and observation aim to achieve in the research and how they contribute to data collection and analysis. Kathy Charmaz (2006: 25) argues that ethnographers are more likely to participate than observe because their aim is to understand something from being inside it rather than trying to look in from the outside. Fieldwork enables us to see people acting informally and spontaneously, and it often forces the fieldworker to learn how to behave according to the rules and norms of the society (Bates, 1996). Participation thus gives an insight into things people may otherwise forget to mention or would not normally want to discuss.

PRACTICAL CONSIDERATIONS

Finally, the extent to which an ethnographer is overt or covert, the participant role, and the level of immersion in the culture of the group, may be as much a practical as an ideological decision. Some settings, doctor/patient consultations for example, do not allow for participation. Sometimes you might hope to participate but not be permitted, as has happened to me on more than one occasion. At other times you may be called on to participate in ways you might not have anticipated, such as when Raymond Firth (1957: 134), in his ethnographic study among the Tikopia, found himself involved in a rather nasty dispute between a husband and wife.

See also: access; fieldnotes; insider ethnographies; key informants and gatekeepers; time; visual ethnography

REFERENCES

General

Bates, D. (1996) *Cultural Anthropology*. Boston and London: Allyn & Bacon.

Charmaz, K. (2006) *Constructing Grounded Theory. A Practical Guide through Qualitative Analysis*. London: Sage.

Ellen, R. F. (1984) *Ethnographic Research: a Guide to General Conduct*. London: Academic Press.

Geertz, C. (1988) *Works and Lives. The Anthropologist as Author*. Cambridge: Polity Press.

Gold, R. L. (1958) 'Roles in sociological fieldwork', *Social Forces*, 36: 217–23.

Junker, B. (1960) *Field Work*. Chicago: University of Chicago Press.

Lareau, A. and Shultz, J. (eds) (1996) *Journeys through Ethnography*. Boulder, CO: Westview Press.

O'Reilly, K. (2005) *Ethnographic Methods*. London: Routledge.

Examples

Adler, P. A. (1985) *Wheeling and Dealing: an Ethnography of an Upper-Level Drug Dealing and Smuggling Community*. New York: Columbia University Press.

Ditton, J. (1977) *Part-Time Crime: an Ethnography of Fiddling and Pilferage*. London: Macmillan.

Estroff, S. E. (1981) *Making It Crazy. An Ethnography of Psychiatric Clients in an American Community*. Berkeley, CA and London: University of California Press.

Firth, R. (1957) *We, the Tikopia. A Sociological Study of Kinship in Primitive Polynesia*. London: George, Allen & Unwin.

Hochschild, A. R. with A. Machung (1989) *The Second Shift*. London: Piatkus.

Humphreys, L. (1970) *Tea-Room Trade*. Chicago: Aldine.

key concepts in ethnography

Lugosi, P. (2006) 'Between overt and covert research: concealment and disclosure in an ethnographic study of commercial hospitality', *Qualitative Inquiry*, 12(3): 541–61.

Monaghan, L. F. (2002) 'Regulating "unruly" bodies: work tasks, conflict and violence in Britain's night-time economy', *British Journal of Sociology*, 53(3): 403–29.

Murphy, D. J. I. (1986) *Customers and Thieves: an Ethnography of Shoplifting.* Aldershot: Gower.

O'Reilly, K. (2000) *The British on the Costa del Sol.* London: Routledge.

Powdermaker, H. (1966) *Stranger and Friend.* New York: W. W. Norton.

Smith, G. J. D. (2007) 'Exploring relations between watchers and watched in control(led) systems: strategies and tactics', *Surveillance and Society*, 4(4): 280–313.

The Participant Observer Oxymoron

The term 'oxymoron' acknowledges the juxtaposition of two terms, such as participant and observer, that are essentially opposed in meaning.

Outline: Participant observation as a contradiction in terms. The tension between detached observer and empathetic participant. The traditional emphasis on the role of observation, with participation as a means of access. Participation as a means of gathering data, through subjective experience. The contemporary need to be aware of the researcher's own role and the advantages of balancing destrangement and estrangement. Practical and philosophical considerations, and the participant observation continuum.

THE CONTRADICTION IN TERMS

Participant observation is an oxymoron: a contradiction in terms; a concept with an inherent tension. As discussed under other concepts, it involves gaining **access**, adopting an insider role, gaining **rapport**, becoming accepted, building relationships, even sometimes making friends. It can be disturbing, finding oneself surrounded by new people in new surroundings and trying not only to fit in but to understand what is going on, and even write about it. Hoping people accept you in their world yet at the same time trying to access groups you would not normally access (such as when I spent time getting to know a group of women whose husbands were all in prison), and **asking questions** people do not normally ask, can make an ethnographer feel insecure and act apologetically. The tension between subjectivity and objectivity, detached observer and participant, group member and ethnographer, always remain whether one is literally adapting to a strange and 'other' culture or observing a parallel culture from a mental distance. As Alfred Schutz (1971) so aptly described in his essay about the stranger in phenomenological sociology, the challenge is to balance attempts to make the strange familiar and the familiar strange. However, the tension remains in the fact that you only really understand a group when you act within it without thinking, but the very act of trying to do that prevents you from ever truly being a member.

EMPHASIS ON OBSERVATION

Ethnography was first established as a method within the context of anthropology, which was then a fledgling discipline trying to establish itself as one of the sciences of society. Natural science, at the time, had earned huge respect as a discipline that could generate reliable and representative facts about phenomena and, even more, could effect change. The promise of sociology and anthropology, then, lay in the potential of science to yield information that could be used to change society for the better. A key element of the scientific approach of **positivism** was the application of empiricist views of natural science to the study of human societies. In turn, this meant that all knowledge about real phenomena had to be gained through direct experience of it using the senses. Anthropologists like **Malinowski** thus began to argue that the best way to understand exotic, 'native' societies was through direct and systematic observation. However, such observation was meant to be detached and objective, and used to record typical ways of thinking and feeling, not individual impressions or reactions. For these early anthropologists, participation was meant to aid this detached observation but was to be kept separate analytically. The goal was to be in the surroundings long enough for people to act naturally, to forget and thus ignore the presence of the anthropologist. Being there enables one to ask not about general rules and abstract principles but how certain cases may be treated or events responded to, and to draw generalisations from such observations. Participation itself was not a means of gathering data but a means of access in order that data could be gathered through observation.

EMPHASIS ON PARTICIPATION

These ideas can also be seen to some extent in the naturalism of the **Chicago School** ethnographers. Here, naturalism is a perspective that sees the world as real, and acknowledges that it can be studied scientifically, but challenges some of the assumptions of empiricism. It is more interpretive (**interpretivism**). Chicago sociologists conducted their research in the natural worlds of social interaction. They drew on ideas from phenomenology, hermeneutics, and symbolic interactionism in their understandings of how society works. Participation therefore had more of a central role in participant observation since it was essential to begin to interpret and understand respondents' meanings. However, there remained a desire to abstract and generalise beyond the specific case (Denzin, 1989). As philosophies of social science have moved increasingly towards a theory of the social world as co-constructed, so ethnographers have argued that it is essential to take part in this construction in order to understand it (see Ellen, 1984; Hammersley and Atkinson, 1995). According to this approach, the social world is indeterminate and does not exist independently of our desire to understand it. As Denzin (1989: 26) states: 'meaningful interpretations of human experience can only come from those persons who have thoroughly immersed themselves in the phenomenon they wish to interpret and understand'. Critical, feminist, and post-positivist ethnographers now want to reclaim some emphasis on the reality of the external world while acknowledging the need to understand its impacts from the perspective of those experiencing it (see **realism**).

THE AIMS OF PARTICIPATION

It is, I believe, futile to attempt to resolve the participant observation oxymoron and to come down on the side of either participation or observation, objectivity or subjectivity. We have reached a point where it is crucial to acknowledge the role, value, and contribution of scientific endeavour while remaining fully aware that humans (including ethnographers) make their worlds. Like Schutz (1971) and Maso (2001), I believe the tension is exactly the point. Ethnographers need to both empathise and sympathise, to balance destrangement and estrangement. Participating enables the strange to become familiar, observing enables the familiar to appear strange. The important thing is for ethnographers to consider why they want to use participation – to what ends. The reasons for participating will affect the extent to which one participates rather than observes. In fact, ethnographers now disagree about the extent to which we can learn through participation.

For some the role of participation is to get close enough to be able to collect data in an objective, detached way, through observation, informal interviews, collecting statistical data, taking photographic evidence, and so on. Participation can be used to enable access to different groups of people at different times, in a variety of settings within which questions can be asked as they occur to the ethnographer. Events can be observed as and when they take place rather than being remembered to be reconstructed at a later date through other means. When Laud Humphreys studied anonymous sexual encounters in a men's toilet in a public park in Chicago, his aim was to observe acts in an undisturbed form. He says 'To employ … any strategies that might distort either the activity observed or the profile of those who engage in it would be foreign to my scientific philosophy' (1970: 21). Thus participant observation enables direct observation rather than a reliance on informants' accounts. More recently, Gavin Smith (2007) has given similar justification for his participation role in CCTV control rooms. Smith saw himself as a 'sociological voyeur', using participation to limit his effect on the natural setting.

Participation enables the ethnographer to learn about events, feelings, rules, and norms in context rather than asking about them. It enables a focus on what actually happens rather than what tends to happen. It enables the entire context of an event to be included in the observation, rather than relying on the interpretation, recollection, and reordering of events that tend to go with reporting. But it can be more involved than this. Some ethnographers turn their ethnographic gaze onto a field in which they are already implicated, sometimes as participants. Aid workers or relief workers, for example, may use their personal commitment to the group as the focus for a **critical ethnography**. Here participation might come before observation, with an insider role already well established (**insider ethnographies**).

For others still, as with Sue Estroff (1981), the role of participation is to sensitise oneself to the world of others through experience and through the co-construction of that world. In her ethnographic study of psychic disorder among clinical outpatients, Estroff talks about learning *from* research participants rather than *about* them. Her aim was for herself and then her readers to 'discover their worlds', not to attempt to impose coherence or order on their lives. Similarly, Matthew Desmond (2006), for his ethnography of high-risk occupations, 'Becoming a firefighter', not only shared experiences with the research participants but his body bore the scars of what we might call acculturation. Desmond, who collected data while working as a wildland firefighter in northern Arizona, explains:

> By taking the 'participant' in 'participant observation' seriously, by offering up my mind and body, day and night, to the practices, rituals and thoughts of the crew, I gained insights into the universe of firefighting, insights I gleaned when I bent my back to thrust a pulaski into the dirt during a direct assault on a fire or when I moved my fingers through new warm ash to dig for hot spots. My body became a field note, for in order to comprehend the contours of the firefighting habitus as deeply as possible, I had to feel it growing inside of me. (Desmond, 2006: 392)

THE PARTICIPANT OBSERVATION CONTINUUM

In contemporary ethnography the extent and role of participation can vary dramatically between and within studies. The distinction between participation and observation takes place on a continuum from full immersion in the setting or culture to very minimal participation, not only between but also within individual studies. In my research in Spain (O'Reilly, 2000) the balance between observer and participant shifted constantly. On one occasion, crippled from having fallen down concrete steps the previous day and with a huge swelling on my right eye from a mosquito bite, I resolutely turned up for a pre-arranged interview only to find the couple on their way out for a swim. Unperturbed they invited me to join them saying, 'the water will do you good'. On this occasion I was a participant rather than an observer, learning from experience about various aspects of life in Spain as well as the pain and disappointment felt by (and the flexibility required of) an ethnographer. On another occasion, a council meeting with expatriate organisations, I was not permitted to participate but was allocated a seat at the edge of the room.

As is discussed in **participant observation**, these decisions are often practical ones as well as theoretical and ethical. There may be times when a reflexive ethnographer who aims to experience and participate in the co-construction of the social world is cast in the role of researcher, or even journalist, and times when the detached observer is drawn in against her will and asked to adjudicate, help out, or otherwise become involved. The important thing is to know why you want to become involved before pursuing (or not) a fully participant role, and then to reconcile your intentions with practical issues on the ground.

See also: *insider ethnographies; interpretivism; Malinowski; positivism; realism*

REFERENCES

General

Denzin, N. (1989) *Interpretive Interactionism*. London: Sage.

Ellen, R. F. (1984) *Ethnographic Research: a Guide to General Conduct*. London: Academic.

Hammersley, M. and Atkinson, P. (1995) *Ethnography. Principles in Practice*, 2nd edn. London: Routledge.

Maso, I. (2001) 'Phenomenology and ethnography', in P. Atkinson, A. Coffey, S. Delamont, J. Lofland and L. Lofland (eds) *Handbook of Ethnography*. London: Sage, pp. 136–44.

Schutz, A. (1971) 'The stranger: an essay in social psychology', in A. Broderson (ed.) *Alfred Schutz: Collected Papers II: Studies in Social Theory*. The Hague: Martinus Nijhoff.

Examples

Desmond, M. (2006) 'Becoming a firefighter', *Ethnography*, 7(4): 387–421.

Estroff, S. E. (1981) *Making It Crazy. An Ethnography of Psychiatric Clients in an American Community*. Berkeley, CA, and London: University of California Press.

Humphreys, L. (1970) *Tea-Room Trade*. Chicago: Aldine.

O'Reilly, K. (2000) *The British on the Costa del Sol*. London: Routledge.

Smith, G. J. D. (2007) 'Exploring relations between watchers and watched in control(led) systems: strategies and tactics', *Surveillance and Society*, 4(4): 280–313.

Positivism

Positivism is the application of empiricist views of natural science to the study of society and the development of policy. It is a denigrated but misunderstood term.

Outline: Positivism and the empiricist model of natural science. Problems with the empiricist view of science and criticisms of empiricist ethnography. Criticisms of applying the natural science approach to ethnography. Warnings against monolithic attacks on science and a call for a post-positivist or subtle realist approach. Recognising the complex nature of ethnographic practice.

POSITIVISM AND EMPIRICISM

The term 'positivism' came from the nineteenth-century French philosopher Auguste Comte in his attempt to label a scientific approach to social science that could emulate natural science. Specifically, he hoped (like many of his contemporaries) that sociology and anthropology would be able, like the natural sciences, to produce reliable, objective knowledge which could be acted on in order to improve society in the future – a positive knowledge from a positive science. However, positivism was based on a specific, empiricist view of natural science rather than on many other available approaches to science that were and increasingly are available. So when social scientists are accused of being 'positivist' they are being accused of being empiricist rather than scientific. There has been no real justification to abandon a scientific approach to social science as a direct result of the attack of empiricism. Let us begin with what empiricism is and its problems.

Positivism is the application of the empiricist model of natural science to the study of society. Empiricism has seven basic doctrines (Benton and Craib, 2001: 14):

positivism

163

1   The individual human mind starts out as a 'blank sheet' on which knowledge is later written. All our knowledge of the world is received through our senses as we experience the world around us and interact with it.

2   Anything we claim to be true can be tested by observation or experiment (by experience).

3   We cannot know about anything that cannot be observed.

4   General recurring patterns of experience can be stated as scientific laws.

5   Explanation of phenomena involves demonstrating that they are instances of such scientific laws.

6   If explaining a phenomenon is a matter of showing that it is an example or 'instance' of a general law, then knowing the law should enable us to predict future occurrences of phenomena of that type. The logic of prediction and explanation are the same.

7   Scientific objectivity rests on a clear separation of (testable) factual statements from (subjective) value judgements.

PROBLEMS WITH EMPIRICISM

Positivism, and especially the empiricism on which it is based, have been heavily criticised to the extent that positivism has become something of a term of abuse and few ethnographers would now call themselves positivist. However, the extent to which positivism has ever been applied systematically to ethnographic research is debatable. Indeed, it has probably been severely misunderstood so that criticisms of empiricism have been directed wholesale towards what are actually realist ethnographies that do not adhere to the empiricist canons (Benton, 1977). It is important that we know exactly what we are attacking when we accuse something of being positivist. There are serious problems with the empiricist view of science, which I shall discuss below. There are also difficulties with the very attempt to view the social world and the study of it using the same models as natural science. This is discussed more under the concept of **interpretivism**. But there is an attempt to reconcile the desire to be somewhat scientific, the belief in a real world external to our thoughts about it, with the lessons of both interpretivism and **reflexivity**; this is discussed more under the concept of **realism**.

A key criticism of empiricism is the idea that the human mind starts as a blank sheet. Implicit in this is the argument that we can put all prior assumptions aside and see the world for what it is. This has seeped through into naïve inductivism, informs some approaches to **grounded theory**, and was what motivated **Malinowski** (1992 [1922]: 9) to insist on setting aside preconceived ideas, which he considered 'pernicious in any scientific work'. Critics of this approach believe that we never simply receive stimuli through our senses in all its complexity but, using the brain's innate capacities, instantly order it, categorise it, and try to make sense of it in relation to other experience. The eighteenth-century German philosopher Immanuel Kant argued that our ability to judge difference, to conceptualise time and space, to think in terms of cause and effect are all innate, universal capacities that impose themselves on the external world through our perceptions rather than existing out there as real. Similarly, Noam Chomsky identified innate dispositions to learn a language and acquire grammatical competence. What we know is therefore the outcome of the interaction between the human mind, and its capacities, and experience of the world beyond.

A further criticism of empiricism is the leap of faith from observation of regularities and patterns to predictions about the future. Empiricist science can in fact only describe constant correlations of events; it cannot demonstrate causes through experience and observation, nor can predictions come from sense experience alone. Causes and predictions are implied from what is observed and calculated by the brain, not concluded from the sense data. We can *reason* that the fact we have seen the sun rise every morning (a correlation of events) might suggest it will rise tomorrow, but we cannot come to that conclusion through observation because we cannot see tomorrow.

The empiricist model of science depends on testing hypotheses generated from a series of observations, by collecting more empirical data. But it is difficult to know what to do with data that apparently falsify the hypothesis. Empiricists tend first to question whether maybe the conditions were different or the observed things measured wrongly so that external factors produced the unexpected outcome. They then ask whether the hypothesis itself needs refining to take account of the new evidence. In other words the findings have to be *interpreted*, and such interpretations, Thomas Kuhn (1970) has argued, are often based on prevailing paradigms, conventions, theoretical perspectives, or even fashions. Clear evidence that what has been labelled positivist has not always faithfully or strictly adhered to an empiricist model is in the reliance by many authors (including **Malinowski**) on theoretical interpretations of concrete observations. This has led relativists to argue that no interpretation of what is observed is any more meaningful or true than any other. But I do not believe that simply because decisions are based on prior experience, shared ideas, and other assumptions this means that all interpretations are therefore equal.

Finally, there are significant difficulties with the assumption that we cannot know about anything that cannot be observed. Much natural science actually relies on the positing of entities which *if they exist* would explain outcomes. Many entities which are relied on for explanation in natural science have therefore never been observed, except in terms of their effects. Take an electrical current, for example. It is not possible to observe an electrical current but only its effects; it is therefore proposed into existence on account of its observable effects. In the philosophy of science, the position that argues that things do exist independently of our ideas about them, independently of how they are perceived, is called realism. Realist philosophers of natural science look for observable phenomena, ask what might explain these, posit the existence of underlying structures or mechanisms, then test hypotheses based on those. Realist views of science have been drawn on to inform a social science that comes between positivism and interpretivism.

PROBLEMS WITH SCIENCE

Other criticisms of positivism question the assumption that science produces the most reliable knowledge. Feyerabend (1981), for example, contends that 'tacit' knowledge, intuition, and moral values have an important role in understanding the world. Others are critical of attempts to apply social scientific knowledge in a practical way, given the messy, unpredictable, and complex nature of the social world. These authors are concerned that we can never be sure of the consequences of interventions and so cannot justify such practice. Ted Benton and Ian Craib (2001), however, cite several important advances social science has been able to make. There have been further criticisms of empiricist views of science and of the idea of using science to study society at all; these are discussed in **interpretivism**. There have also been accusations that even these approaches ignored the role of the researcher and this led to the reflexivity debate.

But the attack on science has been somewhat monolithic in its attempt to challenge science per se rather than distinct scientific epistemologies. It has also been muddled, in that many ethnographers do still want to claim the existence of a real world, and usually claim some authority for their texts. I therefore call for a reflexive-realist position. This I believe is a more ethical position than the defeatism of postmodernism (**postmodern ethnographies**) and the narcissism of some contemporary ethnography.

CONTEMPORARY ETHNOGRAPHY

Rather than try to determine whether or not an ethnography is positivist, it is better to use philosophies of science in their underlabourer role (as a way to consider practical problems that arise in the field) and to interpret the texts we read with some awareness of the epistemologies that are influencing them. It is, for example, quite easy to see the influence of positivist ideas on Malinowski's work. He insisted on 'striving after the objective, scientific view of things' (1992: 6). He was intent on the systematic collection of facts and concrete data, on remaining to some extent detached, on separating thoughts and opinions from facts and observations (hence the use of his diary for such personal reflections). He said, 'the main endeavour must be to let facts speak for themselves' (1992: 20). However, we cannot label as positivist someone who believed that theoretical studies must be prior to observations, and are important in guiding one's work. Nor can we label positivist someone who insists on acquiring 'the feeling' of native manners (no matter with what little success he might have achieved this).

Early social anthropologists were anxious that their discipline would be given the respect and credibility of the natural sciences and so attempted to mimic their methods. But this was not as systematic as is often thought. Similarly, later ethnographers who claim to have abandoned positivism have not necessarily abandoned all attempts to be objective, detached, or to posit the existence of a real world. Jan Savage (2006), for example, believes interpretive ethnographic enquiry can produce solid evidence on which future practice (in this case in healthcare) can be based. Ethnographic research is particularly good at describing patient experiences of treatment and services, and understanding health beliefs and the impact of cultural issues. While my own work has been described as interpretivist, I discuss my discomfort at having to suppress my own thoughts and opinions at times in order not to affect the natural surroundings in which I find myself (O'Reilly, 2000). Margaret Nelson and Rebecca Schutz's (2007) ethnographic approach could not be described as positivist, yet they confidently describe the (real) role of child daycare centres in the reproduction of (real) social class differences in the US.

See also: analysis; interpretivism; participant observer oxymoron; realism; reflexivity

positivism

REFERENCES

General

Benton, T. (1977) *Philosophical Foundations of the Three Sociologies*. London: Taylor & Francis.

Benton, T. and Craib, I. (2001) *Philosophy of Social Science: the Philosophical Foundations of Social Thought*. Basingstoke: Palgrave.

Feyerabend, P. K. (1981) *Problems of Empiricism*. Cambridge: Cambridge University Press.

Kuhn, T. S. (1970) *The Structure of Scientific Revolutions*. Chicago: University of Chicago Press.

Savage, J. (2006) 'Ethnographic evidence. The value of applied ethnography in healthcare', *Journal of Nursing Research*, 11(5): 383–93.

Examples

Malinowski, B. (1992 [1922]) *Argonauts of the Western Pacific: an Account of Native Enterprise and Adventure in the Archipelagoes of Melanesian New Guinea*. London: Routledge.

Nelson, M. K. and Schutz, R. (2007) 'Day care differences and the reproduction of social class', *Journal of Contemporary Ethnography*, 36: 281–317.

O'Reilly, K. (2000) *The British on the Costa del Sol*. London: Routledge.

Postmodern Ethnographies

key concepts in ethnography

The postmodern response to the reflexive turn has been to attempt to approach and write ethnography in ways that accept and celebrate the messy, ambiguous nature of the social world, in postmodern ethnographies.

Outline: The implications of postmodernism for ethnography and the attempt to abandon objective, ordered, authoritative accounts. Types of postmodern presentational style: dialogic and polyphonic accounts, auto-ethnography and performance. Postmodernism and social science, and failed attempts not to privilege the author's voice. 'Responsible' ethnography beyond postmodernism and reflexivity.

INTRODUCTION

Postmodernists often conclude that no single account of any reality is of any more value than any other, and therefore that ethnographic accounts cannot claim to be any more trustworthy, reliable, or representative than a story or tale anyone else might create (Spencer, 1989). Indeed, some go so far as to say that there is no such thing as reality, just different versions of different experiences. Those who drew inspiration from poststructuralist authors such as Foucault and Derrida are pessimistic about the opportunity to obtain any objective knowledge and for knowledge to lead (as modernists hoped) to the eventual improvement of society. These ethnographers abandoned ethnography altogether. Other postmodernist ethnographers have abandoned attempts to provide objective, ordered, authoritative accounts and instead attempt to create ethnographies that reflect and celebrate the complex, ambiguous, messy nature of the social world and of research itself (Hammersley and Atkinson, 1995).

Postmodernist critiques of modernist ethnography have thus led to experimental pieces employing a variety of literary and textual devices including dance, poetry, film, autobiography, and audience participation. The point is to challenge the realist (**realism**) view that there is a reality that exists external to the way we think about and experience it. Max Travers (2001) introduces four such experimental ethnographies: the dialogic ethnography, polyphonic accounts, auto-ethnography, and performance. Of course, these styles of presentation are not mutually exclusive, and so we may find dialogic performances or auto-ethnography with layered accounts.

A DIALOGIC ETHNOGRAPHY

Here the ethnography is presented as a dialogue between the researcher and the researched, thus honestly reflecting the difficulties of interpreting another person's world, the dialogic nature of research itself, and the involved, messy, subjective, and emotional nature of ethnographic research. Travers describes the study of Tuhami by Vincent Crapanzano (1980), who began interviewing Tuhami over a period of time about Moroccan religious brotherhoods but Tuhami gradually took over the interviews and began telling his life story. As one reads the conversation between the researcher and Tuhami, one is transported to the setting, learning about his life through his own words. One also gains an insight into Crapanzano's attempts to make sense of what Tuhami is telling him, especially given that he is often contradictory, discusses demons and saints in the same terms as 'real' people in his life, and slowly reveals a rather sad story. Crapanzano also reveals in the ethnography that the encounter had been an emotional one for him, at times feeling like a mutual therapy session more than an interview.

These sorts of experimental piece can be enjoyable to read and can raise all sorts of issues around who is portraying whom, and whom has power to present who in what ways. However, it may not be as novel as first appears. Way back in the 1930s, Clifford Shaw gave Stanley his own voice, asking that he write his autobiography in his own words, and it was perhaps more empowering for Stanley, who was engaged throughout the process, than it was for Tuhami.

POLYPHONIC OR LAYERED ACCOUNTS

In polyphonic accounts the narrator pieces together disparate passages of data (documents, fieldnotes, interviews), paraphrasing in an attempt to paint a rather abstract theory rather than tell a coherent story. The aim is often to avoid the privileging of one voice over another, so that the narrative is not a social science one, or the author's own, or even that of a single respondent. Travers describes Susan Krieger's (1983) *The Mirror Dance*, which drew on ethnographic research in a lesbian community, using participant observation, interviews, and the researcher's own diary. Krieger was interested in the way there is a pressure to conform even in this alternative community, but she was also keen not to present her work in her own authorial voice. She has experimented with styles of presentation and here she attempts to simply portray the words of her respondents, remaining almost absent herself in the text.

Interestingly, Krieger has been criticised for her work being too abstract and, alternatively, for nevertheless imposing her own interpretation on events via her editing. It is actually very difficult not to be present in this kind of text in the introduction, description of methodology, conclusion, or even simply the editing. Ultimately even if all the data were to be presented in their entirety (which would amount to volumes of work in many cases), the researcher has had to decide what to collect and what to write down, and has collected the data in interaction with the research participants. It can also be frustrating, Travers argues, never to get to know the various authors of the disparate voices in the text. In Krieger's work, 70 women's voices are presented as disembodied text. One cannot help wondering how the women themselves feel about being represented in such an experiment, and I cannot help feeling uncomfortable about the ethics of such an exercise.

Carol Rambo Ronai (1995) has also experimented with various styles of representation. In one very moving, even horrendous article, she presents her own reflections on her experiences of child sex abuse, weaving abstract theory, emotional experience, fantasies, dreams, and statistics in order that none of these presentations is given priority. When I have shown this to my own students, they have generally been more impressed by the powerful ability of the shocking language to overwhelmingly privilege the author's voice than they are by the achievement of a postmodern text to challenge modernist assumptions.

AUTOBIOGRAPHY AND AUTO-ETHNOGRAPHY

Here ethnographers present personal accounts of their own experiences (sometimes alongside those of others) in order to convey their experiential and autobiographical understanding of a phenomenon. It could be seen as a mere contemporary version of 'being there' (see **reflexivity**), since the implicit argument is: I know this because I experienced it myself. It is often, however, a sincere attempt to acknowledge the intimate relationship between researcher and researched. Auto-ethnographers challenge the absent authorial voice of much realist ethnography by front-staging their own character and experiences. In some cases the self is the only data source, as in autobiography, in others the author's voice is one amongst many. Just as with other life histories, the story can be used to illuminate sociological themes and illustrate discourses but always in a self-reflexive manner. Travers describes Carolyn Ellis's (1995) autobiographical story of her relationship with her partner who died from emphysema after a long and painful period of illness. She tells the story from how they met to how he died and their journey together along the way. Travers relates how some American students were so moved when their course tutor got them to read the text that they either 'could not put it down' or had to put it down because it was too painful to bear. Another auto-ethnographic account is that of Sparkes (1996), who tells the emotional story of the back injury that cut short his career as an elite athlete, powerfully evoking common experiences that are later framed in academic discourses around a 'body project'. However, like myself, Travers is not sure of the point of this sort of work for social science and several responses have labelled it sheer self-indulgence. As has been said before, one has to be careful when experimenting with styles that the work does not simply become about oneself.

POETRY, DANCE, AND PERFORMANCE

There are a variety of ways in which an ethnography can now be presented, including all sorts of performance. Travers describes Laurel Richardson's (1997) poem *Louisa May's Story of her Life*, which is based on an interview with a single mother who grew up in the Southern United States. Using the poem, Richardson celebrates an attempt to break away from social science rhetoric entirely, avoiding what she deems the boring, repetitive, authorial statements so typical of realist work. Travers kindly describes the poem as not particularly remarkable literature. But maybe this is not the point: Richardson is experimenting with styles of presentation, not trying to conform to any given genre.

POSTMODERNISM AND SOCIAL SCIENCE

The abiding concern I have with all of these attempts not to privilege any voice or style is that they are doomed to failure. The more one tries to remove or curtail the voice of the author, the more authorial he or she becomes in determining how something is portrayed, and the more dishonest the inevitable representation of the 'other'. Rarely has one gained access to the lives of others in order to play games with representation and there is a shared understanding of how things will be represented that is undermined by attempts to create new styles. In the end most of these techniques tend towards a version of **realism**; the reader is expected to believe the events really happened. Furthermore, and as Travers notes, the 'author always has the last word'. Surely it is more honest to present a consciously authorial voice than a subconscious, thinly disguised one.

POST POSTMODERNISM

Jonathon Spencer (2001) has written a useful chapter titled 'Ethnography after postmodernism', in which he distinguishes text and context. He says it is one thing to tear the text apart in a form of literary criticism and experiment with new forms of textual representation, but another thing altogether to exclude from one's text all core context – that is background, history, and methods. There is a tendency, in Geertz's work on the Balinese cockfight, for example, to seize on a metaphor and sustain it through flashes of description and then to 'climax in a kind of adjectival blizzard' (Spencer, 2001: 445). This sort of work may be enjoyable to read but does not give the reader sufficient information with which to judge its value or relevance; it does not separate the researcher's interpretations from theirs. It should be a mere nicety, Spencer argues, to at least show whose words we are using when and where interpretations come from. Furthermore, while the postmodern argument that everything is interpretation might lead to the abandonment of truth and the privileging of the academic voice, it need not mean abandoning all clarity.

After *Writing Culture* (Clifford and Marcus, 1986), reflexivity is now taken for granted, and no one baulks when they see people writing in the first person. But what reflexivity is, Spencer argues, is not so clear. For some it is postmodern presentation of experimental prose as discussed above (and some people forgetting that the people they are talking to are more interesting than those asking the questions). For others it means no longer seeing cultures as homogeneous, isolated groups but acknowledging broader influences and relationships. In some ways it has inspired participatory research and the inclusion of the voice of the people. Overall, there is more responsibility for the consequences of ways of representing and this sense of responsibility is being seen as a source of liberation rather than merely a burden. Most ethnographers have not responded to the call for reflexivity with the extreme forms explored above. The result of a more moderate response is rich ethnographies that are open about their limitations and partiality; ethnographies that acknowledge the complexity of the social world, and thus the difficulty of rendering it clear and coherent without over-simplifying it.

See also: ethics; multi-sited and mobile ethnographies; realism; reflexivity; virtual ethnography; visual ethnography

REFERENCES

General

Clifford, J. and Marcus, G. E. (1986) *Writing Culture. The Poetics and Politics of Ethnography*. Berkeley, CA: University of California Press.

Hammersley, M. and Atkinson, P. (1995) *Ethnography. Principles in Practice*, 2nd edn. London: Routledge.

Spencer, J. (1989) 'Anthropology as a kind of writing', *Man*, 24(1): 145–64.

Spencer, J. (2001) 'Ethnography after postmodernism', in P. Atkinson, A. Coffey, S. Delamont, J. Lofland and L. Lofland (eds) *Handbook of Ethnography*. London: Sage, pp. 443–52.

Travers, M. (2001) *Qualitative Research through Case Studies*. London: Sage.

Examples

Crapanzano, V. (1980) *Tuhami: Portrait of a Moroccan*. Chicago: University of Chicago Press.

Ellis, C. (1995) *Final Negotiations: a Story of Love, Loss and Chronic Illness*. Philadelphia: Temple University Press.

Krieger, S. (1983) *The Mirror Dance: Identity in a Woman's Community*. Philadelphia: Temple University Press.

Richardson, L. (1997) *Fields of Play: Constructing an Academic Life*. Brunswick, NJ: Rutgers University Press.

Ronai, C. R. (1995) 'Multiple reflections of child sex abuse. An argument for a layered account', *Journal of Contemporary Ethnography*, 23(4): 395–425.

Shaw, C. (1966 [1930]) *The Jack Roller. A Delinquent Boy's Own Story*. Chicago: University of Chicago Press.

Sparkes, C. (1996) 'The fatal flaw: a narrative of the fragile body-self', *Qualitative Inquiry*, 2(4): 463–94.

Rapport

> *Fieldwork entails a long-term commitment on the part of both researcher and participants, which involves establishing reciprocal relationships based on mutual trust and understanding, or rapport.*

> *Outline: The importance of rapport for the quality and ethics of ethnography. The gradual building of trust and its relationship to disclosure. Gaining access, recruitment and rapport. Ongoing relationships, intimacy and conflict. 'Passing' as an insider. Going home and maintaining trust.*

INTRODUCTION

Ethnographic research entails a long-term commitment both on the part of the ethnographer and the participants in the field. It involves establishing reciprocal relationships based on mutual trust and understanding, which in turn demands a certain rapport. The kinds of relationship built in the field can affect the quality and range of access achieved (and vice versa) and the data collected, or constructed. These relationships of course will be predetermined or limited by certain norms and expectations in the field. It would not be possible to gain much rapport in a public setting such as a park or café, for example, or with day visitors in a hospital. However, in most private settings or with the individuals involved on a daily basis in public settings, it is impossible to deny the role of the researcher and the relationship between her and the researched, nor the potential impact of these on the quality of the ethnography.

Many earlier textbooks have spent considerable time considering the issue of rapport. The edited collection by Roy Ellen (1984), for example, has 16 entries under the indexed term 'rapport' and a further two under 'reciprocity'. It was clearly seen as an important issue. Nigel Fielding (2006) says the idea of building trust and gaining rapport were initially seen as methods to gain insights into members' perspectives; it was associated with naturalism and the attempt to reach and faithfully report 'the truth'. He says that 'Wittgensteinian and Winchian perspectives have problematized naturalism' (p. 286) so that now it is crucial to be more reflexive about our role as ethnographers and the relationships we build (see **interpretivism**). Nevertheless, ethnographers continue to concern themselves with issues of trust, truth, and moral imperatives, and to explore the nature of the long-term relationship that is fieldwork.

THE GRADUAL BUILDING OF TRUST

It is crucial that ethnographers build mutually trusting relationships, both for ethical reasons as well as to ensure the quality of the ethnography. We have no reason to trust the ethnography produced by someone with whom the respondents remained suspicious or distant, any more than we can admire or value an ethnography that has been fleetingly constructed out of superficial relationships. But how do we build and retain trust? For John Brewer (2000), shy, reticent, uncommunicative people do not make good ethnographers. Ethnography demands an open friendly demeanour, honesty, communicativeness, and an easy smile. We need to build confidence in our abilities and our trustworthiness. This can be achieved nonverbally as we shake hands (or kiss), smile, make eye contact, and pay due attention to others (Fetterman, 1989). But it can also be more active. We earn trust over **time**, by being there day in, day out, empathising with people in their actions, sharing food, learning the language, adopting cultural habits, and by demonstrating that we have a genuine interest in them and (sometimes) a commitment to their causes.

Trust is linked to how much is disclosed about the research and therefore how much research participants can trust us. It has to be built slowly and carefully, so some people gradually enter the field, spending increasing amounts of time there, progressively becoming more active and overt. This is true of Browner and Preloran (2006) (see below), who decided to build rapport before introducing their research and requesting more active involvement, but for others it is more a matter of the *extent* of overtness and participation. It is common to gradually reveal more in-depth information about research intentions and to be increasingly active in the research goals as time goes on and participants trust you more. In her study of psychiatric out-patients, which took place both in the clinical setting and then, later, in the streets, cafés, homes, and private settings of their daily lives, Sue Estroff (1981) found the building of trust tortuously slow. Clients (as she calls them) were suspicious about her source of income and why she was not working. To explain that her work involved studying them aligned her too much with the staff at the clinic, so she had to demonstrate through her actions that her position was different. She used body language and dress to appear not too staff-like and was sure to keep confidences that were shared with her. Yet, she also had to teach clients and hospital staff to accept that she would also keep confidences *from* them. 'In the end', she says 'I suspect I remain an enigma, a friend, or just another strange person who says she's writing a book about them and their treatment program' (1981: 6). This position of the accepted stranger is one many ethnographers will recognise.

RECRUITMENT AND RAPPORT

Rapport can be an important element in encouraging people to be involved in a study (see **access**). Browner and Preloran (2006) wanted to understand how couples and expectant mothers make the decision whether or not to have an amniocentesis test, given that the test carries its own risk and, furthermore, is offered just as they have been informed there is an increased risk, in their case, of foetal anomaly. In other words, they were hoping to recruit people at a very sensitive and emotional time. However, to make things even more complicated, the community of people they were interested in targeting was immigrant couples, who tend to have a very low level of participation in social research. They eventually recruited 122 couples and 27 single women but only as a result of painstaking building of rapport and trust. First of all they undertook **participant observation** in the clinic, attending regularly, taking on volunteer roles, or simply sitting and chatting with the women as they attended clinic. They would talk about the women's other children, or ask about the sex of the unborn child, or engage in other 'ice-breaking' informal chats. Then, finding women were often anxious, reluctant to ask questions of clinical staff, or struggling with the care of other young children, Browner and Preloran took on more active roles. They listened to the woman sympathetically, helped them fill in forms, watched their children as they attended to medical or administrative details, and offered information where they could on such things as where they might find a pay-phone. Eventually, they found they could explain to women why they were there and managed to motivate them not only to take part in the study but also to persuade their male partners to take part as well. They discuss the recruitment of men as being a sort of second-hand recruitment process.

Access, recruitment, and building rapport are not separate from the research itself. We learn from our attempts to become insiders, to gain trust, to access people and ideas, about how people view things, what they want us to see and what they don't. We may find that something we thought very private will be spoken about easily whereas something we expected to observe openly is taboo. Browner and Preloran (2006: 100) say: 'The difficulty we had recruiting for our study was in itself instructive, casting a revealing light upon some of the attitudes we hoped to investigate'.

RAPPORT AND REPAIR

Trust-building is ongoing. People may test you or you may experience things you do not like, see things you do not approve of, or be encouraged to take part in activities you find abhorrent. You may make mistakes or say things that are misunderstood. People may find your constant attention, questions, and note-taking irritating and unnerving. Trust is *relationship work*, as Jennifer Mason (1996) says. Sometimes research participants will put you to a test or through a rite of passage (see Brewer, 2000: 86). It is crucial to try to be as non-judgemental as possible. However, it is quite natural for people to try to second-guess what you are thinking and the mere fact of you writing about them suggests you are being judgemental. Your questions or your attitude can imply opinions or make participants feel insecure. Indeed, as we write and think and observe, we are standing back and thinking critically about what people say, and so are being judgemental in a way. We think we can summarise what we observe better than they can, and this must come out at some point, either as we ask questions or as we leave the setting to write it all up. The trust participants have in us and we are able to share with them, is therefore carefully and painstakingly established. Roles and statuses must be negotiated and re-negotiated; and friendships will go through trials and tribulations, and even break-ups and make-ups. Precisely because trust and rapport can be so easily undermined, relationships must be continually worked at, even after we leave the field.

TEAM WORK

While it is crucial that participants can trust us, this can cause difficulties in working relationships and even friendships out of the field. Janet Theophano and Karen Curtis (1996), for example, were together studying food use in an Italian American community. Doing **team ethnography**, they built a very strong relationship, writing fieldnotes for and to each other, and sharing them regularly. Then one respondent asked Theophano to keep something to herself and not to tell Curtis. She was torn between loyalty to the respondent and loyalty to her colleague and friend. Eventually she decided the respondent's trust was paramount, that it was more important to retain that confidence than to betray it for the sake of her friendship and relationship with Curtis. She therefore kept the fieldnotes from this time to herself for a while, which became very uncomfortable because she had to try to explain why she was not sharing. Later, fortunately, the respondent allowed her to share but looking back both ethnographers admit this was a very difficult fieldwork experience that taught them a lot about how conflictual trust can be.

INTIMACY AND CONFLICT

The relationships built in the field can become very intimate and, like any close relationships, may go through difficult or tense periods. There may, for example, be conflicts of interest. William Foote Whyte (1993) was studying gangs and was therefore painfully aware that empathising with one gang will exclude acceptance into another. He argues that long-term participant observation usually entails only accessing one group at a time, and only a few in total, but sometimes it becomes clear you have sympathies with competing sides. Whyte found himself playing softball for a team which was matched *against* the Norton Gang, with whom he had previously managed to build good relations. The Norton Gang members were so outraged to see him playing for the other side, that when the match with them came up he decided, literally, it would be safer to sit on the sidelines.

Others remain marginalised or are seen as partisan, even when they try not to be. Whyte (1993) mentions (but does not reference) someone called Jason, who conducted participant observation in a prison and found that, at first, white prisoners were pleased to take him into their confidence, viewing him as a white sympathiser. However, when he refused to take sides in disputes or act as their advocate in difficult situations, he found himself angrily labelled a 'nigger lover'. It depends in the end what level of access is required and how involved a participant you need to become (see **participant observer oxymoron**). It may be necessary (or you may want) to become politically active, or adopt advocacy roles, or to become a fully-fledged member of a faction even where this does restrict access. Alternatively, you may prefer to at least attempt to remain neutral and detached. Most ethnographers need to balance involvement and detachment. Peter Lugosi (2006) found for his research on 'hosts' and 'guests' in the hospitality industry that he sometimes used an *abrupt* approach, interviewing people quickly and spontaneously without the luxury of establishing rapport. Other times he built up his knowledge of and familiarity with a person *incrementally*, involving at least some amount of covertness in the process (**covert**).

'PASSING' AND 'MAKING IT STICK'

Gaining and building quality relationships built on trust and rapport is not just about access but also about remaining for a long period of time in the field. Once you have found a place, you have to make it work in practice. For his covert research into homosexual acts, Humphreys (1970) had first of all to 'pass as a deviant', entering the subculture 'under guise of being another gay guy'. This raises ethical issues but also issues about how overt one really is, even when the research is ostensibly overt. After all, it is quite common for ethnographers to adopt an attitude, hide their feelings, or suppress their socialisation altogether. Humphreys also talks about how difficult it can be to maintain ongoing access, or 'making the contact stick'. For him this involved building more lasting relationships, getting accepted, and eventually being invited to private parties. However, it is important to note that fitting in does not have to mean being exactly the same as the participants. Sometimes it is better to acknowledge your difference. William Foote Whyte says that he learned people did not expect him to be just like them one evening as he was walking down the street with the Norton Gang:

> Trying to enter into the spirit of the small talk, I cut loose with a string of obscenities and profanity. The walk came to a momentary halt as they all stopped to look at me in surprise. Doc shook his head and said: 'Bill, you're not supposed to talk like that. That doesn't sound like you'. (Whyte, 1993: 304)

Whyte goes on to describe how, later, he could easily have been arrested and therefore jeopardised not only his research but his entire career when he voted four times for the same candidate in a single election. If you establish trust with participants on the understanding that you are trustworthy and reliable, you need to stick to this and *be* trustworthy and reliable. As Whyte says, it is as important that the fieldworker is able to live with him or herself as to live with other people.

Finally, there is likely to come a time when the ethnographer ends the research and goes home. Leaving and finishing can be truly problematic depending on the kinds of relationship that have been built. It reminds people of the real purpose of your time in the field and leaves them anxious to know what you found out. Silverman (2000) says that, in organisations especially, it is not just about curiosity or intellectual interest but a concern for the implications of the research for them or their organisation. Leaving need not mean severing all ties and bonds, however, especially if you have arranged follow-up visits, to take back findings to share with research participants, or intend (as often happens) to continue to pursue an intellectual as well as a personal interest in the field and the people. After all, for many ethnographers their field becomes a lifetime passion.

See also: ethics; going 'native'; insider ethnographies; participant observer oxymoron; time

REFERENCES

General

Brewer, J. (2000) *Ethnography*. Buckingham: Open University Press.
Ellen, R. F. (1984) *Ethnographic Research: a Guide to General Conduct*. London: Academic Press.
Fetterman, D. M. (1989) *Ethnography Step by Step*. London: Sage.

Mason, J. (1996) *Qualitative Researching*. London: Sage.

Silverman, D. (2000) *Doing Qualitative Research. A Practical Handbook*. London: Sage.

Examples

Browner, C. H. and Preloran, H. M. (2006) 'Entering the field: recruiting Latinos for ethnographic research', in D. Hobbs and R. Wright (eds) *Handbook of Fieldwork*. London: Sage, pp. 93–106.

Estroff, S. E. (1981) *Making It Crazy. An Ethnography of Psychiatric Clients in an American Community*. Berkeley, CA and London: University of California Press.

Fielding, N. (2006) 'Fieldwork and policework', in D. Hobbs and R. Wright (eds) *Handbook of Fieldwork*. London: Sage, pp. 277–292.

Humphreys, L. (1970) *Tea-Room Trade*. Chicago: Aldine.

Lugosi, P. (2006) 'Between overt and covert research: concealment and disclosure in an ethnographic study of commercial hospitality', *Qualitative Inquiry*, 12(3): 541–61.

Theophana, J. and Curtis, K. (1996) 'Reflections on a tale told twice', in A. Lareau and J. Shultz (eds) *Journeys through Ethnography*. Boulder, CO: Westview, pp. 149–76.

Whyte, W. F. (1993) *Street Corner Society: the Social Structure of an Italian Slum*, 4th edn. Chicago: University of Chicago Press.

Realism

realism

> *Realism is the belief that things exist in the (social) world that are independent of thought or perceptions. Realist ethnographies thus posit the existence of a real world external to the ethnographer.*

> *Outline: What are naturalism and realism and why are they seen as problematic? Assuming realism is the same as other scientific approaches such as empiricism. Interpretivist critiques of realism and the reflexive turn. Post-positivist, past-modern and subtle realist attempts to reconcile the desire to be scientific with lessons learned in recent decades. Critical realist and reflexive-realist ethnographies.*

NATURALISM AND REALISM

Martyn Hammersley and Paul Atkinson (1995) accuse many early ethnographers of a rather naïve naturalism. Naturalism believes the social world can be treated as though it were a natural phenomenon (like the natural world) and should be observed in its natural state, with as little interference from the ethnographer as possible. This naturalism infused other approaches, such as symbolic interactionism, hermeneutics, and phenomenology, which understood the social world as constructed and reconstructed based on people's interactions and interpretations. It saw the goal of ethnography to learn the culture of the group in order to understand its basic social processes, but it ignored the role of the ethnographer in the interpretive act.

The way other cultures were supposedly learned was by adopting the ambiguous role of the stranger (Schutz, 1971), who is able to become enough of an insider to learn the rules of the game, yet retain sufficient objectivity and distance to stand back and see things as an outsider. Thus the complex process of interpreting a world that the participants themselves are trying to make sense of is achieved by suspending (as does the stranger in a new land) all preconceptions, all taken-for-granted knowledge. We have to learn, as does a stranger, how to behave in the new environment. But, like the stranger, we will never become such an insider that we lose the ability to see what is going on. Hammersley and Atkinson suggest this naturalism appeals to a form of natural science yet is naïve in its assumptions that the social world can objectively be known. In my opinion, it is better to describe these ethnographies as to some extent *realist* (van Maanen, 1988). That is to say, that they posit the existence of a real world that is independent of our ideas about it. Indeed, many traditional and contemporary ethnographies draw from interpretivism, constructionism, postmodernism, and even relativism yet aim to give realist accounts (Benton, 1977).

Gavin Smith's ethnographic study of CCTV operators, which explores the lived realities of both watchers and watched as mediated through 'texts' (the words, images, and sounds transmitted via closed-circuit television) is clearly interpretivist (**interpretivism**). In order to attempt to understand the 'multiple layers of reality underpinning CCTV monitoring' Smith *interprets* the ways the operators in turn interpret the images and texts they perceive. Nevertheless the influence of a more naturalistic or realist approach is in evidence when he defends his collection of data *in situ* without checking details later with CCTV operators for accuracy or validity.

key concepts in
ethnography

It was the aim of this researcher from the outset to limit unnecessary disturbance of the settings' socially constructed nature and interaction order. …
It was felt more scientifically accurate to collect and record data in as natural and free flowing a format as possible. (Smith, 2007: 289)

REFLEXIVITY

The reason Hammersley and Atkinson accuse such works of naturalism is that they lack the **reflexivity** of much recent work. This is because in the last two to three decades constructivism and relativism, as well as some literary criticism and textual analysis, have been turned on to the ethnographers themselves, attacking the naïve construction of their authoritative ethnographic accounts, which lack any acknowledgement of their own role in the collection and interpretation of evidence and in the creative act of writing ethnography (see **postmodern ethnographies**). Similarly the sustained attacks on positivism have been applied piecemeal to all scientific approaches, and so have been assumed to apply equally to realist as to empiricist ethnography. While for some, the result has been to abandon all attempts at objectivity and claims to scientific status, for others realism has not been abandoned altogether. Instead they recognise that realist ethnographies must account for the role of interpretation and interaction between researcher and researched.

REALISM AND SUBTLE REALISM

Put simply, realism is the belief that things exist in the (social) world that are independent of thought or our perceptions of them. In other words, there is a real world external to our ideas about it. Naïve realism is now considered inadequate for ethnography, for the reasons rehearsed under the concepts of **positivism** and **reflexivity**. But several authors are proposing subtle or limited versions that take account of the lessons of the past decades (and see **interpretivism**). Clive Seale (1999: 26), for example, believes there are now several examples of attempts to reconcile realism with various forms of interpretivism (and relativism), all of which accept that 'although we always perceive the world from a particular viewpoint, the world acts back on us to constrain the points of view that are possible'. Even protagonists of the reflexive turn (for example, Atkinson, 1992; Clifford and Marcus, 1986) reveal attempts to be somewhat realist. Seale prefers a pragmatic approach to research,

realism

where the craft skill is learned through practice and through an appreciation of excellence in existing studies. Seale also draws on Popper's ideas about falsification, to argue for realist ethnographies that remain falsifiable and for active attempts to falsify as a means of seeking validity. Martyn Hammersley (1998) similarly calls for a subtle realism that makes tentative truth claims, which remain provisional until sufficient evidence has been gathered to demonstrate otherwise. He argues that rather than attempt to *reproduce* reality in our ethnographic accounts, we admit the best we can do is make attempts to *represent* it.

PAST-MODERN REALISM

Rob Stones (1996) has similarly attempted to reclaim some ground for realism in reaction to what he calls the defeatism of the postmodern approach. Acknowledging the problems inherent in naïve realism and in positivism's empiricist base, he seeks a critical role for social science that is lacking in postmodernism's emphasis on the equal validity of all knowledge claims. For Stones, a past-modern realism is confident to make judgements about the status of competing claims to knowledge and will allow itself to judge which stories are more fictional, which are falsifiable, and which have an evidential base. Past-modern realism recognises the complexity of the real social world, as well as the limitations of all attempts to know this world. However, through constant reflexive elaboration, and the focused collection of evidence, it is still possible to achieve limited and falsifiable knowledge.

CRITICAL REALISM

Finally, critical realists combine a version of critical theory with a depth realism in order to inform **critical ethnographies**. Depth realism (Benton and Craib, 2001) posits the existence of phenomena, in the form of mechanisms and tendencies, that exist in the social world beyond the surface of appearances. For critical realists, such as Roy Bhaskar (1998), studying what people *think* they believe is unlikely to provide us with all the answers. Social scientific understanding requires both empirical evidence and theoretical argument, and may lead to the description of social structures that differ from or even contradict those described by the actors themselves. One direction in which critical theory has led research is towards action research, which 'attempts an iterative cycle between practical struggles, the formulation of research questions and the reporting of research findings in a way that informs further practical struggle' (Seale, 1999: 10). This involves raising awareness in participants of the underlying mechanisms affecting their lives. Critical ethnographies include Barbara Ehrenreich's *Nickel and Dimed* (2001) and Nancy Scheper-Hughes's *Death without Weeping* (1993).

REFLEXIVE-REALIST ETHNOGRAPHY FOR THE TWENTY-FIRST CENTURY

Gary Alan Fine contends it is important to recognise that all ethnographies are in a sense realist: 'all empirical work is grounded in the assertion that readers can rely on the claims of the writer' (1999: 535). Even postmodern arguments expect to be believed. He recalls Carolyn Ellis's (1995) impressionistic ethnography, in which she recounts the death of her partner. The reader is expected to believe the death and the accompanying emotions were indeed real, not fictions. What is required for what we might call a contemporary, *reflexive-realist* ethnography is faith in the power of knowledge, accompanied by acknowledgement of the limitations of ourselves as data collection instruments. The fact that we cannot achieve absolute truth need not lead us to abandon all attempts at incomplete knowledge. Fine believes a self-confident ethnography can seek solace in three kinds of defence:

1 An *intersubjective defence* says realist ethnographies gain value and significance as they meet other accounts of similar (or the same) settings and contribute to a plausible, collective account.
2 An *epistemological defence* acknowledges humans who are scholars in the world are no different than humans as citizens in seeing the world as real and having confidence in those perceptions.
3 A *pragmatic defence* argues that it is possible to evaluate knowledge in terms of its outcomes.

Surely, Fine argues, such realist accounts as *Asylums* (Goffman, 1961), *Boys in White* (Becker et al., 1961) and *Tearoom Trade* (Humphreys, 1970) have earned their reputation as valid for their long-term impact on other scholars and the fields of research on which their work has impacted. To paraphrase Fine, if any casual observation is as adequate as labour-intensive understanding of communities, why should we bother to do ethnographic work at all? We have to be able to claim some authority for the ethnographic text that represents aspects of the world

realism

that are to some extent external to our ways of thinking about them. We can do this through reflexive-realist ethnography.

See also: critical ethnography; interpretivism; positivism; postmodern ethnographies; reflexivity

REFERENCES

General

Atkinson, P. (1992) *Understanding Ethnographic Texts.* London: Sage.

Benton, T. (1977) *Philosophical Foundations of the Three Sociologies.* London: Taylor & Francis.

Benton, T. and Craib, I. (2001) *Philosophy of Social Science: the Philosophical Foundations of Social Thought.* Basingstoke: Palgrave.

Bhaskar, R. (1998) *The Possibility of Naturalism: Philosophical Critique of the Contemporary Human Sciences.* London: Routledge.

Clifford, J. and Marcus, G. E. (1986) *Writing Culture. The Poetics and Politics of Ethnography.* Berkeley, CA: University of California Press.

Fine, G. A. (1999) 'Field labour and ethnographic reality', *Journal of Contemporary Ethnography*, 28(5): 532–9.

Hammersley, M. (1998) *Reading Ethnographic Research*, 2nd edn. London: Longman.

Hammersley, M. and Atkinson, P. (1995) *Ethnography. Principles in Practice*, 2nd edn. London: Routledge.

Schutz, A. (1971) 'The stranger: an essay in social psychology', in A. Broderson (ed.) *Alfred Schutz: Collected Papers II: Studies in Social Theory.* The Hague: Martinus Nijhoff.

Seale, C. (1999) *The Quality of Qualitative Research.* London: Sage.

Stones, R. (1996) *Sociological Reasoning. Towards a Past-modern Sociology.* London: Macmillan.

van Maanen, J. (1988) *Tales of the Field: on Writing Ethnography.* Chicago: University of Chicago Press.

Examples

Becker, H. S., Geer, B., Hughes, E. C. and Strauss, A. (1961) *Boys in White. Student Culture in Medical School.* Chicago: University of Chicago Press.

Ehrenreich, B. (2001) *Nickel and Dimed. On (Not) Getting by in America.* New York: Metropolitan Books.

Ellis, C. (1995) *Final Negotiations: a Story of Love, Loss and Chronic Illness.* Philadelphia: Temple University Press.

Goffman, E. (1961) *Asylums: Essays on the Social Situation of Mental Patients and Other Inmates.* New York: Doubleday.

Humphreys, L. (1970) *Tea-Room Trade.* Chicago: Aldine.

Scheper-Hughes, N. (1993) *Death without Weeping: the Violence of Everyday Life in Brazil.* Berkeley, CA: University of California Press.

Smith, G. J. D. (2007) 'Exploring relations between watchers and watched in control(led) systems: strategies and tactics', *Surveillance and Society*, 4(4): 280–313.

key concepts in ethnography

Reflexivity means thinking reflexively about who has conducted and written ethnographic research, how, and under what conditions, and what impact these might have on the value of the ethnography produced.

Outline: The reflexive turn of the 1980s and 1990s. The postmodern response and the modernist reaction. Reflexivity in contemporary fieldwork studies. The requirement to think critically about the context and practice of research and writing. Locating oneself in ethnographic research. Self-reflexive fieldwork accounts. Providing methodological detail.

THE REFLEXIVE TURN

For a long time no one thought much about how fieldwork was written up into descriptions of other cultures. Then, during the 1980s, armed with ideas from textual criticism, cultural theory, and literary theory, and informed by philosophical ideas and political debate about the social construction of reality, fieldworkers began to look critically at the way in which fieldwork is produced and written. They began to explore the wider political contexts in which ethnographic texts had been produced (including colonialism, see Asad, 1973), and to consider the power (and gendered) relationship between the researcher and researched, the role of institutional and disciplinary constraints, and the influence of scientific paradigms. Key texts in what became known as the 'reflexive turn' included the edited volume *Writing Culture*, by James Clifford and George Marcus (1986), which exposed the artificial and constructed nature of descriptions of other cultures by exploring the use of rhetoric in classic texts; Clifford's (1988) *The Predicament of Culture*, which critically explores how western fieldwork studies have tended to construct fictions about other societies rather than simply portray them; and Clifford Geertz's *Works and Lives* (1988), which considers the work of classical authors, including Bronislaw **Malinowski** and Ruth Benedict, in light of their personal biographies. The culmination of these trends was that writing and construction were suddenly seen as central to the fieldwork enterprise.

POSTMODERN ETHNOGRAPHIES

The postmodern response to such criticism and analysis has been to destabilise the power of the ethnographer, and sometimes to conclude that no one voice is of any more value than any other and no ethnography any more trustworthy than any other account (Spencer, 2001). Postmodernists accept and celebrate the complex, ambiguous, messy nature of the social world and of ethnographic research; they self-consciously abandon attempts to provide neat, ordered narrative accounts written in an authoritative voice. Postmodernist and feminist critiques of modernist ethnography have thus led to experimental pieces employing a variety of literary and textual devices, some more avant-garde than others. The postmodern response to the reflexive turn, however, seems doomed to failure. Crucially, **postmodern ethnography** evokes rather than represents. It 'emerges through the reflexivity of text–author–reader and privileges no member of this trinity' (Tyler, 1986: 153). It is fragmentary because it is conscious of the fragmentary nature of the postmodern world. It might take any form, Tyler suggests, but can never be completely realised because consensus can only be transcended by imperfection!

MODERNIST REACTION

For others, the reflexive turn led to a 'crisis in representation'. Modernist researchers considered writing to be the simple presentation of facts and feared that analysing how ethnography is *constructed* completely undermines the scientific enterprise – as if 'exposing how the thing is done is to suggest that, like the lady sawed in half, it isn't done at all' (Geertz, 1988: 2). These fears led to accusations that textual analysis and reflexivity are mere navel-gazing, narcissism and self-adoration, and Ernest Gellner (1988, cited in Okely and Callaway, 1992) even suggested Geertz's book should be locked away from students unless they were mature enough to cope with it.

REFLEXIVITY IN CONTEMPORARY ETHNOGRAPHY

The truth is, though, our relationship to our research and to the researched has changed as a result of this intellectual movement and it is no longer possible to pretend we are not part of the world we study. A less defeatist response has involved serious consideration of the politics of representation; to reclaim some authority for the academic ethnographer, while retaining what was beneficial, intelligent, and insightful from the reflexive turn. That is, an awareness that ethnographies are constructed by human beings who make choices about what to research, interpret what they see and hear, decide what to write and how, and that they do all this in the context of their own personal biographies and often ensconced in scientific and disciplinary environments (Spencer, 2001). Ethnographers have since attempted to confront the challenges of the reflexive turn and the colonial encounter by locating their ethnographies historically, spatially, and structurally in relations of politics and power, time, global political and technological developments, and by including unbounded, fragmented, and mobile communities (see Humphrey, 1993 and **multi-sited and mobile ethnographies**).

Reflexivity in contemporary fieldwork studies is the requirement to think critically about the context and the acts of research and **writing**, and involves thinking about what we read (and an awareness that ethnography is constructed); thinking about what we write and how; and acknowledging we are part of the world we study. Critics in the reflexive turn, for example, noted the tendency of ethnographers to write as if their account were the one true account, the one true voice of authority, thereby effectively silencing all other voices (Hammersley and Atkinson, 1995). This was not achieved by offering a full and explicit description of methods so much as through the use of rhetorical devices. Traditional ethnographies do not express doubt nor hint that what they describe is a matter of interpretation; they draw authority simply from the fact of the author 'being there' and being a scientist. As Geertz (1988:17) argues, there are very few 'anonymous murmurs', almost all ethnographers somehow manage to get themselves into their text, sometimes through the descriptive preamble, describing the setting, their feelings of strangeness on arriving; at other times by simply writing an occasional piece of text in the first person.

A further technique is what has been called 'the ethnographic present'; treating the community as if it were frozen in time, neglecting history, process, and social change. A piece of ethnographic work written in the present tense, for example, carries much more authority than the past tense would evoke. Many ethnographers are using the same techniques now, but some find ways to also acknowledge the tentative, provisional nature of their interpretation of events (e.g. Humphrey, 1993).

Ethnographers need not abandon any attempt to write with authority, or to write in the accepted style of their genre. Hammersley and Atkinson (1995) rightly warn against experimentation for the sake of it and even Marcus (1994), one of the early protagonists of the writing as construction camp, has more recently argued that postmodern responses have gone too far. The legacy of the reflexive turn is the demand to think consciously about writing styles and the nature of argument. All writing is construction and there are various ways in which what is produced could have been constructed (Richardson, 1997). We necessarily use rhetorical devices, but can do so consciously and overtly. We should ask ourselves some questions before and as we write: would a chapter describing methods undermine the authority of the work or enable the evaluation of our findings? Should it be a separate section/chapter or directly linked to the work and threaded through it? Should we write in the past or present tense? Should we write in an authoritative voice or display a rigorous sense of partiality (Clifford and Marcus, 1986)?

Finally, you might also think about the order in which you write. Why should we assume that the social world is best represented in a series of chapters? You may want to leave some sense of the disordered nature of reality in your writing, like Patricia Adler (1985:9), who didn't want to 'make too much rational sense out of this irrational world'.

However, whatever is decided about writing, our responsibility is to those we study. Studies can be rich, evocative, colourful, and a pleasure to read, but should retain authoritative status as a piece of scholarly research if this is what we have told our participants (and supervisors, colleagues, or funding agencies). Similarly, we cannot become so radical in our writing that we forget that there was a social world out there that we studied, social actors who allowed us into their lives to do so, and maybe *gatekeepers* who permitted access to the group. Too much focus on the text as a construction disembodies the account from the fieldwork, whereas for most ethnographers writing is inextricably bound up with data collection.

LOCATING ONESELF IN ETHNOGRAPHIC WRITING

Finally, reflexivity demands critical analysis of the *practice* of ethnography as well of as the ethnographer's own role, a demand that has led to the emergence of a sub-genre of ethnographic writing: the self-reflexive fieldwork account (Clifford and Marcus, 1986:14). Some of these were written as, or in the style of, fictional accounts of fieldwork experience (Barley, 1983; Gardner, 1991), while others followed Geertz, by exploring fieldwork practice in the light of the ethnographers' autobiographies (Okely and Callaway, 1992; Watson, 1993). In a special edition of *Sociology* on autobiography, Cotterill and Letherby (1993), for example, offered autobiographical accounts of their own academic development and their experiences of **feminist ethnography**. However, autobiography can be more of the same if we are not careful; more exoticising, fictionalising, sensationalising, and constructing the 'other' on which we can gaze with wonder. It is not enough merely to acknowledge that the self intrudes upon ethnography. We need to view the 'intrusive self' as a resource; one that constrains the temptation to generalise and simplify other people's lives. What is needed is to be able to locate ourselves in our studies honestly and openly, in an admission that observations are filtered through our own experience, rather than seeking to provide the detached voice of authority.

This does not mean the text becomes one about you. It means confronting your relationship with others, it means conveying the context and your place in it. It also involves noting who your research is for; even impartial access is not always guaranteed. For example, Judith Okely (1983), who studied traveller gypsies, was given access by local council officers who were thinking about introducing sedentarisation. This causes us to subvert the idea of the observer as a detached, impersonal research tool; but rather than undermining the scientific enterprise, it means we are being increasingly rigorous, increasingly sceptical.

reflexivity

METHODOLOGICAL DETAIL

Whatever creative styles or techniques ethnographers attempt, we still need above all to know how researchers did what they did. Many anthropology books do not even have a methodology section, and where they do, this is often distinct from the rest of the book and may be very brief. Some simply offer a paragraph or two stating that the person did fieldwork. This is because anthropologists share a common understanding about what fieldwork is, but in sociology and other disciplines it is not so clear what is meant by ethnography or ethnographic methods. Similarly, in contemporary research on youth and culture, Andy Bennett (2002) has criticised the tendency now to write overtly subjective accounts that lack methodological detail. It is not sufficient, he argues, to be apparently reflexive, what is required are sustained accounts of the impacts of the relationship between the researcher and the researched. I would argue that in any case, the reader should be offered as full a description as possible of where the ethnography was done and how, with what misgivings, what mistakes, what expectations and disappointments, what revelations and what pleasures, to enable the reader not only to enjoy but also to evaluate the written product. For excellent examples of how full and reflexive accounts of the field research and subsequent report writing can serve to illuminate rather than undermine the process, see the fourth edition of William Foote Whyte's (1993) *Street Corner Society*, and Bernadette Barton (2007).

See also: *analysis; ethics; feminist ethnography; interpretivism; positivism; postmodern ethnographies; realism*

REFERENCES

General

Asad, T. (ed.) (1973) *Anthropology and the Colonial Encounter.* London: Ithaca Press.

Clifford, J. (1988) *The Predicament of Culture.* Cambridge, MA: Harvard University Press.

Clifford, J. and Marcus, G. E. (1986) *Writing Culture. The Poetics and Politics of Ethnography.* Berkeley, CA: University of California Press.

Cotterill, P. and Letherby, G. (1993) 'Weaving stories: personal auto/biographies in feminist research', *Sociology*, 27(1): 67–80.

Geertz, C. (1988) *Works and Lives. The Anthropologist as Author.* Cambridge: Polity Press.

Hammersley, M. and Atkinson, P. (1995) *Ethnography. Principles in Practice*, 2nd edn. London: Routledge.

Marcus, G. E. (1994) 'What comes (just) after the "post"? The case of ethnography', in N. K. Denzin and Y. S. Lincoln (eds) *Handbook of Qualitative Research.* Thousand Oaks, CA: Sage.

Okely, J. and Callaway, H. (eds) (1992) *Anthropology and Autobiography*. London: Routledge.

Spencer, J. (2001). 'Ethnography after postmodernism', in P. Atkinson, A. Coffey, S. Delamont, J. Lofland and L. Lofland (eds) *Handbook of Ethnography*. London: Sage, pp. 443–52.

Tyler, S. A. (1986) 'Post-modern ethnography: from document of the occult to occult document', in J. Clifford and G. Marcus (eds) *Writing Culture: The Poetics and Politics of Ethnography*. Berkeley: University of California Press, pp. 122–40.

Watson, C. W. (ed.) (1993) *Being There. Fieldwork in Anthropology*. London: Pluto Press.

Examples

Adler, P. A. (1985) *Wheeling and Dealing: an Ethnography of an Upper-Level Drug Dealing and Smuggling Community*. New York: Columbia University Press.

Barley, N. (1983) *The Innocent Anthropologist. Notes from a Mud Hut*. London: Penguin.

Barton, B. (2007) 'Managing the toll of stripping: boundary setting among exotic dancers', *Journal of Contemporary Ethnography*, 36(5): 571–96.

Bennett, A. (2002) 'Researching youth culture and popular music: a methodological critique', *British Journal of Sociology*, 53(3): 451–66.

Gardner, K. (1991) *Songs at the River's Edge. Stories from a Bangladeshi Village*. London: Virago Press.

Humphrey, R. (1993) 'Life stories and social careers: ageing and social life in an ex-mining town', *Sociology*, 27(1): 166–78.

Okely, J. (1983) *The Traveller-Gypsies*. Cambridge: Cambridge University Press.

Richardson, L. (1997) *Fields of Play: Constructing an Academic Life*. New Brurswick, NJ: Rutgers University Press.

Whyte, W. F. (1993) *Street Corner Society: the Social Structure of an Italian Slum*, 4th edn. Chicago: University of Chicago Press.

reflexivity

Sampling

> *Sampling involves selecting cases from a broader set of choices in such a way that the subset (or sample) chosen is in some ways representative of the broader set, or is in some ways illustrative or even atypical.*

> *Outline: Probability and non-probability samples. Sampling for representativeness and practical issues. Selecting settings, contexts, times, and people. Types of sampling: purposive, theoretical, opportunistic, and snowball. Sampling as an ongoing part of the iterative-inductive process. Issues of representativeness.*

PROBABILITY AND NON-PROBABILITY SAMPLES

In social research generally, sampling involves selecting a group or setting (or times or people) from a broader set of choices in such a way that the subset (or sample) chosen is in some ways representative of the broader set. The terminology of sampling is imported from quantitative research, where a probability sample is considered the best approach and anything else is a less than adequate version of it: hence the blanket term 'non-probability sample' for all other approaches (Brewer, 2000).

A *probability sample* is a sample, or subset, of the population selected in order that every member of the population has an equal, or at least calculable, probability of being selected. The idea is that the sample represents the whole in all important or relevant characteristics. Here the population is any broad, overall group in which the research is interested. It could be all Polish migrants in Aberdeen, all men aged between 18 and 24, all total institutions in the UK, or any other broad set.

Ethnographers rarely appear to worry about sampling for representativeness in this way and talk little in their ethnographies of their sampling procedures. Many make the argument that this is not what qualitative research is all about and that the unique case is often more interesting and enlightening than the typical case (**case study**). However, it is not unusual that an ethnographer is overtly researching one group

key concepts in ethnography

or sample as a 'case' that is illustrative of something broader and many ethnographers do want their research to have wider relevance. Even where this is not the case, choices have to be made where to study, with whom, of what and when. And once in the setting, since it is impossible to be in all places at all times, some sampling choices are inevitable. In practice, 'cases' – people, settings, places, and times – are usually selected *deliberately* for a variety of reasons.

THEORY AND PRACTICE

These choices should be theoretically informed where possible, but may have to be made on the basis of practical limitations. How do we know who to select for our research? The selection of participants will often be quite clear and will have been part of the research design, and initial puzzle. For example, when I decided to research British migration to the Costa del Sol, it was quite easy for me to select the town I knew had received a large number of such migrants. In many cases the research question itself includes the group or the place. When I returned to Andalucía ten years after the first study, to focus more on rural migration, it was clear that I would go to rural areas which had attracted large numbers of migrants. But even here there is the issue of where to draw the boundaries of the group. Should migrant networks that extend beyond the group or locality be included, for example? Would it not be as important to explore migration in a place that attracted few migrants? Will one setting be enough? (see O'Reilly, 2000 and 2007).

In other cases, the overall research question is quite general: how do psychiatric out-patients experience their daily lives? (Estroff, 1981); an ethnography of the routine, every night work of 'bouncers' and 'door supervisors' (Monaghan, 2002). These do not include an actual place or field; this has to be chosen. Often the choice is practical. Studying outpatients in an outpatient setting involved for Sue Estroff (1981) simply driving ten minutes down the road, first to meetings to join in group activities and, later, to drugstores, coffee shops, indeed anywhere she could find clients hanging out together. Later still, fieldwork settings included double-dating with clients and friends, shopping trips, bar-hopping, and a camping trip. At other times an attempt is made to research in a range of settings to enable comparisons, but with similarities, to enable generalisations. Lee Monaghan (2002: 410) has worked as a door supervisor or bouncer in six different establishments, all of which served a predominantly white, heterosexual, young clientele, but which varied in size, mood, appearance, opening times, and the number of door staff. These descriptions of settings

sampling

are implicitly giving the reader an idea of the extent to which his findings can be generalised (see **generalisation**).

WHAT TO SAMPLE

Ethnographers sample (participate and observe in) settings, with people and groups, in various contexts, and at different times of the day, month, and year (Hammersley and Atkinson, 1995). Settings may be chosen because they are representative of other settings, or because they are atypical (and we can therefore learn from their strangeness); they may be chosen because they have been studied previously (Lewis, 1951), or simply because they are accessible (Hicks, 1984). Sometimes a group and a setting are the same thing, but it is important not to be bound by either; flexibility is important.

Having selected a field or setting, we then need to sample situations and people to talk to, spend time with, and observe. Some ethnographers, as Hammersley and Atkinson suggest, use their own categories to sample; for example, they may wish to ensure they access people of different nationalities or ages. Others sample according to the categories of the researched, as ways the group divides itself become apparent. It is likely that sampling is addressed in an ongoing process as ideas are developed and analyses shaped. Some ethnographers go so far as to ask the research participants themselves who and what should be included in the study.

There may be different contexts within the setting that are relevant. For example, when I conducted a small study of schoolchildren of different nationality groups I discovered that the school staff room was very interesting, as it revealed a mix of nationalities of staff and I began to wonder how their various relationships with the children were experienced. Later on in the study, I began to realise that if I wanted to understand how the different national groups mixed, I would have to spend time in the streets and the playground as well as the classrooms. It is also necessary to decide *when* to do the research, and to consider that different times of the day or the year might be relevant (see **time**). Generally (hopefully) we select purposively – with a purpose in mind, and theoretically – with theories, or ideas about how the world works, informing our purpose.

PURPOSIVE SAMPLING

Here the sample is chosen for a purpose, in order to access people, times, and settings that are representative of given criteria (Ritchie and Lewis,

2003). One key purpose is to ensure that all criteria of relevance are included. A second key purpose is to access a diverse sample, as a means of testing how another given criterion varies across categories. It is fairly common, for example, to ensure a sample includes the criteria of gender, age, ethnicity, and social class background. In my research in Spain I became aware of an important criterion of time spent in Spain, during the year. I wanted as a result to ensure my research included the various migration trajectories (seasonal visitors, peripatetic migrants, even returning tourists) so that all were represented and so that comparisons could be made for the various groups. It has been a common misunderstanding that migration is a one-off move to a new destination for purposes of starting a new life. My research has now helped challenge that firm definition of migration.

THEORETICAL SAMPLING

Purposive sampling is used more commonly in applied policy research, while theoretical sampling (explicitly) is more often used for exploratory or basic, blue-skies research. Theoretical sampling developed out of the work of Glaser and Strauss (1967) and, later, Strauss and Corbin (1998). It is in some ways even more purposive than purposive sampling, in that the aim is to directly sample in order to address or test emerging theories. An initial sample is selected on the basis of a loose, working hypothesis. Then, in an iterative-inductive manner, the theoretical explanation that emerges from the first responses are tested, refined, and elaborated in the field by new and ongoing samples (see **grounded theory**).

In theoretical sampling, a sample is generated for the purpose of generating and refining theory; people, settings, and times are included because of their relevance for the developing theoretical explanations and as a means of checking for contradictory cases that delimit the theory. However, I would argue that all purposive sampling is theoretical, in as much as samples are sought (people contacted, time spent) based on the ideas we have (theories) about how the world works and as a means of elaborating such explanations. Whether we are explicitly generating 'grounded theory' or are more iteratively testing and refining and contributing to existing theory, we should not simply choose people and places arbitrarily.

sampling

197

OPPORTUNISTIC AND CONVENIENCE SAMPLING

It seems to me that some academics seek labels in a desperate attempt to make credible something essential and unavoidable, but not ideal.

This is the case with what are called opportunistic or convenience samples. I do not find it particularly helpful to consider these sampling procedures. On the other hand, it is important to acknowledge that sometimes whom we to talk to and where we go is not so much our choice as that of the participants. Opportunistic sampling can be viewed in a positive light if it means that the researcher is led by the demands of the research and by the feelings and thoughts of the participants to sample people and places that arise as an opportunity. This would mean that the selection of items to sample remains close to the research field and to the criteria of (developing) interest. However, I would still hope that if an opportunity arose to spend some time somewhere and with someone, the opportunity was taken not simply because it was there but because it gave access to a facet of life the researcher was interested in (whether that was a result of his or her own theorising or the participants' persuasion).

Convenience sampling is even more problematic if it simply means the researcher spent time with whoever he or she could. However, I doubt (and hope) this rarely happens in practice, and there is usually some level of selection based on theoretical ideas about what the research is about. The result of such convenience or opportunistic sampling is that the ethnographer will have to consider carefully the extent to which any findings are representative. I would recommend not using the language of convenience or opportunistic sampling, and instead give a thorough description of who was included or excluded, how and why.

SNOWBALL SAMPLING

Many purposive and theoretical samples also use an element of snow-balling. Here the researcher begins with a small sample or group of initial contacts – maybe someone he or she already knows or can locate easily. The researcher uses these contacts to snowball the sample out to other people these individuals know and will introduce them to. I began with people in bars and restaurants (and other public spaces), and once I got to know these people, they would introduce me to others. In this way I thus gained access to private spaces. The disadvantage is that the final sample will be limited by the contacts and networks of the initial sample and will tend toward homogeneity; isolated or lonesome people will be excluded. Deborah Lupton and John Tulloch (2002), for their research on the meaning of the 'risk society' for Australian interviewees, snowballed from the pre-existing networks of their local research assistants, and ended up with a sample dominated by well-educated, young, and middle-aged adults of British ancestry. However, such difficulties can be overcome by purposively selecting an initial sample that represents key criteria of interest in the population (and adding to the initial sample as key criteria emerge as relevant), and by making a special effort to use other techniques to include relevant individuals/groups that might be relevant yet excluded.

ONGOING SAMPLING

In ethnographic research, samples are selected and built as the research progresses. As with gaining **access**, sampling is not a one-off event but something that is part of the entire process. This is because ethnographic research is usually iterative-inductive; it evolves gradually with stages overlapping or even running concurrently. Sampling over time and making constant comparisons are important so that as analyses develop, we can distinguish the special but typical from the atypical (Brewer, 2000). For this sort of close intimate study, familiarity and time are required, so that we can gradually come to know who are the relevant people to talk to, and can follow leads and pursue hunches by gathering more information from various avenues. Often an ethnographer simply has to start somewhere and then change direction several times. Or at least the boundaries we draw around our setting may change to include other places, people and things. You might want to include teachers when you thought you would only look at children, for example, or go out into the streets when you thought the school would be the field. Interviewees may well recommend other people you should talk to, which leads to a snowballing of your sample, but which of course is also ongoing. Nancy Scheper-Hughes's (2004) research on organs trafficking quite simply had a sampling method she called 'follow the bodies'. It took her eventually to several continents.

REPRESENTATIVENESS

In ethnographic research there may be an attempt to be representative, but not in a statistical way. Ethnographers often research a setting that is representative of a type of institution or a type of behaviour (for example, the fashion industry or football hooliganism). Or they join a group that represents a sector of society (such as disabled women or domestic labour migrants). I suggest that most ethnographers hope their findings will, at least to some extent, be representative of a wider group, but they make the link through a leap of faith rather than explicit discussion. There is clear evidence of this in the title of journal articles, which tend to refer to the wider population rather than the specific group. For example, Rachel Sherman's (2005) article is about 'luxury hotel workers', not simply those hotel workers she spoke to, and Lanita Jacobs-Huey (2007) talks about African-American cosmetologists in general not just in the one school she visited. In order to confidently (albeit modestly) generalise (see **generalisation**) at some point, it is important to sample carefully, or at least to think systematically about the extent to which the group or setting in which you have participated can be generalised or transferred to others of the same type.

See also: access; case study; generalisation; key informants and gatekeepers; time

REFERENCES

General

Brewer, J. (2000) *Ethnography*. Buckingham: Open University Press.

Glaser, B. G. and Strauss, A. L. (1967) *The Discovery of Grounded Theory : Strategies for Qualitative Research*. Chicago: Aldine de Gruyter.

Hammersley, M. and Atkinson, P. (1995) *Ethnography. Principles in Practice*, 2nd edn. London: Routledge.

Hicks, D. (1984) 'Getting into the field and establishing routines', in R. Ellen (ed.) *Ethnographic Research: A Guide to General Conduct*, London: Academic Press.

Lewis, O. (1951) *Life in a Mexican Village: Tepoztlan Restudied*. Urbana: University of Illinois Press.

Ritchie, J. and Lewis, J. (2003) *Qualitative Research Practice*. London: Sage.

Strauss, A. and Corbin, J. (eds) (1998) *Basics of Qualitative Research*, 2nd edn. London: Sage.

Examples

Estroff, S. E. (1981) *Making It Crazy. An Ethnography of Psychiatric Clients in an American Community*. Berkeley, CA and London: University of California Press.

Jacobs-Huey, L. (2007) 'Learning through the breach: language socialization among African American cosmetologists', *Ethnography*, 8: 171–203

Lupton, D. and Tulloch, J. (2002) '"Risk is part of your life": Risk epistemologies among a group of Australians', *Sociology*, 36(2): 317–34

Monaghan, L. F. (2002) 'Regulating "unruly" bodies: work tasks, conflict and violence in Britain's night-time economy', *British Journal of Sociology*, 53(3): 403–29.

O'Reilly, K. (2000) *The British on the Costa del Sol*. London: Routledge.

O'Reilly, K. (2007) 'Intra-European migration and the mobility–enclosure dialectic', *Sociology*, 41(2): 277–93.

Scheper-Hughes, N. (2004) 'Parts unknown: undercover ethnography of the organs-trafficking underworld', *Ethnography*, 5(1): 29–73.

Sherman, R. (2005) 'Producing the superior self: strategic comparison and symbolic boundaries among luxury hotel workers', *Ethnography*, 6(2): 131–158.

Team Ethnography

> **Though ethnography is often depicted as the achievement of a lone researcher living in a remote place, team ethnography has its own tradition, and its advantages and difficulties.**

> *Outline: A history of team ethnography. Some difficulties and benefits. Team building, project design, and allocating responsibility. Sharing fieldwork experiences through witnessing events together, sharing notes, and debriefing sessions. Encouraging and maintaining a team spirit. Writing team ethnography.*

A HISTORY OF TEAM ETHNOGRAPHY

Team research is not new to ethnography; indeed it has a long tradition, especially in British anthropology, in the form of ethnographic expeditions. The famous Torres Straits Expedition, for example, which set out to conduct an ethnographic survey of the islanders between Australia and New Guinea, was a team effort from the start. Led by Alfred Haddon, it involved seven researchers, including W. H. R. Rivers, Charles Seligman, two other psychologists, a linguist, and a photographer (see Herle and Rouse, 1998). However, though this expedition approach was common, the model was later replaced by that of the lone investigator blazing a trail on *his* own, so that we are now left with the implicit assumption in many ethnographic methods texts and journals that ethnographic research is a solitary enterprise (Benford, 2004). Ethnographers 'earn their spurs' in the field. Being there, doing fieldwork on one's own, is a rite of passage, especially for anthropologists, who need a response to the question asked when they attend conferences or meetings: 'What is your field?' This stance has been passed down from **Malinowski** (1922 [1922]), who insisted the ethnographer should not only camp right in the village but also extolled the virtues of cutting oneself off from the company of other men (by which he meant men of his own kind).

Of course, the main method of ethnography is **participant observation**, and in order to participate one has to be there, but not necessarily alone. Team ethnographies have continued to take place and may be becoming more common, especially with the spread of ethnography to other disciplines such as organisational, health, educational, and applied ethnography. Now, with the burgeoning in the publication of methods texts, and what might be called methods fetishism, attention has been drawn to the advantages and difficulties of this approach. On the one hand, 'ethnographers engaged in team research must sacrifice some of the immersion in another culture we value so highly' (Erickson and Stull, 1997: 55). On the other hand, there are benefits. There is less of the loneliness, anxiety, depression, and self-doubt that so often accompany being alone in the field. There is the pleasure of debriefing sessions (or social gatherings) that generate enthusiasm, debate, new ideas, and challenges to our own perceptions and interpretations. Then there is the intellectual benefit of working in a multi-disciplinary team or at least with others who contribute their own specialisms and offer alternative views of the same scenario.

Janet Theophano and Karen Curtis (1996) experienced these same benefits when they did their joint ethnographic research, studying the relationship between food and ethnicity in an Italian-American community. In contrast to earlier studies on the topic, they looked at the entire system of food use within a community and particularly at women and food. This involved spending time on a daily basis with four families, but rather than see these families as discrete units, they decided to study them together and simultaneously. So they alternated days with the families, copied all their fieldnotes and shared them, met frequently to discuss ideas and in the process developed a long-lasting friendship. However, the two team members were of different ethnic and family backgrounds, different religions, and had different temperaments.

They had their difficulties – jealousies, competition, anxieties that were not shared – but also their triumphs. For example, they noticed after a while that one of them was always cooked fresh food while the other was consistently fed leftovers. On closer analysis they discovered something they could not have discovered alone. Their differential treatment was not because one was liked more than the other but because Theophano was married and therefore treated as a woman and mother, while Curtis, who was single, was treated as a daughter, who needed care and attention.

TEAM BUILDING

Team ethnography can be difficult to manage, especially if people have not worked together before or come from very different perspectives or research traditions. Ken Erickson and Donald Stull, in their insightful book on team ethnography, demonstrate this by sharing with the reader the joys, trials, and tribulations of team research they have experienced. They have had to replace people because of internal strife. They have also built lasting relationships. Careful management or organisation needs to be considered from the outset, from the project's inception. A team has to be carefully built and thought must go in to who is included. 'If ethnography is about discovering – and creating – a story, then the narrative task at the beginning is to come up with a shared story that explains "what we are doing here"' (Erickson and Stull, 1997: 11).

In other words, members of a team may have slightly different focuses, goals, and expectations, but they need to be able to tell a coherent story about what they want to learn from the research. This often has to be negotiated within limitations on time, budget, space, and even focus which are set externally (by, for example, the people in the community, funding agents, and one's own academic community). The team may want to consider including various disciplinary but also personal perspectives. It is important to bring out into the open individual approaches and to consider how these fit into the overall project, to acknowledge the work of others in the team and its contribution to the whole. It is crucial to air and get to know each other's style of work, methodological preferences, any competing loyalties, and to establish lines of authority and responsibility. Studies have been known to break apart on the rocks of difference (Erickson and Stull, 1997: 15).

It is important to consider too how responsibility is allocated and shared. Some teams have hierarchical structures clearly built in or which

team ethnography

203

precede them. Nancy Scheper-Hughes's work on organs trafficking, for example, is indebted to the work of numerous young anthropologists, local researchers, human rights workers, and 'fixers', but it remains her work first and foremost and many of the 'voyages into the darker side of organs procurement' (2004: 33) were undertaken alone. Other teams are more loosely hierarchical or egalitarian. However, it can work well for a team to formalise their structure and establish clearly who is responsible for what, who has which roles and duties, and who has the final decision-making role. Sometimes the division of labour comes almost naturally; for other teams it needs working on. Teams might also establish in the early stages who has ownership of data, guidelines for authorship of papers and who has the right to publish what, the regularity of team meetings, and other details. When I worked in a team in the early stages of my career, I was surprised to find I did not have the right to publish work I had been doing alone on data collected jointly without first consulting the team and the funding agency.

SHARING FIELDWORK

It is common, in team fieldwork, for different team members to take on different groups or sites, events, or time periods (see Mackinem and Higgins, 2007). In other words, fieldwork is often divided up between the team in order to maximise coverage. They must then find ways to bring back the individual findings to the team. Erickson and Stull say there are three key ways to do this: *witnessing an event together* and then discussing it; *sharing fieldnotes*; and *general debriefing*.

Though team members usually work separately, they may sometimes decide to participate in and observe an event together, or to spend time in a setting together and then share their reflections. This approach acknowledges that each and every one of us perceives the world around us through a filter of our own past experiences, our preconceptions, and our gendered, aged, and ethnically framed identities. So comparing our interpretations of events, and even what was seen and what was not, will lead to richer and fuller views.

Another way that a team becomes a team is by sharing and discussing **fieldnotes.** Many ethnographers do not feel comfortable sharing their notes. This could be because they are very personal, or they feel they are inadequate, or it highlights the very individual-level interpretation that is part of what might appear to be the innocent recording of events. However, sharing fieldnotes with a team does encourage you to make fuller and more comprehensive notes which an ethnographer might find more satisfactory at a later date. The function of the fieldnotes thus alters: they become something to share; they need to be full and to contain more context than otherwise; they can rely less on memory; they must be *full* not *scratch* notes. Theophano and Curtis (1996) got around this by writing fieldnotes *to* and *for* each other (and interestingly their chapter, which reflects on their experiences of team ethnography, is also written in the form of notes to each other).

Each of the above depends on joint team sessions in which ideas are shared and discussed. Teams may also have general debriefs, where they discuss findings and emergent analyses. These may be presented as working papers or short reports. A debriefing session tends to act like a focus group. They are creative, encouraging team members to think of things they had not considered before, pursuing new lines of inquiry, bringing new insights, and contributing different views.

TEAM SPIRIT

Teams should attempt to encourage some sort of team spirit. Debriefing sessions can do this, but teams should also have some social, or at least informal gatherings. These give a relaxed opportunity for ideas to develop and for relationships to strengthen. They can involve food and drink, and be for pleasure as much as for work. However, care should be taken as to where these take place. A team of ethnographers who have hit a community *en masse*, seen huddled around a bar giggling privately amongst themselves, could easily cause consternation. It is also important to consider who might be excluded from such gatherings (women? people with young children? those who do not drink?) and to ensure no one is left out as some members manage to meet more often than others, or overhear team communications they were not involved in.

WRITING

Just as with any ethnographic research, the work is not over until it is in some way disseminated to a wider audience; then (unless the authors intend to present film, photograph, dance, or poetry) the issue is one of **writing**. Since the reflexive turn **(reflexivity)**, it is now accepted that there are many ways to write, many potential authors, and multiple audiences. But still few people are talking about co-authorship, even given the extent to which it is becoming so common for ethnography, especially in more applied fields. A team has many options open to them. They can write as one voice, or as many, produce a joint monograph, or report, several discrete articles, or an edited volume. However, the choices do have limitations. Polyvocality will not be appreciated in applied research. Book publishers are not keen on edited volumes. Funding agencies often demand a full and joint report. Performance texts have limited dissemination outlets. And some researchers, like Theophano and Curtis (1996), feel the need to independently 'own' some portion of their data.

The situation is fraught with difficulties. Erickson and Stull admit that on one project their team failed to produce a joint monograph because team members had dispersed, transferring their commitments to new projects, or otherwise moving on. When I worked in a team on a supposedly integrated study of economic competitiveness and social cohesion in London, the team decided that what had essentially been written as separate articles would be published as a monograph with ten authors. However, when the book from the study was eventually published, five authors' names appeared on the front cover, while the five researchers' names were relegated to the inside.

Joint publication can be hampered by differences of opinion or perspectives. Some teams reflect the way the work was divided in the field by writing up their own parts, for their own discipline, on their own 'people' or setting. Some write a series of papers or contribute as a team to a journal's special issue. Theophano and Curtis felt a desire to write something coherent and yet at the same time had to develop their ideas independently as part of their rite of passage to fully fledged (and published) ethnographers. However, many teams do manage to successfully produce joint papers, reports, and monographs. Here either one person writes most of the draft and passes it 'down' to colleagues, or team members write their individual parts separately and then one author is left with the responsibility of providing post-hoc coherence.

SOME TEAM ETHNOGRAPHIES

Pierre Bourdieu has been a keen 'team ethnographer'. Under his direction a whole team of researchers set out to describe and understand everyday suffering in contemporary societies. The result (*The Weight of the World*, 1999) is a series of short stories about factory workers and immigrants, struggling families, unemployed workers, discrimination, and prejudice in late twentieth-century France. Individual authors of sections get the recognition they deserve, while overall the book has a coherence achieved through careful editing.

Boys in White (Becker et al., 1961) is another teamwork classic. A study of how medical students progress from boys in white coats to professional doctors, it explores the transmission of culture as well as medical knowledge that students acquire throughout their training. The authors went with students to lectures and laboratories, accompanied them on their rounds, chatted with them over meals, and sat with them during oral examinations. Fortunately, they had been conducting running analyses while in the field, so sorting their 5,000 pages of shared notes was not such a mammoth task as it might have been if left to the end (see **analysis**).

Patricia and Peter Adler have often worked together. For their (2007) study of the hidden practice of self-injury, they used in-depth interviews and email conversations, joined Internet discussion groups, joint support groups, and built lasting friendships. Being a couple has meant their ethnography can impinge on their lives in ways other teams may not be able to permit. Finally, some participatory and postmodern ethnographies could be seen as team ethnographies, where the researchers and participants together constitute the team.

See also: *grounded theory; postmodern ethnographies; rapport*

REFERENCES

Key text

Erickson, K. and Stull, D. (1997) *Doing Team Ethnography. Warnings and Advice.* Qualitative Research Methods Series, no. 42. London: Sage.

General

Benford, R. (2004) 'Reflections on the state of JCE from the outgoing editor', *Journal of Contemporary Ethnography*, 33(6): 767–71.

Herle, A. and Rouse, S. (eds) (1998) *Cambridge and the Torres Strait: Centenary Essays on the 1898 Anthropological Expedition.* Cambridge: Cambridge University Press.

Malinowski, B. (1992 [1922]) *Argonauts of the Western Pacific: an Account of Native Enterprise and Adventure in the Archipelagoes of Melanesian New Guinea.* London: Routledge.

Examples

Adler, P. and Adler, P. (2007) 'The demedicalization of self-injury: from psychopathology to sociological deviance', *Journal of Contemporary Ethnography*, 36(5): 537–70.

Becker, H. S., Geer, B., Hughes, E. C. and Strauss, A. (1961) *Boys in White. Student Culture in Medical School.* Chicago: University of Chicago Press.

Bourdieu, P. et al. (1999) *The Weight of the World. Social Suffering in Contemporary Society*. Stanford, CA: Stanford University Press.

Mackinem, M. B. and Higgins, P. (2007) 'Tell me about the test: the construction of truth and lies in drug court', *Journal of Contemporary Ethnography*, 36(3): 223–51.

Scheper-Hughes, N. (2004) 'Parts unknown: undercover ethnography of the organs-trafficking underworld', *Ethnography*, 5(1): 29–73.

Theophana, J. and Curtis, K. (1996) 'Reflections on a tale told twice', in A. Lareau and J. Shultz (eds) *Journeys through Ethnography*. Boulder, CO: Westview press, pp. 149–76.

Time

Ethnography is usually undertaken long term, for various reasons, but it is important to consider how much time is needed and why.

Outline: A consideration of time and its relationship to the quality of ethnography. Time and becoming an insider, or making the strange familiar. Time and the Hawthorne Effect. Time to observe change and process. Time to build quality relationships. Time for iterative-inductive reasoning, and simultaneous data collection and analysis. Avoiding a smash-and-grab approach.

MAKING THE STRANGE FAMILIAR AND THE FAMILIAR STRANGE

Certain subtle peculiarities, which make an impression as long as they are novel, cease to be noticed as soon as they become familiar. Others again can only be perceived with a better knowledge of the local conditions. (Malinowski 1992 [1922]: 21)

The point **Malinowski** is making above is that ethnographers need to take time in the field for a variety of reasons, not least of which is in order that the strange may become familiar and the familiar strange. When you are a newcomer in a field or you start to study a culture for the first time, even as an insider, all sorts of strange and wonderful things begin to reveal themselves. You are hyper-sensitive to your surroundings, to sights, smells, and sounds, and especially to the strange and exotic, challenging and unique. As a fieldworker you will take notes furiously on the weird and wonderful things you are seeing (or noticing) for the first time. You will have had some foreshadowed problems and these will direct your gaze to some extent but you may not yet be clear what aspects of the new world that you are witnessing light end up as the focus of the eventual study. It is usual to retain an open mind at this stage, remaining receptive to all avenues of intrigue (see **inductive and deductive**). This is a crucial phase of fieldwork, when senses are heightened, awareness of things is sharp, and the level of fascination is high. It is crucial to note down all the observations you are making, however disparate they appear, because you are witnessing things with a critical and fresh perspective that will be lost with time and is difficult to access once analyses become more developed.

However, this perspective of the newcomer is only part of the fieldwork story. If we were to stop there and write up what we had found, all our studies would be superficial, and would focus on the exotic and peculiar at the cost of the rich insights and deep analysis that come with time and diligence. The ethnographer must take full advantage of this early phase but then stay in the field long enough for those things that can only be perceived with time and with a better knowledge of local conditions to be revealed. Furthermore, one of the strangest outcomes of time in the field is that some of those things that you at first took for granted and ignored come to take on new significance or seem to have a relevance you had overlooked when linked to other events and emotions.

TIME AND THE HAWTHORNE EFFECT

A further good reason for spending more than a fleeting moment in the field is to give research participants time to become familiar with your presence. Many ethnographers worry about what has become known as the Hawthorne Effect. The term actually has nothing to do with ethnography, but is taken from a factory, the Hawthorne Works, where experiments were carried out during the 1920s to test the effects of environmental factors on workers. However, it has come to imply behavioural changes caused by changes outside of the individual (like having a newcomer in your midst and knowing they are watching you!). Fortunately, the effects are limited by time. When the ethnographer has hung around long enough he or she becomes part of the setting, and part of the background that others are taking for granted. However, this does mean we must acknowledge that we are now part of this setting, however tiny, and may need to consider what the long-term effects of our presence might be, depending of course on the extent to which we participate.

For many ethnographers, the response to concerns about the Hawthorne Effect is to try to be as unobtrusive or invisible as possible. However, one ethnographer more recently has actually used obtrusiveness as a technique. Michael Schwalbe (1996) undertook three years' intensive fieldwork with the men's movement as an insider and full participant, and in many ways his ethnography is quite traditional. But he was able to illustrate his argument, that the group was mostly progressive but hampered by anti-intellectualism, purely because he dared occasionally to be deliberately provocative, and to express, and watch the reaction to, feminist sociological arguments in men's group meetings. In other words, he discovered that obtrusiveness could be a useful strategy (Harrington, 2002). Of course, Schwalbe was perhaps only able to carry this off because the rest of the time he had been at pains to establish himself as a committed insider.

TIME AND CHANGE

A wonderful by-product of spending enough time in the field is that rather than a focus on static and unconnected elements of people's lives (as often occurs with interview methods), it is possible to witness first-hand the complex interweaving of events, interactions, and interpretations; their role in the gradual process of the construction of events, and their subsequent incorporation into the culture of the community. Time in the field also creates space for the **sampling** of times of day, times of the week/month/year; time to be in different places at the same point for different events; time to witness and engage in the unravelling of culture.

Sue Estroff's (1981) research with psychiatric outpatients, for example, took place in two phases. During the first phase, which lasted 18 months, she regularly attended the clinical setting, gradually spending more time with 'clients' outside the clinic on social activities, but managing to maintain some kind of daily routine and regular time off for herself. During the second phase, for six months, she gave up all routine and moved to live amongst the psychiatric outpatients in a downtown area, spending time in their homes, going out shopping, playing pool, and hanging out in coffee bars. Like William Foote Whyte (1993), she saw the need to move right into the neighbourhood and spend time out of routine and with her community.

TIME AND RAPPORT

Time is an essential component in the building of **rapport**. Participants in a research project need time to learn they can trust you, time to understand your methodology and to empathise with your goals sufficiently to want to share their lives, thoughts and experiences with you. Ethnographers often speak of the quality of the relationships they have developed in the field and the depth of understanding they yield.

Time was thus very important for one particular insight in my own research. In the early stages of fieldwork, I noted the tendency for British migrants to compare Britain negatively with Spain. It was almost taboo to say anything bad about Spain and certainly to admit to ever feeling any desire to go home. However, as time went on, a few women came to feel they could trust me enough to confide in me the loneliness they sometimes felt, and the yearning for home they occasionally shared, but hid from others. With time I came to understand the role that such a positive image of Spain had for migrants who felt they had made a choice to move rather than being forced to leave their home countries. Admitting any discontent was tantamount to admitting (to themselves as well as to me) that they had made a mistake. In recognition of the trust placed in me when these confidences were shared, I have not drawn the conclusion that women in Spain were really lonely and desperate to go home, but acknowledged this is merely an aspect of their complex of experiences (O'Reilly, 2000).

TIME AND ITERATIVE-INDUCTIVE REASONING

Ethnographic research tends more towards inductive than deductive reasoning. This is to say, ethnographers often begin with some foreshadowed problems or a set of sensitising concepts but beyond that the focus is neither fixed nor predetermined. Indeed, some ethnographers merely choose a field site or a vague topic, arrive, and wait to see what turns up. In these cases time is an essential tool in the development of a focus and

time

ongoing hypotheses, pursuing hunches and following leads, and constructing the ongoing analysis. In the pursuit of what I call iterative-inductive reasoning, data analysis and collection run simultaneously and take time. Indeed, as for Malinowski (1922), you might even need to return to the field a few times to do more observations once you start to write up your research. Many ethnographers see their fieldwork as a lifetime commitment.

HOW MUCH TIME?

The question remains: how much time is sufficient? Of course, the credibility of an ethnography depends on being able to satisfy a reader that a serious effort has been made and the ethnographer is speaking from a secure and solid foundation of observations. Kathy Charmaz (2006: 18) believes it is important to gather sufficient data (in extent and quality) to give as full a picture as possible of the field. She maintains that this cannot be achieved with a 'smash and grab' approach, where data collection has been directed to a specific, brief task. What we might consider an ethnographic understanding of a group or situation takes time. This does not mean to say, however, that time is *all* it takes. It can be just as important to leave the field and begin writing up as to stay there collecting more and more irrelevant information. Whyte (1993) describes his reluctance to leave the field and begin writing, believing that even after 18 months, he needed at least another three years before he could even begin to understand the community. Funding and other commitments did not permit this luxury however, and luckily he was forced to begin writing. Looking back, he sees this as a positive thing, and now many ethnographers argue for a period of time out of the field, to get some perspective, and maybe make a return visit later.

Anthropologists traditionally believed that at least a year in the field was essential but some have spent much longer while others have produced very good, rich ethnographies in far less time. In the early days of ethnography when people were travelling to strange lands to observe the 'natives', the first few days or weeks were often spent engaged in the basic tasks of finding somewhere to live and how to obtain food. Now, however, short periods of participant observation can make an important contribution to ongoing studies using a range of methods, or can be used to supplement long-term fieldwork conducted by others or by yourself in other circumstances. Daniel Murphy (1986), for instance, describes his 'summative ethnography', in which short bursts of fieldwork in a range of settings over time contribute to a complex understanding of a broad phenomenon (in this case shoplifting). Gary Alan Fine (2004), however, spent years on his study of self-taught artists, attending annual meetings and art fairs, auctions, and tours, organising events, acting as a guide, and even sharing in an email discussion group for a two-year period. And Phillipe Bourgois and Jeff Schonberg (2007) built their understanding of 'intimate apartheid' among homeless heroin users on ten years' participant observation fieldwork and photography.

Of course, it is not only how much time but what times of day, year, month, and so on, that matter. This becomes particularly crucial for organisational ethnographies, that tend to take place in institutional settings. It becomes important to consider which times of day, which settings, which meetings, which informal gatherings to attend (see **sampling**). Should you go home with the boss and participate in the part of his or her life where some major decisions might be made? Do you join the cleaners on their annual trip to the seaside? The answers depend on the research problem as well as on the practical and ethical situation, and the extent and range of the analysis, but the time spent and the thoroughness with which ethnographic research was undertaken will in turn impact on the quality of the ethnography written.

See also: *going 'native; inductive and deductive; interviews and conversations; participant observation; rapport;*

REFERENCES

General

Charmaz, K. (2006) *Constructing Grounded Theory. A Practical Guide through Qualitative Analysis.* London: Sage.
Malinowski, B. (1992 [1922]) *Argonauts of the Western Pacific: an Account of Native Enterprise and Adventure in the Archipelagoes of Melanesian New Guinea.* London: Routledge.

Examples

Bourgois, P. and Schonberg, J. (2007) 'Intimate apartheid. Ethnic dimensions of habitus among homeless heroin injectors', *Ethnography*, 8(1): 7–31.
Estroff, S. E. (1981) *Making It Crazy. An Ethnography of Psychiatric Clients in an American Community.* Berkeley, CA and London: University of California Press.
Fine, G. A. (2004) *Everyday Genius. Self-Taught Art and the Culture of Authenticity.* London and Chicago: University of Chicago Press.

time

Harrington, B. (2002) 'Obtrusiveness as strategy in ethnographic research', *Qualitative Sociology*, 25(1): 49–61.

Murphy, D. J. I. (1986) *Customers and Thieves: an Ethnography of Shoplifting*. Aldershot: Gower.

O'Reilly, K. (2000) 'Trading intimacy for liberty: British women on the Costa del Sol', in F. Anthias and G. Lazaridis (eds) *Gender and Migration in Southern Europe*. Oxford: Berg Publications.

Schwalbe, M. (1996) *Unlocking the Iron Cage*. Oxford and New York: Oxford University Press.

Whyte, W. F. (1993) *Street Corner Society: the Social Structure of an Italian Slum*, 4th edn. Chicago: University of Chicago Press.

Virtual Ethnography

As the virtual world and new technologies impact increasingly on our daily lives, so ethnographers need to consider the implications for the social world and for their research methodologies.

Outline: The Internet as a field site transforming and transformed by culture. The Internet as both artefact and cultural domain. The implications for ethnographic methods: virtual participation, virtual interviews, virtual respondents, and virtual ethnographers. Ethical issues and reflexivity. Online and offline research.

VIRTUAL SITES

Ethnographers are becomingly progressively more interested in the virtual world as a new kind of field site at the same time as increasingly innovative uses of digital media impact the daily lives of various sectors of our communities (Dicks et al., 2005; Hine, 2005). However, there are several challenges to be met with the application of traditional methodologies, analytic procedures, and modes of representation to the online world. The main difficulty for an ethnography of the Internet is the selection of a field site. Christine Hine (2000) uses as a case study, or focus, the trial of Louise Woodward, a British nanny accused of murdering the child in her care in the US. The trial stimulated massive media and Internet interest, and Hine centres much of her ethnography on the construction and use of the Internet sites around this topic. So, for her, the media event becomes the field site. However, Hine argues that the Internet can be seen as a 'place' (cyberspace), a culture, or a thing (the Internet as artefact). Ethnography has already moved on from its earlier preoccupation with distant and bounded cultures and now engages in ethnography 'at home' or in multiple locations (see **insider ethnographies** and **multi-sited and mobile ethnographies**). Even though she cannot travel to a remote field and engage in face-to-face interaction, an ethnographer will 'gain a reflexive understanding of what it is to be part of the Internet' (Hine, 2000: 54) by sharing similar experiences to the research participants.

Ethnographic studies of online settings have made a major contribution to the view of the Internet as 'place' where culture is formed and transformed, and this has led to the acceptance of cyberspace as a plausible field site (Hine, 2000: 9). But the Internet can also be seen as culturally produced; an outcome shaped by external social forces. Hine argues that both perspectives are important in studies of, in, and through the Internet. Virtual ethnography has to think itself out of the idea of the bounded unit and question traditional notions of the field (Gupta and Ferguson, 1998) as well as challenge the implicit conception of community behind much traditional ethnography (Ward, 1999).

THE INTERNET AS CULTURE AND ARTEFACT

Research has shown that online groups can and do form virtual communities (Rheingold, 1993), and meaningful relationships can exist in cyberspace. This opened up the field to qualitative researchers in the fields of anthropology, cultural and media studies, and sociology. There have also been quantitative, discourse, and ethno-methodological studies. Researchers also explore the concept of identity-play or identity-work. Ethnographic studies, however, have a particular interest in the daily, lived experiential interaction with and interpretation of the technology. Many of those studies that call themselves ethnographic are very partially so, but others are nevertheless long-term, engage in real-time discussion, and use other means of communication such as email and face-to-face interviews to study online communities and cultures (see Baym, 2000; Correll, 1995).

However, Hine warns against separating the online and offline too distinctly as if they were entirely separate. A broader perspective sees the Internet as socially shaped in development, use, meanings, and interpretations. This involves analysis of its history and development, and how it has been represented or understood by different groups. Steve Woolgar and Keith Grint (1997), for example, see the Internet as inherently social, and explore not only the impact of designers but also of users. That is to say, they look at both production and consumption of the Internet and the articulation of the two. The problem is that both producers and users are broad categories and of course users also produce web pages, newsgroups, and so on. Woolgar and Grint used a computer construction company as their field 'site'. Hine (2000) though looks at the production and consumption of a particular 'use' of the Internet, arguing that we can start the trail from there, and be creative with the notion or idea of a 'site' (and see Dicks and Mason, 1998).

VIRTUAL(LY) ETHNOGRAPHY: ADAPTING THE METHODS

Similar to concerns expressed by those conducting multi-sited and mobile ethnography, virtual ethnographers sometimes feel the methodology is being stretched beyond recognition, to a virtual (not quite real) ethnography rather than simply an ethnography of the virtual. Hine believes that because methods have to be adapted to fit the new media, we end up with a partial ethnography. Crucially, ethnography of the Internet challenges the ethnographic 'ethos of engagement with events as they happen in the field, and of a holistic attention to all practices as constitutive of a distinct culture' (2000: 21). How can one engage with Internet use in the field, as it occurs, when there is no single place to be? Even if you choose to take part in a chat room, for example, you cannot be there all the time, and you need to accept that all those who take part are not there all the time either. One possibility is to simply access the archives. These are easily available and can be accessed when you are ready, in your own time and at your leisure. But this will not give you **access** to the culture of use and construction of the Internet. If you want to understand the experience of the Internet as others have, then you will have to consider how they use it. Do they consult newsgroups as messages arrive or visit them later? You may need to experience the delays in a chat room, see the message appear in bits, and sit and wait for new messages. This means that instead of thinking in terms of places or locations, an Internet ethnographer looks to connections between things. Like ethnographies of mobility or travel, they may start in one 'place' then follow leads and networks to other places and spaces.

Ethnographers are adapting **participant observation** for use in virtual settings by ensuring they meet certain criteria, such as acquiring insider knowledge about the rules governing interaction, 'moving' about the site in acceptable ways, and even being socialised into the culture (Markham, 1998). Participant observation here involves observing identity performances, rule and norm enforcement, learning acceptable behaviour, witnessing transgressions (and corrections), sharing exchanges, coming to understand power structures and to recognise hierarchies. In-depth, qualitative email interviews are becoming more widely used to good advantage, often combined with other methods (see Adler and Adler, 2007; Coco and Woodward, 2007). Miller and Slater (2000) suggest some people find it easier to be intimate in virtual than in face-to-face settings. They are also a useful way to snowball, as respondents can forward emails effortlessly to family and friends. And, of course, there are huge advantages in email interviews being already in digital format, ready to copy, share, or import into software for analysis with no transcription costs or time.

VIRTUAL PARTICIPANTS

It might also be necessary to suspend doubts about who the participants might 'really be'. One thing people tend to get anxious about with the Internet is that we can have no idea who is contributing, what is their 'real' identity, or whether what they are saying has any validity. Some attempt to verify online performances (Orgad, 2005). But how relevant are these concerns in this situation? Ethnographic studies should be undertaken, Hine argues, just as studies of other cultures, with ethnocentric views left behind. The search for authenticity should be put aside unless or until it reveals itself as a problem for the inhabitants of cyberspace. Engaging thus with the practice of users enables a more reflexive understanding of their role, and gives us the chance to develop iterative-inductive research, where research questions surface, insights emerge, and analyses are developed as part of the long-term process.

Similarly, how can one tap into other users, such as those who read but do not participate in newsgroups (known as lurkers)? The ethnographer needs to consider their role and impact. Do they affect the community? Are they engaging in any sort of identity play? Are others aware they are there? If so, what impact might that have? However, if it is the lurkers as a group that are the focus of a study, then that is a different matter. They will need to somehow be located and included.

VIRTUALLY COVERT

Finally, virtual research raises ethical issues of its own, as well as those relevant for all ethnography (**ethics**). Should, or even can, virtual ethnography be overt? How an ethnographer presents him or herself online remains a difficult question. It is possible to stay invisible, researching by 'cyberstealth' (Ebo, 1998), or constructing 'avatars' that are never direct representations. Several researchers have already reported on work gathered as they merely 'lurked' in the background or collected data after the event (Denzin, 1999). Nevertheless, the ethnographer is there, selecting whom to listen to, what to collect or record, imposing their research agenda in subtle ways. Hine argues that if we believe a virtual community is real enough to research, then they are real enough for us to harm or infringe their privacy. Neither real names nor user names should be used without permission, for example, as these are patently of relevance to the participants.

ETHNOGRAPHY ONLINE AND OFFLINE

To defend virtual ethnography in terms of traditional expectations, Hine says that although Internet ethnographers do not travel in order to gain the perceptual distance that used to be considered necessary, neither do insider ethnographers. On the other hand, they do have to travel experientially. They even have to learn a new (technical) language. They too can gain the authority of 'being there' by interacting and participating, and this can bring surprises, challenges, and new insights in a world that can seem just as strange as a foreign land. However, the Internet consists of interactions and connections, and also texts. Unlike speech or observations, texts are co-produced, are mobile, divorced from the context and the producer, are less ephemeral (can time-travel and be adapted, revisited or lost), and are consumed in a variety of ways. These present ongoing challenges for this developing ethnography that are often paralleled by those engaging in multi-sited ethnography and using visual and other forms of data. There is no reason to feel you need to select either/or virtual or 'real' ethnography, a single or fixed site, or even textual versus visual data. Ethnographers are combining elements such as online interviews and participation in networking sites with face-to-face interviews and household surveys (Miller and Slater, 2000; Orgad, 2005).

See also: covert; holism; insider ethnographies; interviews and conversations; multi-sited and mobile ethnographies

REFERENCES

General

Dicks, B. and Mason, B. (1998) 'Hypermedia and ethnography: reflections on the construction of a research approach', *Sociological Research Online*, 3(3).

Dicks, B, Mason, B., Coffey, A. and Atkinson, P. (2005) *Qualitative Research and Hypermedia: Ethnography for the Digital Age*. London: Sage.

Ebo, B. (1998) 'Internet or outernet?', in B. Ebo (ed.) *Cyberghetto or Cybertopia? Race, Class and Gender on the Internet*. Westport, CT: Praeger Publishers, pp. 1–14.

Hine, C. (2000) *Virtual Ethnography*. London: Sage

Hine, C. (ed.) (2005) *Virtual Methods: Issues in Social Research on the Internet*. Oxford: Berg.

Markham, A. (1998) *Life Online: Researching Real Experience in Virtual Space*. Walnut Creek, CA: Altamira Press.

Miller, D. and Slater, D. (2000) *The Internet: an Ethnographic Approach*. Oxford: Berg.

Examples

Adler, P. and Adler, P. (2007) 'The demedicalization of self-injury: from psychopathology to sociological deviance', *Journal of Contemporary Ethnography*, 36(5): 537–70.

Baym, N. K. (2000) *Tune In, Log On: Soaps, Fandom, and Online Community*. Thousand Oaks, CA: Sage.

Coco, A. and Woodward, I. (2007) 'Discourses of authenticity within a pagan community: the emergence of the "Fluffy Bunny" sanction', *Journal of Contemporary Ethnography*, 36(5): 479-504.

Correll, S. (1995) 'The ethnography of an electronic bar: the lesbian café', *Journal of Contemporary Ethnography*, 24(3): 270–98.

Denzin, N. K. (1999) 'Cybertalk and the method of instances', in S. G. Jones (ed.) *Doing Internet Research: Critical Issues and Methods for Examining the Net*. Thousand Oaks, CA: Sage, pp. 107–26.

Gupta, A. and Ferguson, J. (1998) 'Discipline and practice: "the field" as site, method, and location in anthropology', in A. Gupta and J. Ferguson (eds) *Anthropological Locations: Boundaries and Grounds of a Field Science*. Berkeley, CA: University of California Press.

Orgad, S. (2005) 'From online to offline and back: moving from online to offline relationships with research informants', in C. Hine (ed.) *Virtual Methods*. Oxford: Berg.

Rheingold, H. (1993) *The Virtual Community: Homesteading on the Electric Frontier*. Reading, MA: Addison-Wesley.

Ward, K. (1999) 'Cyber-ethnography and the emergence of the virtually new community', *Journal of Information Technology*, 14(1): 95–105.

Woolgar, S. and Grint, K. (1997) *The Machine at Work: Technology, Work and Organization*. Cambridge: Polity Press.

Visual Ethnography

> The term visual ethnography is ambiguous. It relates to both the study and use of visual media and material, but also to the incorporation of a visual lens into mainstream ethnography.

> Outline: Technological developments and the increasing relevance of the visual. The hegemony of the text. Images as 'writing', found images, and creative uses of images. Photo analysis and photo elicitation. Auto-ethnography. Writing the visual after the reflexive turn.

NEW TECHNOLOGIES

Though I have not used visual media much in my own research, reading and thinking about them for *Ethnographic Methods* (O'Reilly, 2005) got me thinking much more about visuality and its role in research; I hope that reading about the concept here will do the same for the readers of this book. There is no doubt that the role of the visual in ethnography is becoming more important, for various reasons. Technological advances mean that there are more things that can be achieved, more creative ways that visual images can be produced and used. As a result, the cultures we research are using photography, film, and hypermedia in more diverse ways, while, simultaneously, ethnographers are improving their own skills in the use of these technologies. The development of a field of visual ethnography has raised awareness of the role of visuality for cultural (re)production, analysis, and representation. This is an exciting time, with the creative uses of visual (and digital) media for research only just being realized, while at the same time the impact of the technologies on local and global cultures is escalating. Visual ethnography thus opens up whole new ways of seeing the worlds we study, enabling a focus on the emotions, the sensual, the artistic, and creative elements that digital media, especially, are providing entire new ways to represent.

THE HEGEMONY OF THE TEXT

There has been a tendency in all ethnographic research to concentrate on words and texts rather than on images. This is strange given that a crucial element of ethnographic fieldwork is observation. However, I think it can be explained to some extent by the fact that it is a more familiar medium of representation for ideas, thoughts, and opinions. Articles, books and other texts give writers the opportunity to describe in depth, to explain their thinking to a variety of audiences, and to guide them in how to interpret what they are saying and **writing.** Images are more like art, and open to interpretation by the viewer, which would have seemed problematic for the positivist or naïve realist ethnographer trying to faithfully portray a true scene (**realism**). Of course, several early ethnographers, such as Bronislaw **Malinowski** (see Wright, 1994) and Gregory Bateson and Margaret Mead (1942), used images extensively, but these were often meant as realist representations of the cultures they faithfully represented and were used as evidence to support textual descriptions (Ball and Smith, 2001). Even though Bateson and Mead present 759 photographs to support their argument that Balinese character is better portrayed through images than words, still they were at pains to randomly and spontaneously capture *natural* events. There is no **reflexivity** about who took what pictures for which purposes, and the photographs rely on the supporting text.

The production of images is also expensive and requires technological skills that can be time-consuming to learn, and publishers have thus been reluctant to accept them in finished texts. It is interesting to note that even Sarah Pink's latest edition of *Doing Visual Ethnography* (2007) still only has a limited number of black and white photographs as illustration. It would be radical indeed to include film, colour slides, moving animation, or hypermedia. Of course, such developments are taking place through the Internet, but these then raise issues of dissemination and copyright. There are also difficult legal and ethical issues to consider with photograph and film, not least of which is how to ensure anonymity (an immensely interesting phenomenon for a sociology of the visual is that an individual can be anonymised by altering names, descriptions, and other details, but the idea of altering a visual image of a face is hugely problematic). Using and analysing images therefore poses ethical, technical, and economic challenges (Emmison and Smith, 2000).

A VISUAL LENS

When I reflect on fieldwork I have done in the past, I realise that there are many elements I overlooked that a *visual lens* would have illuminated. I have never managed to describe the way elderly British migrants appear to the eye: the colourful clothes, the golden-brown suntans, healthy glow, smiles, and strong bodies that lack the frailty and pallor of their counterparts in the UK. These seem important now I think about them. Similarly, the visual presentation of the newer migrants was important in the characterisation of them as 'the wrong sort of Brits' (O'Reilly, 2007). Here I would need to portray younger people with families, men with shaved heads and tattoos, women in short skirts bought from the market. Then I am afraid I would need some aural representation (film would be best) to present the localised accents, the shouting and swearing, that other migrants refer to when positioning these migrants in a class category. How strange it is that ethnography has often used the analogy of the camera (see Peacock, 1986) to discuss a perspective that has concentrated so wholeheartedly on words and text.

IMAGES AS WRITING

As visual ethnography developed, it has been useful to distinguish images as *writing*, from *found* images, and the more recent and diverse *creative* uses of images. Where images are used as a form of writing, the visual makes or supports a point or conveys a message. The sorts of things I have been talking about above would fit here, taking full advantage of the golden opportunity to portray 'life as it is lived accurately recorded as it happens, and constantly available for playback and analysis' (Plummer, 2001: 66). Photographs and film have historically been used as evidence to support an argument made in the presentation of findings. Sometimes these have been realistic representations, collected 'spontaneously and naturally'. At other times (and perhaps it is not that easy to distinguish the two), events have been staged in order to appear real (Ball and Smith, 2001). Either way the visual is used here in the sprit of the notion that 'a picture paints a thousand words'. For a poignant example I recommend leafing through Michael Jacobson-Hardy's (2002) photographs taken in prisons in the United States. There is very little accompanying text, but the brief captions unite the images into a powerful argument about race and class in contemporary western societies.

FOUND IMAGES

Found images refer to those visual data produced and presented by the research participants themselves, and can include all manner of things from photographs and film to posters and even building design. Worth (1980) distinguishes these data that are found in the field from those an ethnographer might create or co-create. Rather than being used by the ethnographer for the presentation of ideas, these data may be analysed, interpreted, questioned, challenged, and searched for their implicit meanings, for the way cultural norms are inscribed in them, or the way relationships are portrayed, or hidden hierarchies revealed. *Photoanalysis* (Plummer, 2001) is a technique for asking questions about such data, and directs the ethnographer's gaze to what the image portrays, what it does not portray, how it achieves this, what is going on in the image, what is being said by the way it is displayed, and so on. This takes the ethnographer somewhat into the realm of content, discourse or semiotic analysis. It also fits well with interpretive analysis more broadly (**interpretivism**). Though I have not used visual media much in my research to date, I have always collected posters, advertisements, and even letters, and have tried to make sense of these in the context of the developing analysis. For example, the fact that a new migrant theatre group presented itself as inter-cultural yet produced all its posters in English contributed to my understanding of the ambivalence of identity (O'Reilly, 2007). Interestingly, such analysis can lead us to challenge (indirectly) what a participant has said and can lead the research in different directions.

However, realist presentation of visual data or the interpretation of 'found' data are both being challenged by creative and co-constructive developments in fieldwork. Photographs may once have been viewed as truthful and verifiable representations of reality, but the reflexive turn challenged any attempt on the part of ethnography to represent objectively. Some have responded with attempts to employ visual media in more rigorous, scientific ways. Others, such as Elizabeth Chaplin (1994), suggest that rather than 'reading' or interpreting found visual media, or using them uncritically to support authoritative statements, we should use them to create knowledge. The development of digital technologies has drastically altered the potential for visual representation and critically challenged any idea that the camera never lies. Images can be cut, sliced, merged, altered, and enhanced. Backgrounds can be added or removed, montages created, along with any number of other improvements or deceits. These developments are available to ethnographers and research participants alike. In journalism, television and film-making, documentary and fiction have merged, so that we need to be critical of everything we see. As a result, the visual is increasingly being used as a critical tool influenced by philosophical debates around realism, postmodernism, and social constructionism (Plummer, 2001).

Photo elicitation (Collier and Collier, 1986) is one such creative use, in which visual images are explored and/or created with participants in an attempt to elicit rather than impose feelings, responses, and interpretations. Participants are asked to sit down with the ethnographer and to talk through what, for example, a family photograph album means: who is represented, why and how, why particular settings were chosen, and so on. Other researchers have given cameras to their research participants and asked them to take photographs that they feel illustrate elements of their lives. Radley and Taylor (2003) used this technique for a study with homeless people in Britain and then discussed the photographs afterwards. They found people articulate experiences and emotions through images that may have been repressed during a standard interview (see Pink, 2007). Photo elicitation is also a useful technique to use with children or people who feel uncomfortable talking face-to-face with an interviewer. Phil Mizen (2005), for example, for his study of the place of work in children's lives in England and Wales, asked children to make video-diaries that represented and reflected on their experiences of work in the context of their lives. And Virginia Morrow (2003), for her study of health and social capital, asked children to describe their neighbourhoods through photography, map drawing, and talk.

Auto-ethnography emerged in the 1990s, the visual version of which involved participants using video and still photography to tell stories about their own lives. This is a version of what we think of as the video diary, which is becoming popular with television broadcasters (Russel, 1999). For some ethnographers, the use of the visual is more emancipatory and powerful than the use of text. Ruth Holliday (1999 and 2000) employed the use of video diaries in her study of the performative nature of identity. In a direct and overt engagement of research participants in her study, she asked 'queer subjects' to think about how their identities are constructed and displayed in everyday settings, and to demonstrate this visually as well as through talk, using camcorders. The method, she argues, captured both the visual and processual elements of self-representation more completely than purely aural data. The visual element of the study served two important functions: empowerment of the respondents, who were able to construct their own presentation as well as confront Holliday's own interpretations; and emotional engagement on the part of the academic audience.

WRITING THE VISUAL

Finally, we might think about how to 'write up' these creative uses of visual media without resorting to the naïve realism of early ethnographers. Sarah Pink (2007) notes the tendency to continue to present images unproblematically as supporting evidence for the text. She calls for presentational styles that retain photographic integrity by using images in a combination of realist, expressive, and allusive ways to create and suggest, rather than insist on, an interpretation of the field. Readers and viewers would then make meanings in interaction with the images and text. I feel a little anxious that ethnography then becomes more art than science, and uncomfortable that the outcome might be a powerful presentation of the author's political position disguised as democracy in action. Nevertheless, I welcome the call to consider creative uses of visual and digital technologies and to 'play' with representational styles, as long as we remember who gave us permission to do what with what ends. Furthermore, as Pink (2007: 6) acknowledges, 'visual representations bear an important relationship to, but cannot replace, words in theoretical discussion'. So, while the visual might be given the same *weight* as words in ethnographic work, this is not to say they can do the same work as each other.

See also: interviews and conversations; postmodern ethnographies; reflexivity; writing

visual ethnography

REFERENCES
General

Ball, M. and Smith, G. (2001) 'Technologies of realism? Ethnographic uses of photography and film', in P. Atkinson, A. Coffey, S. Delamont, J. Lofland and L. Lofland (eds) *Handbook of Ethnography*. London: Sage, pp. 302–20.

Chaplin, E. (1994) *Sociology and Visual Representations*. London: Routledge.

Collier, J. and Collier, M. (1986) *Visual Anthropology: Photography as a Research Method*, 2nd edn. Albuquerque: University of New Mexico Press.

Emmison, M. and Smith, P. (2000) *Researching the Visual*. London: Sage.

O'Reilly, K. (2005) *Ethnographic Methods*. London: Routledge.

Peacock, J. (1986) *The Anthropological Lens: Harsh Light, Soft Focus*. Cambridge: Cambridge University Press.

Pink, S. (2007) *Doing Visual Ethnography*, 2nd edn. London: Sage.

Plummer, K. (2001) *Documents of Life 2*, 2nd edn. London: Sage.

Worth, S. (1980) 'Margaret Mead and the shift from "visual anthropology" to the "anthropology of visual communication"', *Studies in Visual Communication*, 6(1): 15–22.

Wright, T. (ed.) (1994) *The Anthropologist as Artist. Malinowski's Trobriand Photographs*. Saarbrücken: Nijmegen Studies in Development and Cultural Change, No. 19.

Examples

Bateson, G. and Mead, M. (1942) *Balinese Character*, vol. II. New York: New York Academy of Science.

Holliday, R. (1999) 'The comfort of identity', *Sexualities*, 2(4): 475–91.

Holliday, R. (2000) 'We've been framed: visualising methodology', *The Sociological Review*, 48(4): 503–21.

Jacobson-Hardy, M. (2002) 'Behind the razor wire. A photographic essay', *Ethnography*, 3(4): 398-415

Mizen, P. (2005) 'A little "light work"? Children's images of their labour', *Visual Studies*, 20(2): 124–39

Morrow, V. (2003) 'No ball games: children's views of their urban environments', *Journal of Epidemiology and Community Health*, 57: 234.

O'Reilly, K. (2007) 'Intra-European migration and the mobility–enclosure dialectic', *Sociology*, 41(2): 277–93.

Radley, A. and Taylor, D. (2003) 'Images of recovery: a photo-elicitation study on the hospital ward', *Qualitative Health Research*, 13(1): 77–99.

Russel, C. (1999) 'Autoethnography: journeys of the self': excerpt from *Experimental Ethnography*. Durham, NC: Duke University Press. available at: www.haussite.net/haus.0/SCRIPT/txt2001/01/russel.html

key concepts in ethnography

Writing

Ethnography literally means 'writing about peoples'. Here we consider what is generally labelled 'writing-up'.

Outline: When and where to start writing up. Retaining links with the field. Selecting what to write while avoiding reductionism. Thinking about writing. Presenting an argument and remembering your audience. Overcoming writer's block: freewriting; having a title; sorting; re-drafting. A standard format for writing up and some non-standard examples.

WHERE TO START WRITING

I like the fact that the concept of writing begins with a 'w', which places it neatly at the end of this book. Of course, writing is part and parcel of ethnographic fieldwork in the shape of fieldnote observations (**field-notes**) and intellectual reflections, notes taken as you read existing literature, memos that elaborate your emerging analyses and the analysis itself as you work through it. However, there comes a time when you need to move from writing things down to writing up. That is to say, there comes a time when you need to prepare what you have learned or understood into a format in which it can be shared with others. Of course, you could prepare film and photos as well as write, but we will leave that thought to one side for a moment as we focus on the act of presentation through writing. Since the act of writing has come under critical scrutiny, it should be done reflexively and with due care and consideration (**reflexivity**).

It is likely that as research and analyses progressed (see **analysis**), as you sorted, coded and wrote memos, and as you read existing literature in light of your findings, you began writing up. In fact the very worst thing you can do in ethnographic research is collect data unthinkingly to bring home at a later date, which you then sort, analyse, and write about. Ethnographic research is iterative-inductive (O'Reilly, 2005). It moves back and forth continually between data collection, analysis, reading, thinking, and writing. Writing up starts as soon as you collect and make sense of data in the field. Writing up polished pieces for presentation to others collates these emergent insights into a coherent story. Bruce Berg (2004) believes you are ready to write up once you have considered all your data, reflected on all your analytical deliberations, and have decided on at least one story to tell. I think there is a chance that you feel ready to write up but may well want to go back and rethink, re-analyse, consult more literature, and even perhaps collect more data once you begin shaping up your ideas into a written piece. For this reason, it is ideal if you can retain some links with the field in order to go back and clarify issues or elaborate details.

WRITING INVOLVES SELECTION

Just as a survey researcher does not present an entire database or the correlation of every variable with every other, neither does an ethnographer present all the fieldnotes, quotations, photographs, emerging insights, analytical notes, and theoretical interpretations he or she has collected or considered. Writing involves selection and presentation. It involves taking what you think you know or understand and deciding how to communicate some of that to others. It can be frustrating to discover that everything you have learned about a setting or group cannot be shared with others in what you write up; that you have to be selective, saving some things for other forums. It can be even more frustrating to find that what you have to say is so complex and convoluted that it takes a whole book to express it. In conferences, meetings, or even down the pub with friends, when people ask what the research is all about, you feel as if you should be able to give a coherent answer briefly and engagingly enough to keep the listeners awake (see Hine, 2000: 147). If you cannot do this, you think, how can you possibly begin to write it all up? But such reduction of the complex, fascinating world you studied is more difficult the nearer you are to having just left the field. Sometimes the ability to tell a coherent story takes not only distance but mental distance, and time. After my first ethnographic project, I spent six months after leaving the field thinking about writing up, and producing very little in the way of polished prose.

WRITING IS DONE FOR A PURPOSE

Writing up, then, is not a matter of preparing everything for presentation but selecting and preparing an argument for a given audience. This is an important point. When writing up, what we write is *for* something; for a particular journal or conference paper, for a book, for an academic or non-academic audience, or perhaps for a dissertation (Agar, 1986). It is always necessary to write up with the audience in mind because this will affect what is written and how. It will affect the extent to which we can use visual and aural media, the style we write in, the amount of supplementary material and explanation required, and the extent to which we focus on description or theoretical insights.

HOW TO OVERCOME WRITER'S BLOCK

Writing up, because it is for an audience, can be very daunting. You find yourself doing everything but getting on with it: writing just a few more notes, collecting a little more data, reading a few more articles, tidying your desk once again, going for a walk, or eating! These are avoidance tactics. The best way to overcome them is to just do it. One of my PhD supervisors told me the best thing to do is to carry the following words around in your head: *don't get it right, get it written*. You can work on it to get it right afterwards, he advised. I find this approach works well for some written pieces, but not all. I tend to write memos or rambling pieces, convincing myself no one will ever read them, then I restructure them and rewrite after a period of doing something completely different.

That does not work for everyone. One of my students only ever writes things once. She builds up her writing slowly and painstakingly, one sentence at a time. Others try freewriting – simply writing whatever comes to mind without checking for grammar or spellings – as a way of breaking writer's block (Wolcott, 2001). I recommend having a title or short passage in front of you as a constant reminder of what you are writing about. I also like to collect and write all sorts of notes, then sort them into paragraphs, code them, and write them in order. Do not expect to get it right first time. With the aid of computers it is now much easier to draft, redraft, reorder, or build up the work in tiny blocks. Most effective and persuasive writing has been through several revisions (Berg, 2004; Walker, 1987).

It seems an obvious point but if you are not sure what you are trying to say, then you will not be able to say it. If writing is not coming easily, try explaining your thinking out loud to someone (or into a voice recorder), or try summarising it into an outline. On the other hand, it is often the very act of writing up that enables thoughts to be organised. Finally, and most importantly, try to enjoy your writing. If you are finding it painful to

writing

write, the chances are it will be painful to read. Even academic writing can be lively and inspirational. Look at the way, in *Myth in Primitive Psychology*, **Malinowski** invites his reader to join him in a 'mental flight' back to the years he spent in New Guinea.

> There paddling on the lagoon, watching the natives under the blazing sun at their garden-work, following them through the patches of jungle, and on the winding beaches and reefs, we shall learn about their life. (1926: 17)

Alternatively, for inspiration, explore the styles of presentation of some contemporary studies and **postmodern ethnographies**.

THE STANDARD FORMAT FOR WRITING UP

It is crucial with contemporary ethnography to think about how we write and what we are doing when we write. The best way to think about writing styles and their impacts is to read as much and as widely as possible; to consider novels and poetry, academic writing (in various disciplines), and newspaper journalism, and to consciously select a style for the purpose intended. Notwithstanding the entire debate about the constructed nature of ethnographic writing and the call for reflexive consideration of writing styles (**reflexivity**), most journal articles, books, reports, and dissertations tend to follow a fairly standard format. It is not essential to follow this format these days, but it can help to be aware of it so that you know what you may be deviating from.

- *Introduction* – The introduction tells the reader what to expect, and locates the overall topic in some scholarly tradition. This is the place to say something about where the work fits theoretically, the intellectual puzzle, how it fits in to an overall scheme, and perhaps to discuss concepts that will be analysed or contributed to later. The introduction is often the last section written, but it makes sense to sketch it out early on.
- *Literature Review* – The review of existing literature can be incorporated into the introduction or can be a separate chapter, and should be both substantive and theoretical/conceptual. A literature review is not a summary of everything that has been read in relation to a field but is a coherent account, critically reviewing related literature, and leading to an argument in support of your own work and its place in the field.

- *The setting and background* – It is crucial to offer the reader some description and background to the study. This may be historical, it may set the scene (taking the reader there with you), or it may describe relevant policies, media representations, or debates. Explain to the reader details that may be familiar to you but not to them. Describe your group, the people, the lifestyles.
- *The methodology and methods* – This section or chapter must outline the epistemological and ontological premises on which the study is based. It must describe the methods used and the reasons for selecting them, difficulties experienced and how they were overcome, strengths and limitations of the data collected. Without such information the reader cannot know to what extent the findings are reliable or valid, or can be transferred to other settings.
- *Findings and analysis* – Though this appears low down in the list, it is of course crucial and the main body of the written piece. As there are so many styles of presentation now available to the ethnographer, I recommend reading and selecting a paper, book, or report (or film or poem) that you have enjoyed and think will work for you and using it as your model. There is little to be gained from reinventing the wheel unless you have a specific argument to make about why your findings should be presented differently. Some ethnographers separate findings into descriptive and more analytical; others intertwine them as they tell their analytical story.
- *The conclusion* – This summarises for the reader what has been said, acting as a sort of précis of the article or book. It is also a useful place to highlight emerging insights, to draw inferences, to make policy recommendations, and to describe future research priorities.

Gavin Smith (2007) follows this format so faithfully as to offer his reader the following subheadings: introduction; situating the study; methods; findings and discussion; and conclusion. In other works the pattern is harder to find. Gary Alan Fine (2003, 2004), for example, intertwines findings, reflections, sociological interpretations, and evidence from elsewhere, each chapter making its own argument and contribution to the whole. However, closer inspection reveals the book's introduction to offer description of the field, a summary of what is known or already understood about the topic, methodology and other background information. Then follow the individual chapters, with their various arguments. The conclusion is finally used to summarise the overarching themes and extrapolate out from the ethnographic data to the wider social system.

Of course, there are numerous ways other than writing that you might consider for presenting your work to others, such as film, photograph, biography, poetry, and even dance (see **postmodern** and **visual ethnography**). The important thing is to remember you have a point to make and an audience to persuade, and were granted access based on certain promises or expectations.

See also: analysis; coding; fieldnotes; grounded theory; inductive and deductive; reflexivity

REFERENCES

General

Agar, M. H. (1986) *Speaking of Ethnography*. Beverley Hills, CA: Sage.

Berg, B. L. (2004) *Qualitative Research Methods for the Social Sciences*, 5th edn. Boston: Pearson.

Hine, C. (2000) *Virtual Ethnography*. London: Sage.

O'Reilly, K. (2005) *Ethnographic Methods*. London: Routledge.

Walker, M. (1987) *Writing Research Papers*, 2nd edn. New York: Norton.

Wolcott, H. F. (2001) *Writing up Qualitative Research*, 2nd edn. Thousand Oaks, CA: Sage.

Examples

Fine, G. A. (2003) *Morel Tales: the Culture of Mushrooming*. Urbana and Chicago: University of Illinois Press.

Fine, G. A. (2004) *Everyday Genius. Self-Taught Art and the Culture of Authenticity*. London and Chicago: University of Chicago Press.

Malinowski, B. (1926) *Myth in Primitive Psychology*. London: Kegan Paul, Trench, Trubner.

Smith, G. J. D. (2007) 'Exploring relations between watchers and watched in control(led) systems: strategies and tactics', *Surveillance and Society*, 4(4): 280–313.

Where to Find Other Ethnographic Concepts

Action or participatory research
   Critical ethnography
   Ethics
   Realism
Auto-ethnography and autobiography
   Chicago School
   Postmodern ethnographies
   Visual ethnography
Diary
   Chicago School
   Fieldnotes
   Malinowski
   Visual ethnography
Documents
   Chicago School
Emic and etic
   Insider ethnographies
Field/fieldwork
   Introduction
   Access
   Sampling
   Malinowski
Functionalism
   Holism
   Malinowski

ethnographic concepts